The BENTEEN-GOLDIN LETTERS ON CUSTER AND HIS LAST BATTLE

Captain Frederick W. Benteen, commander of Troop H, Seventh Cavalry. From the John M. Carroll Collection.

Theodore W. Goldin, who fought in the Battle of the Little Big Horn and won a Medal of Honor. Photo taken about 1911. Courtesy of the State Historical Society of Wisconsin.

The
BENTEEN-GOLDIN LETTERS ON CUSTER AND HIS LAST BATTLE

Edited by
JOHN M. CARROLL

Illustrated by
LORENCE BJORKLUND

UNIVERSITY OF NEBRASKA PRESS
LINCOLN AND LONDON

First Bison Book printing: 1991
Most recent printing indicated by the last digit below:
10   9   8   7   6   5   4   3   2   1

Library of Congress Cataloging-in-Publication Data
The Benteen-Goldin letters on Custer and his last battle / edited by John
M. Carroll; illustrated by Lorence Bjorklund.—1st Bison book print.
p.   cm.
Reprint, with six additional photographs. Originally published: New
York: Liveright, c1974.
Includes index
ISBN 0-8032-6335-X
1. Custer, George Armstrong, 1839–1876.   2. Little Big Horn, Battle of
the, 1876.   3. Benteen, Frederick William, 1834–1898—Correspon-
dence. 4. Goldin, Theodore W.—Correspondence.   I. Benteen, Fre-
derick William, 1834–1898.   II. Goldin, Theodore W.   III. Carroll,
John M. (John Melvin), 1928–   .   IV. Bjorklund, Lorence F.
[E83.876.B47   1991]
973.8'2'092—dc20
90-20012   CIP

Reprinted by arrangement with John M. Carroll

The photographs have been added to this Bison Book edition.

*For my two dear friends,
Jose and Vicenta Cisneros.
To know them is to love
them.*

CONTENTS

Major Marcus A. Reno commanded Companies A, G, and M in the valley and hilltop fights at the Little Big Horn. From the John M. Carroll Collection.

George A. Custer, in early 1876, while still a lieutenant colonel and before his hair was cut short for his last campaign. From the John M. Carroll Collection.

Elizabeth Custer in 1874. She did not escape the scathing comments of Benteen and Goldin. From the John M. Carroll Collection.

An important photograph of enlisted survivors of the Battle of the Little Big Horn, in dress uniform, probably taken at Fort Lincoln in July 1876. The officer standing in the middle is Lieutenant Mathey. From the John M. Carroll Collection.

PREFACE

THE COMPILATION AND PRESENTATION of all these Benteen-
Goldin letters and narratives has long been a personal goal
of mine. Although the reason for this may not be readily dis-
cernible to the casual reader, it is at once obvious to the Custer
student who has not had the advantage of owning a set of
the transcribed letters *in their entirety* or who has had to rely
on the too carefully edited versions in Colonel W. A. Graham's
Custer Myth.

I have gone on record before concerning my views of
Custer's character and the Little Big Horn affair, so it will
come as no surprise to many that I value the Benteen-Goldin
letters only as historic documents *per se* and not as historic
documents filled with historic truths. They are filled with too
much vituperation. Benteen presents himself as a paragon of
diplomatic virtues and an unparalleled military genius who
was mostly misunderstood and envied by all who knew him.
Only he, it seems, could easily win at poker against all odds;
only he could tell Custer off without bias; and only he could
overcome difficulties that defeated other men. At least his
letters to Goldin convey this impression. Colonel Graham
was far too generous when he suggested Benteen was in his

sunset years when the letters were written. This is only a partial truth. The letters spanned a five year period which is an unconscionably long sunset for any man. Benteen was also vindictive and far from being a gallant, as his letters will reveal. Today, a number of his remarks printed here sound strongly racist, but on this score he must be judged by the standards of his times.

I find myself in full agreement only once in all these missives, and that is in the letter from Benteen which suggests Custer divided his command into four units and not the more popular version of three. Everyone, it appears, forgets about Captain McDougall, his forty-eight men and the pack-train. Everything else stated by Benteen, including his denunciation of almost every officer in the army, I take with a grain of salt. I also found it difficult to read these letters objectively when Benteen himself stated categorically in a letter to Goldin that he would write an unbiased evaluation of Custer and then proceeded to assassinate the dead man's character in the most disgusting and graphic terms possible. And then in his May 26, 1896, letter to Goldin he had the gall to state ". . . I do not want a doughboy to speak in any but respectful manner of a dead cavalryman." Evidently he felt he had the right since he was a retired cavalryman. His double standards are confusing! Last but not least, his full force attack on Mrs. Custer (as well as many ladies mentioned throughout the massive correspondence) labels him less than a gentleman and certainly not the paladin he pretends to be.

Benteen also proved to be a most gullible person when it came to Goldin. Colonel Graham made the point most clearly in his introduction to the expurgated letters in his book by stating Benteen believed Goldin to have served longer and participated in more campaigns than he actually did.

Theodore Goldin is yet another enigma. It is difficult for me to give credence to his "story" when none of his letters to Benteen survive and are therefore unavailable to researchers.

There are other factors, however, from which to judge. First, Goldin allowed Benteen to believe a portion of his personal military history which was not true. This had to be a deliberate attitude on his part. Second, he *sold* the letters from Benteen, a very personal correspondence. Third, the Medal of Honor awarded Goldin evidently came to him only after his prodding Benteen into acting on his behalf many, many years after everyone else in that daring "water party" had received theirs. This is made all the more suspect by the literary activities of Fred Dustin and E. A. Brininstool who wrote of Goldin later, more in the way of justification than anything else. Such heroics need no justification. Perhaps these factors would be considered flimsy to most, especially when being used as interpretative tools, but it is interesting to note that many of the Custer "character assassins" accomplished their deeds on lesser substantiation. The reports of Surgeon Lothrop and Lieutenant Colonel McQueen of the First Iowa Cavalry, who served under Custer in Texas in 1865-66, are examples of character assassination without foundation. Both their reports have stood as historical truths for too many years.

Regardless of interpretations and of personal biases, this collection of writings by these two gentlemen and others does constitute a remarkable wealth of historical documentation.

JOHN M. CARROLL

INTRODUCTION

BETWEEN OCTOBER 20, 1891, and August 12, 1896, there was an exchange of many letters between two members of the Seventh Cavalry who were at the Little Big Horn that fateful day—June 25, 1876. What is most remarkable about these letters is the fact they were exchanged between the retired officer who had commanded Company H, Seventh Cavalry, Captain (Brevet Brigadier General) Frederick W. Benteen, and an enlisted man, Private (later Colonel in the Wisconsin National Guard) Theodore W. Goldin (born John Stilwell), of Company G, Seventh Cavalry. This is unusual in that there were stringently observed rules of conduct in the military of those days which frowned upon fraternization of officers and enlisted men. It is true that Captain Benteen had been retired for some years when the communications began. This may have accounted for his relaxed attitude. Another theory, however, and one which seems logical, was that Benteen's knowledge of Theodore Goldin's colonelcy in the State National Guard made the relationship more palatable to him; and also, the two had shared a moment in American warfare which by 1891 had become an important incident in our history. The Battle of the Little Big Horn had already become a legend, and all those who had been connected with it were part of that legend.

To illustrate more fully the characters of the two major figures in this publication, the following biographical information from Kenneth Hammer's *Little Big Horn Biographies*, revised edition, 1965, is offered. To the biography of Theodore Goldin is added additional personal information taken from *Portrait and Biographical Album Of Rock County, Wisconsin*, compiler anonymous, published in Chicago by the Acme Publishing Company in 1889:

FREDERICK WILLIAM BENTEEN, Captain,
Company H

Commanding Company H in the hilltop fight.

Born on August 24, 1834 in Petersburg, Virginia. He entered military service from Missouri as a First Lieutenant, 10th Missouri Volunteer Cavalry on September 1, 1861. He was promoted to Captain on October 1, 1861 and engaged in the action at West Glaze and at Wilson's Creek and the skirmish at Salem. In 1862 he was in the action at Bolivar, the skirmish at Springfield, the skirmish at Sugar Creek, the battle at Pea Ridge, the skirmish at Batesville and at Cotton Plant and Kickapoo Bottom, the defense of Helena, the skirmish at Greenville and the action at Milliken's Bend. He was promoted to Major on December 19, 1862. In 1863 he was in the skirmish at Florence, the siege of Vicksburg, the action at Iuka, the capture of Jackson, the action at Brandon Station and the skirmish at Cane Creek. He was promoted to Lieut. Colonel on February 27, 1864. He was in the actions at Bolivar and Pleasant Hill and the action on the Big Blue and the Little Osage and at Charlot, the skirmish at Montevallo, the assault and capture of Selma and the raid on Columbus. He was honorably mustered out on June 30, 1865 and appointed Colonel, 138th, U.S. Colored Infantry until July 15, 1865. On June 6, 1865 he was recommended for Brig. General brevet, Missouri Militia. He was appointed Captain, 7th Cavalry to rank from July 28, 1866. He was brevetted Major, USA and Lieut. Colonel, USA on March 2, 1867 for his gallant and meritorious services in the battle of Osage and the raid on Columbus. He received the brevet of Colonel for his service in an engagement with hostiles on the Saline River on August 13, 1868. He participated in the Washita River fight on November 28, 1868. He fought in the Little Bighorn River fight on June 25, 1876 and was wounded in the right thumb and contracted malarious dysentry. Engaged in the Nez Perce campaign in 1877. In 1878 he commanded a battalion against hostile Indians. In 1879 he was detailed to appear at the Reno Court of Inquiry. He was promoted to Major, 9th Cavalry on December 17, 1882. He was court martialed at Fort Du Chesne, Utah and suspended from rank for one year at half pay. He retired on July 7, 1888 and resided in Atlanta. He received the brevet of Brig. General on February 27, 1890 for his service at the Little Bighorn and against the Nez Perce at Canyon Creek. General Benteen passed away in Atlanta on June 22, 1898 and was interred in the National Cemetery, Arlington, Virginia.

THEODORE W. GOLDIN, (born John Stilwell), Private, Company G
    In the valley and hilltop fights.
    Born on July 25, 1858 in Green County, Wis-

consin. Enlisted on April 8, 1876 at Chicago by
Lieut. Edmund Luff. Previous occupation was *brake-
man*. Cavalry duty was as headquarters clerk. Discharged on November 13, 1877 in the field in
Dakota Territory per paragraph 3, Special Order
Nr. 174, dated August 16, 1877, AGO, War Department, as a Private of good character, *because
of a concealed minority enlistment*. He had blue
eyes, brown hair, fair complexion and was 5' 7¾"
in height. On December 21, 1895, upon his own
application, he was awarded the Medal of Honor
as one of a party of volunteers who, under heavy
fire from the Indians, went for and brought water
to the wounded in the Little Bighorn River fight.
This medal is on display at Prairie du Chien. In
1904 he was chairman of the Republican Central
Committee in Wisconsin. He became a prominent
attorney and a Colonel in the Wisconsin National
Guard. He died on February 15, 1935. Interred in
King Veteran's Cemetery. Colonel T. W. Goldin,
General Staff, Wisconsin National Guard, was the
author of "Comment On A United States Army,"
Vol. XIII, p. 339 and "Meritorious Discharged Soldiers," May, 1891, Vol. XII, Nr. LI, pp. 660–661
in the Journal of the Military Service Institution.

Theodore W. Goldin, a member of the firm
of Dunwiddie & Goldin, Attorneys and Counsellors-
at-law of Janesville, is a native of Rock County, and
a son of Reuben W. Goldin. The family were
among the pioneers of this country. George Goldin,
the grandfather of our subject having become one
of its residents in 1844. He was a native of the
Empire State, thence emigrating to Rock County,
Wis., with his wife and children. Locating in the

town of Newark, he improved a farm, which he continued to cultivate for a number of years, but later made his home in the town of Spring Valley. About the year 1862 he removed to Green County, Wis., and after three years went to California, where he engaged in mining and other occupations until 1867, when he returned from the Golden State. In the meantime, his family had removed to Kansas, where he joined them and died several years later. He and his wife were the parents of four children— Anna, who married N. S. Gilbert, and resides at Evanston, Ill.; Reuben W., the next in order of birth; Elizabeth, the wife of C. G. Tozier, whose home is at Junction City, Kan.; and James W., who was a soldier in the War of the Rebellion, but several years later went to Black Hills, Mont.

Reuben W. Goldin was born in the State of New York, about the year 1820, and came with the family to Wisconsin. He later returned to the East for a bride and was united in marriage with Miss Elizabeth E. Bradfield a native of Columbiana County, Ohio. Soon after their marriage the young couple returned to Rock County, and began their domestic life upon a farm in Spring Valley Township, which Mr. Goldin engaged in cultivating. Several years later he went to Albany, Green Co., Wis., where he embarked in the harness and saddlery business and subsequently became a resident of Brodhead, where he continued in the same line until his death, which occurred in 1884. His widow is still residing in that city. Like his father, Reuben Goldin was an honorable, upright citzen descended from Quaker ancestry, and inherited the honesty of purpose that characterized that people. He was prominent in advancing the educational interests of the town in which he lived and was identified with those enterprises which tended to promote the best interests of the community.

Theodore W. Goldin, whose name heads this sketch, was the only child of Reuben W. and Elizabeth E. (Bradfield) Goldin. He was born in the town of Spring Valley, Rock Co., Wis., July 29, 1855, and received his primary education in the schools of Brodhead, supplementing it by a course in the Tilton University of Tilton, N. H., where he was a student for four years. Completing his literary studies, he enlisted at Chicago, in April, 1875, to serve in the Regular Army. He was assigned to the 7th Regular Cavalry, commanded by Gen. George A. Custer, who fell with the whole of his immediate army in the battle of Little Big Horn on the 25th day of June, 1876. At the time of the battle, which resulted so fatally to Gen. Custer and his command, Mr. Goldin was with Major Reno, but a short distance from the field of combat. He was present on the field soon after the massacre and assisted in burying the gallant General and his brave comrades. He took part in the fight with the Indians at Carrion Creek and Bear Paw Mountain, Montana. He was twice wounded in the second day's fight of the Little Big Horn, and those wounds resulted in his discharge for disability on the 29th day of September, 1879.

Mr. Goldin began the study of law at Brodhead, Wis., in 1881, with A. M. Randall, Esq., with whom he continued until the fall of 1882, when he was elected Clerk of the Circuit Court of Green County, a position he held until November, 1885, when he came to Janesville, and engaged in the practice of his profession, succeeding Pliny Norcross, as a partner of B. F. Dunwiddie. This is one of the leading law firms of Janesville, and the high reputation which it has won at the bar is well merited. Mr. Goldin was united in marriage with Miss Laura Dunwiddie, a sister of his partner, and a daughter of David Dunwiddie. To them have been born one child, a son—Herbert D. Our subject is a member of the staff of Gov. Hoard, in the capacity of Inspector of rifle practice, and is regarded as one of the leading citizens of Janesville.

Long after Captain Benteen's death, his letters to Theodore Goldin were sold to Mr. E. A. Brininstool of Los Angeles, a famed historian and a Little Big Horn enthusiast. He later sold them to Dr. Phillip G. Cole of New York. They were then sold to the Thomas Gilcrease Foundation after his death. But before the original letters found residence at the Gilcrease Foundation, Mr. Brininstool allowed Colonel W. A. Graham to make copies for his study, and from that typed set several copies have been made and distributed. However, before these famous letters are reviewed, it is important to note that several other people important to the Custer story were in correspondence with Theodore Goldin.

Of the many letters preceding the famed Benteen-Goldin Letters in this publication it would be difficult to opt for the one or group considered most important in the collection; they are all informative and revealing. I believe it is possible to gain a deeper insight into the character of Theodore W. Goldin by simply following his correspondence with others, even though they will appear out of chronological order, before examining those exchanged with Benteen.

[xxi]

As for myself, I have ambivalent feelings about Goldin. At times I became intensely angry at his denunciation of almost all the officers in the Seventh Cavalry and his "teasing" of us all with insinuations rather than with facts supporting his denunciations. At other times I am impressed with his straightforwardness and the way he never seems to stumble or falter when telling a fact for the umpteenth time. I am particularly impressed with his generosity toward Mrs. Custer.

The two letters from Goldin to Brininstool are the only two available for publication, although it is known there was a long period of correspondence between these men. The letters reveal nothing not already well documented, but it is interesting to note Goldin's observations on other people.

The extracts from letters written by Goldin to Albert Johnson are of extreme interest as personalities dominate them. It is difficult to determine who is responsible for the many parentheses, brackets and underlinings in the letters. Often these markings appear to have been part of Goldin's original letters, but throughout it is evident some belong to Fred Dustin, who made the extractions. This makes interpretation a dangerous thing. Nevertheless, lack of an answer to this question in no way lessens the value of the contents. Full capitalization of words and sentences obviously was intended by Dustin to mark immediate points of interest for himself, so they are duplicated here exactly as they appear in the transcription. Since originals of the letters are no longer available, there is no way of knowing their exact form.

The letters to Dr. Phillip Cole are of particular warmth and value, and they reveal a great deal about the "inner" Goldin. They also constitute valuable historical references and descriptions; one or two of them have never been published before.

One letter which still remains a puzzle is that of December 14, 1931—obviously in extract—since no one knows to whom it was addressed. Fred Dustin described it as "An Important Letter" when he made the transcription. It is a pity that he did not detail all the pertinent information at the same time.

Perhaps the most revealing of all the letters—including those from Benteen—was the series from Goldin to Fred Dustin. The first was written in February, 1932; the last in mid-December, 1934, two months prior to Goldin's death. Here, for the first time, is personal information of the kind that might have appeared in his earlier letters to Benteen, if they had not been lost. In reading these it is often possible to believe Goldin's letters were in answer to Benteen rather than to Dustin. Although the exchanges of information regarding the Masons has no pertinent relevance to the Custer story, they do tell us more about Goldin's private personality than is otherwise possible through interpretation of scanty information. This is important for it gives a frame of reference to the reader who has yet to evaluate Goldin's honesty and intention—if ever these were considered important enough for interpretation. And too, the personal insights—asides, as it were—on any number of important members in this drama are extremely valuable as contributions to historical interpretations.

As editor I was gratified to read in the December 31, 1932, letter to Dr. Cole that it was Mr. Goldin's desire that the letters would ". . . some day . . . find a resting place where the contents may be available to real searchers after the history of the Old West." Their publication here is intended for that very purpose. However, Mr. Goldin, then almost blind and residing in the Wisconsin Veterans' Home, had to rely on a touch-type system of corresponding with Brininstool and others and there was little room or care for corrections. This system left much to be desired, as Mr. Goldin states in one of his letters, so I have taken the liberty of correcting *some* punctuation and grammar only to make the letters more easily read and comprehended. Wherever possible I left the narratives within the letters untouched so as to retain and preserve the original flavor Theodore W. Goldin imparted to them.

JOHN M. CARROLL
Editor

THEODORE W. GOLDIN
TO
E. A. BRININSTOOL

Masonic Home, Dousman, Wis.,
December 26, 1927

Dear Mr. Brininstool:

I do not know when I have read anything that listens as good as this Brisbin Letter, which I am returning herewith.

It is the first thing I have ever seen telling of the details of that final conference and the subsequent movements of the Montana Column (as we all called Gibbon's outfit).

It tells a graphic story, *and if given to the world would start a controversy that would put all past ones in the shade,* and some day, possibly after Mrs. Custer has passed away, it may see the light.

While the sergeant major and I were getting our papers ready for storage on the boat, we could catch occasional snatches of the conversation, and from it we formed the idea that the attaching of Brisbin's squadron to the Seventh for that march, came up incidentally in the course of the talk on board the steamer, but what little we overheard might have been after talk, as I have no doubt Brisbin has told things as they were, as his letter was written at a time when there were

[3]

officers living who could have caught him up on any points wherein he misstated the facts, and as nothing of the sort ever came to the surface it is more than likely the facts were about as the old man stated them.

His quotation of the order issued by Terry coincides perfectly with my recollection of it. I believe, too, Mrs. Custer, in one of her books, quotes the order in the same language used by Brisbin, but I am not clear as to that.

We, at headquarters, never saw the order as it came to Custer, as it was retained by him, and was, as I recall it, transmitted to his wife in the last letter he wrote her, which was left at the boat when we hit the trail.

In the winter of '76-7, when we came to write up the records of the expedition in the regimental records, as I recall it, no copy of this order was to be found among the papers brought back from the field, but if I am not very much mistaken a copy was later procured and I think an examination of the old record books of the regiment will show a copy of this order in its proper place in the regimental order book. All this work was done by the regimental clerk, whose name I cannot now recall. He was a new man in the office however as his predecessor went down with Custer. I had nothing to do with the regimental records, aside from the "Letters Forwarded" book and the "Endorsement Book," in which I copied more or less of my own work.

It was well known throughout the Old Seventh, that the relations between Custer and Brisbin, were strained, and I believe I mention, either in my manuscript or a note thereto, what Benteen told me as to the origin of this feeling.

His statement as to what Terry said about what took place at Washington, in the Belknap matter, and which I have no doubt Brisbin states correctly, further the general idea that Custer hoped, by a coup, to redeem himself before the Army

[4]

and the world, and for that reason was disposed to take chances, and preferred to have no one with him who might, at a critical time, defeat his object.

His story of how Herendeen came to be with us, is just as I understood it at the time. The fact that Mitch Bouyer and the Crows had been acting with Gibbon's column was new to me, and yet I had never known definitely how they came to be with us.

You may have heard, or possibly read, of a rumor that was in circulation at Lincoln, even before the expedition left there, of a statement said to have been made by Custer, who was known to have felt chagrined that he was not sent out at the head of this expedition. This statement was to the effect that if the opportunity offered he would give Terry the skip, as he had given it to Stanley in '73, when the Seventh had the fight near the mouth of the Big Horn.

Custer denied this statement at the time it was made, and I never recall hearing of it later, until long after the battle.

Brisbin's story of that night march was entirely new to me in its details, although bits of it came to us at a later date during the summer.

His statement as to their coming up with Curley and the two other Crows who had been in the fight, rather negatives [negates?] the sensational story of Curley's appearance at the boat in an almost exhausted condition and the manner in which he made known the death of Custer's command.

His story of how Gibbon's command was picketing one side of the Yellowstone and the Indians the other, is new matter to me, as was the story of Bradley's trip across to scout out the outfit. Bradley may have made reference to this in some of his articles, but I cannot now recall ever having seen anything of this.

I recall the scout Muggins Taylor very distinctly and

[5]

always understood that it was he who guided Terry and his staff to Reno Hill.

On the whole I think the Old Major told the story as he knew it, and fairly correct. I can recall only a few minor details which are different than my own understanding of the matter, and am disposed to concede that he, being an officer, was more likely to have details straight than a mere man behind the guns.

In any event I surely want to thank you for the privilege of reading this letter.

Naturally Godfrey would not have made use of it, even had Brisbin failed to ask that it be treated as a matter only for officers of the Seventh.

I can imagine several reasons why, during all these years, it has never been made public. A desire to spare Mrs. Custer, a disinclination to further open up a controversy wherein both principals had passed over the divide, may have had its weight.

Again referring to the order issued by Terry, and I believe accurately quoted by Brisbin. Just a word:

I indistinctly recall some talk in the office regarding the necessity for having a copy of this order for the records, and a statement being made that an examination of Custer's effects in his field kit, might disclose such a copy, or if not a duplicate could be procured from department headquarters, but further than this I have no recollection, save a statement, either made in print or in my hearing, that the copy as recorded at department headquarters was not a copy of the order as it reached Custer, but had been changed to relieve Terry from possible responsibility.

All these things were rumors and made but little impression on my mind at the time and in the lapse of years have almost faded from recollection.

Again thanking you for a highly esteemed privilege, and wishing you a Happy and mighty prosperous New Year, I am

Sincerely yours,
Theo. W. Goldin

(Note by Brininstool: "Theodore W. Goldin had been appointed a regimental clerk on this expedition, and he was on the *Far West* in that capacity during the celebrated 'conference' between Terry, Custer and Gibbon. Goldin was a member of "G" Troop, 7th Cavalry.")

December 27, 1932

Dear Brininstool:

We did not finish reading the Pigford-Roberts[1] junk until yesterday but Mrs Goldin has it all tied up, directed and will take it to the office soon, this letter will reach you I hope about the same time, possibly not until 1933. Owing to the fact that Mrs. G. was somewhat under the weather from a persistent attack of some sort of stomach trouble we had to depend on one of her friends, a member of the Home, to read it for us and she was keenly interested and being a good reader we got the most out of the story. It was well written and

[1] The reference here is to the series of articles entitled "Two Men Who Were With Gallant General Custer At The Little Big Horn Battle Are Still Living" as told to Earle R. Forrest by Edward Pigford and George A. Roberts. They appeared in the newspaper, *Morning Observer*, Washington, Pennsylvania, between October 3 and October 19, 1932. Dustin (#107) says of these: "Some facts in these stories are of value, but parts of the Pigford revelation are imaginary; under the known conditions, impossible."

[7]

aside from that fool story about being in sight of the finish of the Custer outfit was, considering the time that has elapsed not so very far from the facts. As I recall it he was plainly in error in the statement that Isaiah Dorman[2] and the Rees comprised the party that pushed toward to the Crows Nest on the night of the 24th. My very distinct recollection is that it was Mich Bouler[3] and the Crows that rode with Varnum that night. As a matter of fact the Rees were in a strange country to them, knew nothing of it, while it was familiar territory to the Crows, but the thing that spilled the beans was that fool story about being sent out by French to get news of Custer and his claim to have reached a point within a few hundred yards of that last stand. You know as well as I do that there was no place within the distance he names where a white man could have remained concealed for a pair of minutes.

We never heard of any such act on the part of French. Weir in a fit of anger was insubordinate enough to move out with his troop and pushed ahead on the trail with some speed, so that in the event Pigford had been sent out he would have had to pass Weir and we know that Weir never reached a point where the fighting was visible to his command and was still pressing forward when the Indians suddenly appeared in his front in large numbers, causing him to retreat in a hurry. To me that part of the Pigford story smells like spoiled fish and makes it very evident that Pigford was not familiar with the terrain in the vicinity of Custer Hill, and it is such stuff as this that is being foisted on the public as history, possibly by men who mean well but who have never taken the trouble to investigate matters and learn actual conditions.

[2] The only black man at the battle.
[3] Mitch Bouyer.

[8]

The Roberts story is even more full of holes than a housewife's skimmer, but he has the honesty to admit that he was not among the last survivors.

His first bad break comes when he tells of arriving at Lincoln just at the time Custer left for the east to appear before that Court of Inquiry, and that his brotherinlaw, Capt. Yates was left in command of the post, and that Yates made him Adjutant. The idea that the regular staff officers were chased off the field for a civilian is laughable to any man at all familiar with Army life. All the way through this story it gives to me evidence of being made up of stories that we have all heard many times. Roberts may have been on the herd as he claims, I only recall Autie Reed and a young fellow named Garland, a son of a lieut. of that name, these were the only two aside from the chief herder who were with the herd so far as I can now recall and they were not in Government employ but in the employ of the beef contractor and paid by him. He also tells of his cayuse getting a dose of glanders[4] while at the Rosebud and that unable to secure another mount he remained behind. Cannot imagine where he stayed at, so far as I can recall after Terry moved out with Gibbon's command and the infantry followed the departure of the Seventh, there was nothing left at the mouth of the Rosebud as Gibbon's wagon train had started down the river to join the main supply camp at or across the mouth of the Powder River. My recollection is that this train was in motion before we left on the 22d, but I am not positive as to this. The Roberts story listens to me like the gathering together of a lot of camp rumors and stories rather than the narrative of the experiences

[4] Goldin has reference to the disease, glanders. This disease is defined as a contagious and destructive one—especially to horses—caused by a bacterium and characterized by caseating nodular lesions that tend to break down and form ulcers.

[9]

of one man, but I can see nothing to be gained on my part
by trying to pick it to pieces, it will be foisted on the public
as history and you and I have learned by bitter experience
how futile is any attempt to get such stuff as this corrected
and how, time and time again so called and considered reputable publications have turned down stories capable of being
proven by the records and grabbed at stuff like the Pigford
and Roberts stories like a hungry trout at a grasshopper.

I imagine you received from Dr. Cole one of his unique
and interesting Christmas cards, one came to me which I
intend to acknowledge.

That makes me think, up to this morning I have not
received returns from the draft left with the Old National
Bank here for collection Dec. 14th. When I took the draft
to the bank they did not seem to want to let go of that amount
of currency but stated that they would prefer accepting it for
collection. It will be two weeks tomorrow since I left it with
them taking their receipt and Saturday when I called up or
had the adjutant call up for me their answer was that they
thought likely they would have returns today. I'll call up
later today and if there is no dough I'll begin to make things
blue around that penny ante bank, not apparently financially
strong enough to cash a $500.00 draft.

I have not heard from or of Ostrander in a long while,
hope he is still with us as the world would be a good bit more
lonesome were I to learn that he had gone west.

Our cold weather left us over a week ago and since then
we have had rain, warm weather, just one flurry of snow, a
kind of weather we are not used to.

Mrs. Goldin joins me in an earnest wish for a Happy and
PROSPEROUS New Year.

Yours till the game is called

Goldin

EXTRACTS FROM LETTERS
WRITTEN BY
THEODORE W. GOLDIN
LATE A MEMBER OF THE
SEVENTH U.S. CAVALRY
WHO TOOK PART IN THE
CUSTER FIGHT JUNE 25-26, 1876
TO
ALBERT W. JOHNSON,
MARINE-ON-ST. CROIX,
MINNESOTA

[First letter dated at Masonic Home, Dousman, Wisconsin.]

April 21, 1928

States that he had completed a story of the campaign in collaboration with E. A. Brininstool.

April 30, 1928

States that he is a Past Grand Commander, Knights Templar, Wisconsin, also is a 33rd Degree Mason.

Was on the roll of McIntosh's troop, "G," but that the greater part of his service was as a clerk at headquarters.

May 18, 1928

States he became a thirty-second Degree Mason in 1896.

May 31, 1928

States that he did not receive the Medal of Honor until many years later, under Grover Cleveland's administration when D. Lamont was Secretary of War, and the investigation was made by Assistant Secretary J. B. Doe, and Lamont, and that it was presented in open court at Janesville, Wisconsin.

[13]

June 10, 1928

"I was at headquarters from the time we left Ft. Lincoln until I turned back on the 25th, with that first message to Reno."

"I have always been at a loss to understand how it was that I was the only one of our party who went after water, who [did not receive] the Congress medal, while members of "D" troop and others were awarded it."

"Many disliked him [Custer]. I liked him much, as I did and do Mrs. Custer . . . but cold facts are hard to controvert . . . I will be sorry if the existing stories and documents see the light, save as they may serve to lift the cloud from the memory of men who are dead, and whose character and motives were assailed by ill-advised friends of Custer, in their attempts to clear him of blame."

July 28, 1928

"Mrs. Custer . . . a loyal, loving wife she was, and every man's heart bled for her . . . this and this alone to-day is and will be as long as she lives, be responsible for the suppression of a lot of matters that may throw a clearer light on that campaign . . . her loving loyalty to the General was respected, even though there were those who felt she was worshipping an image of clay. I do not say this unkindly, as I saw much of Custer, and admired him in many ways. It has been permitted me to read much of this matter that has been suppressed, and you can I think judge something of the regard in which Mrs. Custer is held, when I tell you that for fifty years this matter has been well-known to officers and a few men of the old army.

"I have had men, good soldiers too, write me of their hairbreadth escapes, page after page—AND THEY KNEW THEY WERE LYING WHEN THEY WROTE THEM, AND KNEW THAT I KNEW IT. . . . What gets me . . . is

[14]

that high-class publications will grab and publish this rot and ask for more, while they turn down stories capable of being proved from the records."

Theodore W. Goldin to Albert W. Johnson

August 3, 1928

[Referring to reporters and publishers] "I can sympathize with him [D. F. Barry] in his annoyance at the way the reporters cut his article . . . Twice, on the solemn promise that it [his article] should appear just as it was written, only to see it assaulted, battered, mistreated and maltreated, and a lot of cock and bull stuff inserted to give it thrill stories told by would-be heroes."

October 3, 1928

Mentions a large white cross on Reno Hill, which seems to have been knocked down. "This cross is the center of Reno's final position, and if placed where we set the flag, June 26, 1926, is about where our hospital and corral was located during the fight. . . . The body of the Unknown Soldier . . . was found not very far from the point occupied by "G" Troop in the earliest moments of the fight. THERE IS A BIT OF UNCERTAINTY AS TO HOW CLOSE THIS MARKER IS TO WHERE MCINTOSH WAS REALLY BURIED, as the Indian on whose allotment the grave is located admits having moved the stone once or twice, but claims that where it is located now is where it was when he first moved it, and in any event, the location is approximately correct.

"The ravine down which we went for water was upstream from the one up which Reno's men made their way in retreat. It starts down midway the position occupied by "B" and "H" Troops. Slaper and I located this ravine very definitely and followed its windings down to the river, on the 26th of June, 1926.

"A chapter I was supposed to have written for C. T.

[15]

Brady's book . . . which Brady without my knowledge re-
wrote to meet his ideas of that campaign . . . the article in
question . . . was so different from the one I dictated as to be
to me almost unrecognizable."

October 14, 1928
"The marker for Dr. DeWolfe is correctly placed. In 1926
I went over the lines with Godfrey, and while we may not
have been able to locate them within a few yards, he was not
far off on his designations.

"The ravine used by the Indians in their attack on
Benteen's position, was not the ravine we used in going after
water, but still farther up the stream to the south. There were
several small draws in front of Benteen's position, converging
into one larger one at the point where the Indians massed
for attack. These were the ones used by the Indians and were
in use by them when we went for water. We saw no evidence
that the ravine we used had been occupied by the Indians up
to the time our last trip, but it may have been later; this,
however, would have brought the Indians out at a point between Benteen and McDougall . . . I just returned to Mr.
Brininstool the front case of a hunting case watch, picked
up by him in the bottom, I believe in 1915. No other part of
the watch was found."

October 20, 1928
"As to Russell White Bear there is little to be said. He married
Curley's squaw after Curley died. . . . I had one of his maps.
His locations of the various bands of Indians is fairly good.
I went over the location of the village with a Cheyenne chief
who was in the battle, and who pointed out as well as he
could under present topographical conditions the [?]. There
have been a number of changes in the river since the fight.

I have never been entirely clear . . . where Reno first crossed *Theodore W. Goldin*
to Albert W. Johnson
the Little Big Horn as I did not cross with his outfit, and have
never found two who did, who agree as to the exact point of
his crossing but I think the map made by the engineers in '77
fairly shows it, as it does other points on both the Custer and
Reno fields.

"At the time of the fight the entire bottom was covered
with a growth of high sage brush, clumps of bullberry bushes,
and high, rank grass, making it very difficult at the present
time to determine locations accurately. . . . At the time of
the fight, along back from the river was quite a growth of
cottonwoods, all of which have been cut down, entirely changing the appearance of the valley. I have only an indistinct
recollection of the terrain in the vicinity of the point where
Reno crossed in retreat, only visiting it briefly after the fight
was over. I know at the time of the battle there was a cutbank
on both east and west sides of the stream, which at that time
was from knee deep to belly deep on the horses, and the men
spoke of having trouble in forcing their horses to take the
plunge, and in several instances men reported that in trying
to negotiate the cutbank on the eastern side, where they came
out, a number of horses fell back, but that in a few moments
the bank was pawed off so that a landing could be made.
Herendeen and I forded the river on foot at least 150 and
possibly 200 yards further down stream, finding the water
where we entered fully breast deep and running strong but
shelving up onto a shallow gravel bottom a short distance
below where we crossed [This was the place where the Ree
and Crow scouts crossed—F.D.][1] . . . So far as I could see,
the Indians made no direct rush on the lines (at the ford)

[1] F.D. is Fred Dustin, noted Custer historian.

but seemed to be circling on the flank southward as though
to prevent the men from taking the back trail. Apparently
they were resting their guns across their bodies or ponies and
firing without much attempt at aim. . . . Quite a few men,
including Lieut. Hodgson were killed after they had made the
crossing on that little flat at the foot of the hills up which they
were forcing their way.

"The Hodgson marker was placed almost at the point
were Reno halted after reaching the bluffs.

"Some day when Mrs. Custer has passed away it may be
that the mass of stuff that has been suppressed . . . will find
its way into print, and I can imagine the sensation some of
these would-be historians are going to experience when confronted by indisputable evidence.

"I wish Varnum and Hare might be induced to dictate
their stories ere it is too late. Varnum kicks against it, and
Hare has always even refused to answer letters regarding the
fight, just why I could never understand. I saw a bit of him
during the World War. He talked frankly of everything else
but closed up like the traditional clam when the subject of
the Little Big Horn was brought up."

October 27, 1928
"I had a rather amusing experience with Col. Bates at the
celebration . . . took and read his pamphlet . . . made an
appointment with him, but later gave him my ideas along
certain lines, which were very evidently not in harmony with
his views and plans, as he never kept the appointment. He . . .
was bitter toward Reno and Benteen. . . . I failed to agree
with many of his theories which were untenable. That's been
the trouble all these years.

"I have always given preference to the Maguire map as

it best coincides with my own recollections. Gen. Godfrey and I have never been in accord as to the point where Custer came on the field. . . .

Theodore W. Goldin to Albert W. Johnson

"We found the bodies of a number of men and horses of "E" Troop (the white horse). To all appearance they had angled off across the hillside, finally entering a narrow coulee . . . which proved to be a veritable cul de sac, ending with a high bank in front and on both sides of them. Here they were apparently shot down, men and horses together. It was impossible to reach them and we shoveled dirt from the overhanging bank to cover them.

"If you have studied the topography of the field you will recall that there were only two places where this was possible (for Reno's men to see Custer's column on the other side of the river) one was as they passed the opening that marked the ravine up which Reno afterward retreated, and the other at the point where I have always contended that Custer entered the valley, and near where the two trails shown on the map (Maguire) divided, but I'm doubtful whether at this point any troop movements were visible from Reno's position. [It was not possible for any of Reno's men to see Custer at the latter point, as his command did not get there before Reno left the valley, unless he made much better time than has been reckoned.—F.D.]

"The absence of the heavy timber in the bottoms made it very hard for me to accurately determine locations on my later visits to the field, and it was only by locating the Reynolds marker, the grave of Lieut. McIntosh and lining them with the marker at De Wolf's grave that I was finally able to determine locations of points held by Reno's force.

"The place pointed out to me was not far from the line occupied by McIntosh's troop before he swung back into the heavy timber, and I recall seeing other bodies between the Reynolds marker and the river, most of them not far from McIntosh's grave. These were I believe, as were all who fell near the crossing, buried by the 2nd Cavalry and the 7th Infantry."

November 4, 1928

"Before Custer made his final swing to the right and pushed into the bluffs, we already heard firing in the bottom below us, indicating that Reno had already engaged the enemy, and as I now recall it, it was at about this point where Custer left the head of the column and followed only by Color Sergt. Hughes, and Custer's striker, rode over toward the edge of the bluffs . . . but he was gone only a few moments. [This introduces an interesting *possible* fact, that Custer might naturally do so under the circumstances.—F.D.]

"In the disposition of our command on the bluffs, the formation was much in the shape of a horseshoe, the opening toward the river, but covered by a cross fire from either end of the formation. For a time "G" Troop held one end of this horseshoe, and "H" Troop under Benteen, the other, but the Indians were crowding Benteen hard, and he insisted on reinforcements, and "B" Troop under McDougall moved over and took position near where the ravines broke down hill, the remaining troops were deployed to complete the formation and McDougall was able to afford him substantial aid at critical times.

"I found but few apparent changes in the river from those shown in the Maguire Map.

"From what I have learned from letters from Mrs. Godfrey and others, I much fear that Gen. Godfrey would be apt to err . . . on certain locations, although in 1926 I found him very accurate as to anything within his personal knowledge, but . . . somewhat at sea regarding points where he did not operate."

Theodore W. Goldin
to Albert W. Johnson

November 18, 1928

"In regard to that night march on the 24th of June, I will say that I have talked with officers and men, and found that none of them had a clear recollection as to time, from that time until many hours later, in fact after Reno's retreat to the bluffs . . . Since leaving the Yellowstone each man had carried on his saddle a twelve quart sack of oats . . . but several of us decided that our horses could better carry this supply inside than out, and as soon as it was dark . . . we slipped out and fed the grain to our tired horses. I was not far from headquarters with the Sergeant-Major and old Sergeant Hughes, Color Sergt., but were not near enough to hear any of the conversation . . . Most of our Indians were squatting on the ground near headquarters, and soon after this we saw Lieuts. Varnum and Hare pass us. . . . An hour later . . . we were back on the trail. . . . It must have been well after midnight when we halted and it was at this point close to the base of the high divide between the Rosebud and the Little Big Horn. Near where we halted was an alkali stream or a series of pools, but thirsty as the horses were they refused to drink it. Here as I recollect, an attempt was made to make coffee, but the water was so strongly alkaline, being of the color of strong lye, we could not drink the stuff. Here . . . the final division of the command was announced. . . . From the point where we crossed the divide we thought we could see the smoke from the village, but of course were uncertain."

November 24, 1928

[Wading the river to rejoin his command] "I was hatless and coatless and up to my middle in the water. I reached the top of the bluffs about the time that Benteen's men were dismounting, and the officers were gathered on a slight elevation not far from where the Hodgson marker is now located."

December 8, 1928

"I was with two [water] parties, or rather our little party made two trips. On the first one we saw no Indians save at a distance and were not discovered. On the second trip we were fired upon by a small party from across the river, and one of our men was wounded, but on neither trip did we encounter Indians on our side of the river, but I heard rumors that . . . other parties were fired on from the east side of the river.

". . . Timber conditions in the bottom where Reno first attacked [?]. In the vicinity of the river and along what was probably a former channel of the stream and in which Reno took position after he . . . was forced to change position, there was a forest . . . of good sized cottonwoods, in which there was sagebrush, bullberry thickets and considerable rank grass. When the retreat to the bluffs was decided on, some of the officers and many of the men understood it was to be a charge. It seemed to be the idea that we were to charge through the Indians (between us and the first crossing) in an attempt to reach Benteen . . . but when we rode out of the timber we found the head of the column headed for the bluffs and the Indians swarming in on our right. My horse was tied to a clump of brush some little distance from where I dismounted to deliver my message and where he was pretty well concealed. When I came out in the bottom, I saw the direction the outfit was heading . . . and I headed straight for the river some yards to the left of the main column, and when my horse fell and I made for the brush, I found myself perhaps a hundred yards down river from the Reno crossing, but in plain sight of what was going on. . . . There was quite a party of men whose horses had been killed or stampeded, and they came out later . . . under the leadership of the scout Herendeen. . . . They were discovered working their way through the timber, and Lieut. Hare crept out on the side of the hill and flagged them to come ahead, as at that time there were few Indians in our vicinity. I saw no one in this party who was severely wounded, although *there were* wounded men in the party."

December 16, 1928
"There is no record of any men ever coming back from Custer's column and either joining Reno or Benteen, none save Martin and one man who left just before he did. So far as I have ever been able to learn, there is no record of any such incident . . . Martin told me he saw no Indians at close range except just after he left Custer. . . . Sergt. Wm. Slaper . . . took issue with Thompson at Crow Agency in '26 and came near precipitating a riot, but stood his ground.

"When De Rudio received his captaincy and was assigned to "E" Troop, he secured O'Neil's transfer and made him his first sergeant."

December 16, 1928
"Girard was with us and went out as an interpreter. . . . He was a good interpreter, but very dissipated, so much so that it was hard for him to secure and retain a job in the government service. He died in a hospital in St. Joseph, Mo.

"Godfrey and I have always differed as to the point where Custer came into the valley. I have always contended that he came in at the point on the Maguire map, while he carries the column down behind the bluffs, bringing them on the field not far from where Calhoun's men went down. The

[23]

Maguire map was made in 1877 [the map, the *original*, was made on the ground June 27, 1876, by Maguire and his Sergeant, Becker.—F.D.] from actual surveys and observations. Just where Godfrey got the data for his map I never knew . . . but as I went over the trail with Martin on June 28 . . . going to the point where he said he turned back with the dispatch for Benteen, the trail over which he took me seems to correspond with that shown on the Maguire map."

January 1, 1929

[Goldin says that Godfrey claimed that Girard, Jackson, O'Neil, and De Rudio all came in at the same time, but Goldin says: "I am forced to differ with him," as well he might. Godfrey was too cock-sure.—F.D.]

[There seems to be some mix-up in regard to Girard and Grouard: in a former letter Goldin states that *Girard* died in St. Joseph, Missouri, but in this letter of January 1, 1929, he says it was *Grouard* that died in St. Joseph.] "I understood that Girard went to Minneapolis where he developed into an Indian doctor, and that he died there sometime in the late 80's."

January 17, 1929

Goldin speaks of a review of Frazier Hunt's *The First of the Cavaliers*, by one Capt. Thomason, in which the latter burns up Hunt. Goldin says: "I am sorry that this review will . . . cause Mrs. Custer grief and annoyance. But for years this writer and that, using the slogan 'Save Mrs. Custer annoyance and heart-aches' as a smoke screen, have gone on and on, writing misinformation and calling it history. . . . Some of them, perhaps all of them must know or should know, that held in leash is an overwhelming mass of incontrovertible facts, liable some day to sweep down like an avalanche and engulf their card-board edifices. . . . In their assaults on the characters of men as brave, if not as reckless as Custer . . . They have grown a bit reckless.

Speaking of Varnum, Goldin says: "In Col. Varnum you have an officer and a gentleman of the Old School. He is a man for whom I always entertained a high regard . . . he had the regard and confidence of his fellow officers and of every enlisted man who served under him, as did but few officers of the Seventh."

February 24, 1929

"The only thing I ever heard Martin say regarding Indians (on his lone trip back to Benteen) was that his horse was wounded by a long range shot from somewhere over toward the river."

March 1, 1929

"I have always understood that Custer, at that time [his visit to the Crow's Nest] had no good field glasses, but used a telescope belonging to someone in the scouting party, and in this I am confirmed by a statement in one of Capt. Benteen's letters to me."

Goldin says in this letter, regarding his (Custer) being seen by De Rudio, ". . . we were approaching the point where Reno's intrenchments were later established, and while yet some distance from them I saw Custer leave . . . bearing off to the left. . . . Where he went and what he saw I know not."

March 24, 1929

"I saw a recent letter from Mrs. Godfrey not long ago in which she admitted what I always contended, ie., that Godfrey made a number of changes in his Century article when he re-wrote it for the use of the Battlefield Association in 1922, at

[25]

the unveiling of the medalion monument to Custer at Hardin, Mont. She says that after the publication of the Century article Godfrey talked and corresponded with many of the officers, and when he came to re-write it, he omitted a number of things that were in the original."

September 30, 1929

"You speak of the unexploded cartridge you found near what seemed to be some breastworks thrown up to protect the water parties. I do not recall even seeing these rifle pits, unless they were the ones dug on the night of the 26th when the Indians left us. Our positions were changed that night and pits dug nearer the edge of the bluffs, which would have afforded protection to water-carriers."

November 6, 1929

". . . the wounds in Custer's body as I saw them June 27, were made by a gun of smaller caliber than the .45, and we calculated it may have been from a Winchester or Henry. There were no powder marks about the wounds at all . . . When I visited the field in 1924, we had an old Indian take us across Reno Creek in his wagon, and when on the bluff just south of Reno intrenchments, he pointed out the Crow's Nest."

December 30, 1929

"General Godfrey and I do not agree as to the point where Custer entered the valley. From every indication I have always contended he entered as shown by the Maguire map, while Godfrey shows him going in near the top of the ridge. IN GOING IN THERE WITH THE BURIAL PARTY, AND ALSO WHEN VISITING THE FIELD WITH LIEUT. BRADLEY'S PARTY ON JUNE 27, WE FOLLOWED A WELL-MARKED TRAIL OF SHOD HORSES THROUGH

[26]

THIS DRAW, AS I RECOLLECT IT, THE FIRST BREAK IN THE HIGH BLUFFS . . . IT WAS THERE THAT WE PICKED UP AND FOLLOWED THAT FAINTLY DEFINED TRAIL LEADING OFF TO THE LEFT ALONG THE SIDE OF THE BLUFFS, WHILE THE MAIN TRAIL LED BACK TO THE POINT WHERE CALHOUN'S TROOP WAS FOUND . . . IN GOING BACK OVER THE TRAIL WITH MARTIN ON THE 28TH, HE POINTED TO A PLACE NOT FAR FROM THIS OPENING INTO THE VALLEY, AS THE POINT WHERE HE TURNED BACK, AND SAID THE COLUMN WAS MOVING NORTHWESTERLY WHEN HE LEFT IT."

Theodore W. Goldin
to Albert W. Johnson

January 15, 1930

"I FORMED MY OPINION ON WHAT WE SAW WHEN VISITING THE FIELD ON THE 27TH WITH BRADLEY AND AGAIN . . . ON THE 28TH . . . WE TURNED IN AT AN OPENING [little coulee] FOLLOWING A WELL-MARKED TRAIL OF SHOD HORSES NOT VERY FAR FROM THE SOUTHWEST CORNER OF THE PRESENT FENCED ENCLOSURE. THIS BROUGHT US TO THE FIRST GROUP OF SEVERAL SOLDIERS, NOW MARKED BY HEADSTONES, AND IT WAS FROM THIS POINT WE DISCOVERED THE FAINT TRAIL LEADING ALONG THE LOWER EDGE OF THE BLUFF [Battle Ridge] TO THE POINT WHERE WE FOUND THE MEN AND HORSES OF SMITH'S TROOP IN WHAT PROVED TO THEM TO BE A CUL DE SAC, AND MEN AND HORSES WERE PILED UP TOGETHER, AND THE ODOR WAS SUCH THAT WE DID NOT GET DOWN TO THEM, BUT SHOVELED DIRT FROM THE TOP COVERING THEM IN ONE BIG GRAVE.

"FROM THE POINT WHERE WE FOUND THE

[27]

FIRST BODIES THERE WAS EVIDENCES OF SHOD HORSES IN BROKEN ORDER, LEADING BACK IN THE DIRECTION WHERE WE LATER FOUND CALHOUN'S TROOP.

[Concerning hearing heavy volleys] "Herendeen and I, while still in the river bottom, after being dismounted, heard them, distinctly, and Herendeen remarked: "That's Custer and he has found more Indians than he can handle, just as I expected, and he's asking for help. Later after I had crossed the river and while Herendeen was bringing out his party of dismounted men, I reported these volleys and was a bit surprised to be told they were not heard by the force on the bluffs. This seemed to be strange at the time, but later among a group of officers, and some one remarked that it would be easy to determine by putting a company of infantry on Custer Hill, while officers with compared watches went to Reno Hill, and at an agreed time three volleys were fired, BUT WERE NOT HEARD ON RENO HILL." [Not at all strange! Intervening ridges, and over four miles distance, wind conditions might strongly effect.—F.D.]

January 27, 1930

"Some years ago I talked with two of the men who accompanied Lieut. (now General) Hugh L. Scott when they visited the field to remove the bodies of Custer and the other officers. They told me that after locating the bodies of the officers, Lieut. Scott had a long trench dug right on top of the ridge, and that they went over the field with a wagon gathering up all the bones they could find and placed them in the trench, which was then filled up, and then at the head of the trench built up a monument of rocks surmounted by a buffalo skull, which monument was at the point where the present monument stands.

[28]

"I asked these men at the time if they were at all sure that they recovered the bones of the officers; one of them promptly replied 'No, we took some pains to gather with each body bones enough to make a complete skeleton, but as most of the bodies had been exposed by foxes and coyotes, and in several instances portions of bodies had been dragged away, we were not at all certain as to the identity of any of the bodies, save that we gathered them near the point where the marker indicated they had been originally buried.'

"I could understand this, as I know that on my visit to the field in 1924 I found a hand and forearm, and a foot and lower part of a leg far distant from any marker, and each widely separated from the other, and others, residents and visitors, have told me of similar finds, but I have always felt that it was better not to discuss these features out of regard to the feelings of those who mourned them."

*Theodore W. Goldin
to Albert W. Johnson*

January 27, 1930

"IT MAY BE THAT THERE WAS A DIVISION OF THE COMMAND AND THAT AN ENTRANCE WAS MADE BOTH AT THE POINT NEAR THE SOUTHEAST CORNER OF THE PRESENT FENCED FIELD AND UP ON THE RIDGE AS CONTENDED BY GODFREY. IF THERE WAS SUCH A DIVISION IT TOOK PLACE AFTER MARTIN HAD TURNED BACK."

February 8, 1930

"The bodies were poorly interred for three reasons: . . . we were poorly provided with picks, shovels and axes. . . . In the second place, the ground was so hard it could not be loosened with shovel or spade, and required a pick to make an impression on it; third, the bodies were in such a state of mortification that they could not be handled to move them. I

[29]

saw instances where men taking hold of an arm often found it to come loose from the body, so all we were able to do was to heap dirt or even sagebrush over the remains and leave them to the mercy of the coyotes, wolves and vultures. I believe that in most cases, at least those that came under my observation, extra efforts were made to inter the bodies of officers."

June 1, 1930

"YOU LIKE MYSELF, have often been disgusted by the many stories that have come to you. . . . For many years I made an effort to contradict these stories, but many of them, published by reputable publications, were allowed to stand as the publications declined my articles based on facts and records."

September 11, 1930

"Hare was always adverse to having anything said that would pain Mrs. Custer, although he was not of the Custer faction of the regiment."

September 25, 1930

". . . If you have ever climbed to the Crow's Nest as I have, and have in mind the extent of that village, YOU WILL REALIZE THAT EVEN FROM THIS VANTAGE POINT, THE ENTIRE VILLAGE WAS NOT VISIBLE ANY MORE THAN THE WHOLE PONY HERD AND SOME SMALL COLUMNS OF SMOKE WERE. I have reason to know that Custer, after his return from the Crow's Nest, was warned by Mitch Bouyer that there were more Indians down in that valley than he, Custer, could handle with his force. I OVER-HEARD THAT MUCH, but did not hear the remark of Bouyer that he was not afraid to go wherever Custer went, but if they went down in that valley they would wake up in

Hell the next morning. . . . That came to me through an officer since deceased."

Theodore W. Goldin
to Albert W. Johnson

January 1, 1931

"I recall both Half Yellow Face and White Swan, and if my memory serves me right it was the former who threw me the end of his rope when I had lost my footing in fording the river and could not regain it owing to the swiftness of the current, and the many smooth rocks in the river bottom. I saw him just as I lost my footing, and took him at first for an enemy and remember that I said my 'Now I lay me down to sleep,' expecting nothing but a shot. He was on the bank of the river some distance below where our men crossed on a sort of gravel bar jutting out into the stream. A second glance told me he was a Crow and I sure grabbed that rope as it whirled past me and he pulled me ashore and pointed the way to our men on the bluffs and then rode into the stream signing to me that he was going after hair and horses. I saw him later as I gave White Swan and Half Yellow Face a drink out of my canteen on our return from the second trip for water. I saw him again in '77 when he was my sponsor in some ceremony of adoption as his 'White Brother' because as he said, I had been good to him and a wounded brave (White Swan) on the hill with Reno. . . . This ceremony took place at the Crow Mission on the Stillwater and Little Rosebud while we were waiting for orders as to our movements against the Nez Perces."

July 13, 1931

Goldin again speaks of Half Yellow Face. He was watering his pony when Goldin lost his footing in the river and Half Yellow Face threw him the end of his lariat. Goldin was seventy-three on July 25, 1931.

[31]

July 27, 1931

" 'I' Troop lay in a slight depression and looked as though it had been formed IN A HOLLOW SQUARE with KEOGH and one or two others in the center . . . Sturgis' marker southward of the monument, a bit east perhaps.

"Madden was wounded between the edge of the river and a clump of brush and a bit of a mound behind which we remained concealed save when in twos with a small camp kettle we made a dash for the river, filling the kettle and dashing back to the shelter and there filling the canteens. We found the ravine hard to negotiate when we were loaded down with canteens, and even worse when we had to get Madden up the hill."

September 11, 1931

Speaking of his disputed "message to Reno from Custer," Goldin says, "I turned back from Custer's column nearly or quite a half-mile down stream from Hodgson's marker."

October 5, 1931

"While on the Mexican border I ran across a Maj. Porter and learned he was the son of Dr. Porter, our only surgeon in the fight, and that the old Doctor was still living in Bismarck. . . . The son is or was constructing quartermaster . . . at Whipple Barracks, Arizona.

"My recollection is that we saw nothing to indicate that the White Horse Troop approached the river much nearer the point where they entered the valley, but the trail seemed to lead . . . diagonally along the hillside and away from the river until it ended in that dead-end ravine where the bodies of men and horses were found.

"WE HAD QUITE A NUMBER OF DISMOUNTED RECRUITS WHO . . . WERE LEFT AT THE SUPPLY CAMP AT POWDER RIVER.

"Martin and myself went back to the point where he turned back with Custer's message to Benteen, WHICH WAS NOT FAR FROM THE POINT WHERE THE TRAIL OF THE WHITE HORSE TROOP LEFT THE MAIN COLUMN AND SWUNG TO THE LEFT AND ENTERED THE VALLEY BY WAY OF WHAT SEEMED TO ME A DRY CREEK BED. The main trail must have kept on northerly, back of the bluffs."

Theodore W. Goldin to Albert W. Johnson

December 14, 1931

"In forming his line, Reno brought "A" Troop on his right, "M" Troop in the center and "G" Troop on the left . . . the Indian scouts on the extreme left. The Indians seem to have regarded this as the weak place in the line and massed for an attack there."

December 29, 1931

"You have several times expressed a wonder at my recollection of incidents and details concerning the Sioux campaign of 1876. . . . I was a young man then, clear-minded and trained from early childhood to habits of keen observation. I of course did not see all that happened, but I did see much, and learned more first-handed from officers and comrades and stored it away in an orderly manner. To that can be added that pretty much ever since I left the service I have been in more or less close contact with the subject . . . written much in a fragmentary way, sought by careful correspondence to clear things up where there was a bit of doubt . . . as to my own memory. Then when you take into consideration that for the past five years I have been unable to read, and forced to live much in the past, all the time keeping more or less in touch with this campaign, I think the matter has solved itself. . . . From time to time I have checked up with official records and reports and found them supporting my own well-formed recollections.

". . . I distinctly recall seeing moccasin tracks in considerable number at the ford where we crossed the river after burying Custer's men . . . we thought they were made by the squaws, old men and boys as they crossed the stream to strip . . . Custer's dead, but the story you wrote of has in it the appearance of truth, and that Indians in considerable numbers crossed the river on foot or more likely were carried across two or three on one pony.

"For a long time there was a report current that the body of 'Jack' Sturgis was not identified, but I later found a stone well down the hillside toward the river marking his grave . . . in 1924, so took it that his body was identified and the location of the grave marked at the time of his burial. (This also applies to Dr. Lord, so that it would seem that Porter and Harrington were really the only ones not identified.—F.D.)

"In burying the bodies we spread out from the point where the first bodies were found . . . (The end of the hogback nearest the gate toward Medicine Tail) in a sort of skirmish line advance we covered the entire field so that only the men in each sector saw the bodies in their front, so that it isn't strange that there were errors of judgment and in failure to report all the bodies who were really identified."

January 6, 1932

"Am just in receipt of a letter from a man [Ghent!—F.D.] in Washington bringing up a new question. He says there is a story that Reno, on the night of June 25 proposed to Benteen to abandon the position, leaving such of the wounded as were unable to ride, to their fate. Inasmuch as he did not have even the courtesy to enclose a stamp, my reply will be brief. I NEVER HEARD SUCH A RUMOR AND DO NOT BELIEVE RENO WAS EVER WEAK ENOUGH TO PROPOSE SUCH A COWARDLY ACTION. *THIS MUCH I DID HEAR*: the enlisted men did talk of taking their horses and endeavoring to escape, but were dissuaded by their officers who pointed out the impossibility of carrying out such a plan. In the end nothing came of it. . . . Reno was inexperienced as an Indian fighter, but he was not a coward."

Theodore W. Goldin to Albert W. Johnson

January 19, 1932

"Brig-Gen. Nicholson . . . you may have heard the story that while he was stationed at Ft. Abercrombie . . . where Reno was in command, he had an altercation with Reno in the club-room, and presumably under the influence of nose-paint, made a slighting remark about the wife of an officer of the garrison. Nicholson . . . resented it and told Reno so in no uncertain terms, with the result that Reno threw a billiard ball at Nicholson who retaliated by breaking a cue over Reno's head. Result, a court-martial with Reno dismissed from the service and Nicholson reprimanded. I am not clear as to whether he lost a file or two or not. This story came to me many years later through an officer now deceased, who was present at the incident." [I think Goldin has the cue-and-ball incident reversed: it seems to me that the record shows that the cue was used by Reno.—F.D.]

"Speaking of Nicholson, reminds me that this man Ghent has come to the front with a new story about the Reno-Benteen incident (abandon the wounded yarn). . . . My answer to his first letter seemed to displease him and he now comes back with the story that Nicholson, at a meeting of Veterans of Indian Wars, repeated the statement regarding Reno's suggestion to Benteen, saying that Benteen told it to him in the winter of '77 while we were at Ft. Buford . . . but asked him never to repeat it as long as he—Benteen—lived." [Goldin was a lawyer, and his many letters indicate a very clear, analytical mind.—F.D.]

January 28, 1932

"From what you write me and what I have learned from other sources, I have formed a very poor opinion of Mr. Ghent and his methods of trying to secure information for purposes of his own. . . . From what I gather . . . he seems to belong to the tribe of muck-rackers . . . for which I have nothing but contempt. As to the matter in which he was interested I can only say that it was never spoken of at the time, or even hinted at, but there was some talk among the enlisted men of trying to break out—a foolish idea and an impossible one which was quickly headed off as soon as it came to the ears of officers versed in Indian fighting."

April 25, 1932

"I had but little correspondence with Gen. Godfrey in these late years . . . but our relations were always pleasant. He told Mrs. Godfrey when we were at Crow Agency (In 1926) that there was one thing he liked about me, and that was the fact that I was never disposed to be unfair in any way, even though we disagreed on many points. I liked Godfrey as a soldier, even though our view points often differed widely."

June 7, 1932

"Ghent wrote me two or three times, but . . . received mighty short answers. Later he tried to pump me through a man named Dustin [Fred Dustin and Theodore Goldin had not yet begun their correspondence.] of Saginaw, Mich., but his hand in this was too plainly disclosed and Dustin got

[36]

nothing. He (Ghent) has characterized me in letters he has written as a liar and a fakir." [Goldin is quite wrong in his impression as to "Dustin" and was naturally suspicious as he didn't know Dustin.—F.D.]

Theodore W. Goldin
to Albert W. Johnson

June 22, 1932

"It is in a way unfortunate that there is not a living officer who knows of what I did on June 25—Custer, Cook, Reno, Moylan and Hodgson all dead, but the fact remains that I carried that message."

July 11, 1932

"My last letter from McWhorter asks for some information I am glad to be able to give him. He has several letters from men in the Seventh who tell of carrying sabers on that campaign in '77. We *did* carry them all summer until the morning we left Tongue River on that campaign; we then turned them in and never saw them again." [This refers to the Nez Perce Campaign, not the campaign of 1876, when the sabers were ALL LEFT AT FT. LINCOLN.]

August 22, 1932

"On June 27, when Lieuts. Wallace and Hare and several enlisted men of the regiment went down to look over the Indian village . . . we crossed the river near the point where I had come out on the 25th, and where there was a considerable bar extending well out into the stream. We first rode back along the line of Reno's retreat, and some of the party ran across and identified the remains of Lieut. McIntosh. I did not see them, but later we found the body of Reynolds and his head was NOT missing. We then rode over into the camps, and at one point we found the ashes and debris of a large fire and near it, in the trodden high grass some one of the party found two human heads, so charred and burned as

[37]

to be beyond recognition. We left the heads where or near where we found them. . . . Later I believe they were found by the 7th Infantry. . . . I was told later that the heads were examined by Dr. H. O. Paulding, a surgeon with Gibbon's command, and he pronounced one to be the head of a white man, and the other an Indian or half-breed."

September 14, 1932

"I cannot now recall just where we crossed Reno Creek . . . but we headed toward that high bluff and the direction where Hodgson's marker is now located. When still some distance from this point, Custer left the column riding rapidly off to the northwest, while the command continued to pursue its same general direction. Custer was lost to sight behind the ridge you mention and judging from what men in Reno's command afterward reported, rode to a point overlooking the valley, but to the west of this low ridge. . . . We continued along behind this ridge . . . to a point where the ridge ran down to more level ground, and had reached the point about where Reno's advance was halted by the enemy, and near where Weir entered the ravine . . . in his advance to find Custer. We had not entered this ravine when Custer rejoined us, and it was shortly after we dipped down into this ravine that I received the message to Reno. I looked up the place in 1924 when visiting the field . . . This point was in a slight widening of the ravine and as near as I could estimate it, about a mile or a little less from where I descended the bluff, forded the river and made my way to Reno. It is my best judgment that I went down a ravine to the right of where Dr. De Wolfe was afterward killed. The ravine was steep in placement but brought me out on a gravel bar. . . . I headed my horse up-stream in making the crossing and across some open ground to where I found the fighting line."

[38]

November 8, 1932

*Theodore W. Goldin
to Albert W. Johnson*

"While Gen. Godfrey always contended our marches as to number of miles per day were not long, he entirely failed to state that they were over a rough, tortuous country that told heavily on horses working on half forage and on men living on insufficient food, and I know that on our first halt after that night march, men and horses were worn out, and hardly had we halted when the men threw themselves to the ground and slept, while horses with heaving sides and drooping heads, stood just where their riders left the saddles, making no effort to crop the scant grass that surrounded them. . . . I think that night march was over a bit of the roughest country I ever rode on."

December 4, 1932

"I presume you have heard the story of the warning given Custer by Bouyer the guide. I did not hear the conversation, but did hear Bouyer say to some of the officers when he left Custer in anger, something to the effect that he told Custer there were more Indians in that bottom than he could handle."

December 27, 1932

"I had a very interesting letter from Dustin, in which . . . he commented . . . on that story of Godfrey's that Reno proposed to Benteen the abandonment of the wounded. . . . Dustin does not believe the story, neither do I. The fact that it never gained circulation until after both Reno and Benteen were dead stamps it as fishy. . . . If such a proposition had been made, it would have certainly have come to the surface long before it did. I cannot believe Godfrey's story that Benteen told him of the proposition while we were burying the dead on the 28th, but that he did not get full details until a considerable later date. Knowing from letters and personal talks with Benteen many years later, that I feel very certain that regarding Godfrey as Benteen regarded Godfrey, he (Godfrey) was the last officer in the regiment to whom Benteen would have told such a story. In both the letters I had from Benteen, and my visit with him at his home, such a thing was never mentioned, although we talked over very intimately practically all the details of the fight, and several times remarks were made that were not very complimentary to Godfrey. I have felt that in his intense partisanship for Custer that Godfrey stopped at nothing his imagination could suggest to belittle Reno and other officers who were not in accord with his views."

January 4, 1933

"You ask as to my recollection as to where Isaiah Dorman fell. As I recall, it was not far from the edge of the timber. . . . When we went over the field on the morning of the 27th before Terry came up, I saw his body together with that of Charley Reynolds, and my recollection is that it lay a bit to the south and east of where Reynolds fell. The body was badly mutilated, scalped but recognizable, as was that of Bloody Knife and Reynolds about as you describe it. I was later told by a sergeant of the Seventh Infantry that Dorman's privates were cut off and stuffed in his mouth. Later I asked one of the Crows (through an interpreter, no doubt) if this was often done, and he replied that where a dead warrior was known and hated by the Sioux or Cheyennes, as was Dorman, it was sometimes done, usually by the squaws, as it was regarded as the deepest insult to send a dead warrior to the Happy Hunting Grounds minus his "working tools." We did not notice this when we saw the body, but no careful examination was made. Dorman's father was said to be a Jamaica negro, and his mother a squaw. He was known as a good interpreter, scout and trailer.

Theodore W. Goldin
to Albert W. Johnson

"I know it was Mitch Bouyer who had hot words with Custer; I was near enough to see them, but not to hear their words, but later that day was told by the Sergeant-Major that Bouyer warned Custer there were too many Indians for his small command, and that Custer replied that he, Bouyer, was not a soldier and did not have to go in, and that Bouyer replied that he wasn't afraid to go anywhere Custer did, but if they went down into the valley of the Little Big Horn, they would both wake up in Hell in the morning, and that Bouyer then turned and walked angrily away. I only know from what I saw that there was a pretty hot exchange of words, but what they were I cannot say."

January 17, 1933

"I knew Sergt. Alexander Brown intimately. He was the senior surviving non-com. officer of Troop "G" and acted as first sergeant after the fight. Our first sergeant had just re-enlisted before we left the south and had taken a six months leave, and gone to England, his old home. Edward Botzer, who acted in his place, was killed at the river crossing on June 25, and Brown succeeded him."

February 5, 1933

"Herendeen was a quiet, unassuming man, a good scout, truthful and reliable so far as I ever heard. He was responsible for bringing out that party of dismounted men which he did soon after seeing me cross the river where I made my own landing a short time previous."

February 16, 1933

"All of those killed in "G" Troop were killed at the crossing except McIntosh and his striker Rapp, WHO WAS

ONE OF THE HORSE-HOLDERS, AND WAS KILLED WITH THE HORSES, thus releasing the Lieutenant's [McIntosh's] horse, and leaving him horseless when the retreat was ordered, until McCormick gave him his horse and remained with the dismounted bunch that later came out with Herendeen. . . . So far as I know, all the others were killed at the ford except Andy Moore who was killed on the hill on the 26th, but Farrier Gid Wells' horse, 'Wild Bill,' bolted with him and the men said dashed right into the advancing Indians."

April 1, 1933

"According to the De Rudio story, he and O'Neil must have worked upstream some distance, but O'Neil does not tell it that way. To take De Rudio's version they must have gone back nearly or quite to Reno's first crossing, but O'Neil's story does not bear this out.

"The mystery to me has always been why all four of them did not come out as I did, or as Herendeen and his party did. There was quite a time after Benteen came up and before the arrival of the packs that there were no Indians on our front, they evidently having left us to take part in the attack on Custer . . . I saw no Indians save a couple of Crows at the time I made my crossing, and men with Herendeen tell the same story, so if those four had been on the alert as we were, they could have come out as we did. . . . I can recall seeing the party as they approached and crossed the stream . . . moving in single file, Herendeen at the head. Lieut. Hare crept to the edge of the bluffs and signaled our position to them. . . . From where I was hidden on the west side of the river I saw a considerable number of Indians leave Reno's front and go off down the valley. . . . Why De Rudio, O'Neil, Gerard and Jackson did not essay a crossing at, or even after that time is more than I can figure out. I am inclined to believe that at that time the squaws were on the field. I could hear a commotion back of me but could not see them owing to the rank grass and sage brush, and it might be that this party were in closer range of the squaws and did not deem it wise to make any move."

Theodore W. Goldin
to Albert W. Johnson

April 5, 1933

"I do not regard it at all strange that he [Herendeen] omitted any mention of our meeting on the bank of the river. At that time he was out scouting for a possible crossing. We were together but a few moments. He watched me cross the river and then returned to where he had his men concealed in the timber. It was not very long after that until we saw him leading his party out just as he described it in his statement. He reached us just a few moments before we began to advance to support Weir whose act of insubordination nearly cost him the loss of his troop. . . . I saw McIntosh when he went down and only noticed that he did not regain his feet. I was perhaps fifty yards to the left and a bit to the rear when I saw his horse go down. . . . I noticed that his lariat was dragging on the ground, once in a while catching in the tall grass or sage brush and then breaking loose and the picket pin bounding into the air. . . . My own horse was on the run, and I was bearing more to the left. . . . A moment or two after that my own horse went down, and I made for the brush.

[An incident after Benteen's charge] "As Benteen was passing along the line one of his sergeants stuck up his head just in time to get a bullet through the top of his hat, spinning it away from him, and Benteen called out, 'Damn you, I told you to keep down; now you do it." The sergeant looked up at him with a grin and asked: 'Why don't you keep

[43]

down, Captain?' Benteen replied, 'Oh, I am all right; Mother [his wife] sewed some good medicine in my blouse before I left home, so they won't get me.' This was said half-laughingly but this exhibition of coolness had a great effect in keeping up the spirits of his men, and his actions all through the fight were a real inspiration. . . . McIntosh's horse was stampeded or killed at the time his striker Rapp was shot down, and when they were mounting for the retreat, Private McCormick surrendered his horse . . . and was one of the party brought out by Herendeen."

April 26, 1933

"The First Sergeant that went to England on a 6-mos. leave was Edward Garlic."

May 2, 1933

"Herendeen was attached to Gibbon's command and when at the conference on the Far West it was decided advisable to scout the upper valley of Tullock's Creek by our column, while Gibbon's cavalry scouted the lower valley. Herendeen was detached from Gibbon's column and sent with Custer for the purpose of bringing back the report of Custer's scout. This scout was never made. I wonder if in his story Herendeen refers to the fact that when they reached the vicinity of this creek, he called Custer's attention to it, but that Custer made no reply, nor did he pause to carry out his instructions? I had this information from Lieut. Cooke, our regimental adjutant, just by way of comment. Herendeen did not mention the matter to Custer again, but receiving no orders, continued on."

May 8, 1933

"Captain Weir was not ORDERED by Reno to go to Custer's assistance, but as a matter of fact was guilty of in-

[44]

subordination in making his forward movement. He must have advanced close to a mile. . . . In 1924 I went over the ground on foot to locate the point where I turned back, which according to my knowledge was very near the point reached by Weir. [From all I can gather it would seem that Custer sent Goldin back to Reno *soon after* he returned from Custer's Lookout. A rather common-sense idea, after seeing what he could from the Lookout, just as he sent Martin back after seeing what he could from Weir's Peak.—F.D.] Dr. Paulding, one of the surgeons with Gibbon's command, told me in 1877, when I was doing some clerical work for him at Ft. Buford, that he personally emptied brandy into the hats of some of the men from the emergency canteen that he carried, and that this with water was given to the horse, Comanche. . . . I saw him [Comanche] at the boat, and there were only FIVE bullet wounds on him.

*Theodore W. Goldin
to Albert W. Johnson*

"With Lieuts. Wallace and Hare, I, with a small party of soldiers, visited the field on the forenoon of the 27th and discovered a tepee standing in the shelter of the timber pretty much out of sight and tightly closed. Curious to see what it contained, Lieut. Wallace slashed a hole in the side of it with his knife, and we were all scared stiff at the howls that came from inside, and lit out for our horses, only to be stopped by the laughter of the horse-holders who pointed back toward the tepee. On looking back we saw just outside the hole made by Wallace, an Indian dog, whose ear was bleeding and we decided that Wallace must have cut him, and that the howls that stampeded us were simply his protest against that sort of treatment. In the tepee were six or seven dead warriors, evidently chiefs or warriors of importance, as two or three had their war bonnets on. . . . We changed our position and occupied better ground and intrenched better after the Indians left on the 26th.

[45]

[Concerning the "water parties"] "We simply picked up a bunch of canteens and a five gallon camp kettle and started from the corral, made a dash for the ravine WHICH WAS LOCATED BETWEEN BENTEEN'S AND MCDOUGAL'S LINES, and possibly forty or fifty yards from the corral."

July 5, 1933

[The Unknown Soldier] "The point where the body (bones) was found was not very far from, if not right at the point, where "H" Troop line was first established. [Was this not the skeleton of O'Hara?—F.D.] This I gathered as to the location of the troop from men who were with it, and with whom I visited the field on the 27th. I of course was not with the troop at any time during the fight nor until I joined them after the retreat, as when I joined with my message I remained near him until the retreat started."

September 6, 1933

Personally I had a high regard for Godfrey, but was entirely out of sympathy with some of the methods he used in his efforts to throw a smoke screen around the memory and record of his leader."

October 16, 1933

"It took me some time to get the right slant on Bruce. . . . I can understand why men like Ghent and Bruce . . . have gathered all their information and leanings through personal contact with Mrs. Custer, than whom no nobler woman ever lived or one more loyal to the memory of a husband who did not deserve such loyalty and devotion. Those of us who knew him knew that he fell far short of being the perfect man Mrs. Custer, Godfrey and others sought to picture him. In all that I have done and written, I studiously avoided any men-

[46]

tion of private life of the man, but always sought to confine myself to his military history."

November 25, 1933

"Godfrey was a good soldier, but for some reason was never a popular officer in the regiment, and particularly so after the death of Custer."

December 8, 1933

"My real reason for hitting the frontier was, I guess, the fact that I failed by just a quarter of a point in winning a scholarship at West Point, and thinking there was a possible chance to win a commission from the ranks I drifted into the service. . . . The fellow who beat me for the Point was a boyhood friend who later joined the Seventh and our friendship bridged over many a rough spot. I never like to think of his end; it was a sad one. He was one of the youngsters in the regiment who took their first lessons in poker from Custer."

December 27, 1933

"Van de Water writes me that he did not find Gen. Scott (Hugh) much of an admirer of Custer, but that he was guarded but frank in what he said."

January 16, 1934

". . . Our party identified the body of Bloody Knife. It was not far from where he fell or was last seen alive. He was scalped and there were a number of arrows in his body. . . . He was not decapitated. Reynolds was scalped but not mutilated, as he lay some distance from any of the others partly hidden by a clump of brush."

January 28, 1934

"McIntosh showed the Indian blood in his features very plainly. . . . I saw the horse of Farrier Gideon Wells break

[47]

from the lines and charge directly into the ranks of the pursuing Indians. I did not see him go down, but later we found his body, stripped, scalped and mutilated, some distance to the right, or south of the trail of the retreating column."

[A QUESTION: The "grave" of McIntosh has always struck me as being TOO FAR SOUTHWARD. While Goldin states that the Indian who owned the land had admitted that the marker was moved more than once, he claimed that it was *now* (1926) on the right spot. *Is it?* Is it not possibly the "grave" of Wells that was marked by mistake?—F.D.]

[Concerning Windolph's story about the "water parties"] "The temptation to add a few thrills to a story of an old-timer in telling is mighty strong. I know, because I have had to fight it time and time again. Many little details pop into a fellow's imagination that might have happened, that the temptation to relate them as really happening, in my judgment, accounts for a lot of the fairy stories that creep into print; added to this is the fact that the average enlisted man of the old army had both a vivid imagination and a willingness to use it, accounts for a lot of false history."

April 21, 1934

"As a matter of fact, the Custer column passed over the ground where Reno made his first halt (on the bluffs) as well as where he made his final stand. They passed to the left and along the base of that high bluff, and on down to where they entered the ravine."

July 26, 1934

"As you know, I was temporarily attached to Custer's column. . . . When it crossed to the northerly side of Reno Creek and headed downstream behind the bluffs along the L.B.H., I was riding on the left flank of the column about midway from its front to rear. This was about the time Custer left the column and rode over toward the edge of the bluffs . . . where he was seen by men in Reno's outfit. Two or three times at the least as we crossed that open country between Reno Creek and that high bluff, I looked back in an effort to locate the pack train and Benteen column. I could see what I was satisfied was the pack train a long distance in our rear, and away over farther to the southwest a dust cloud that must have been made by Benteen's outfit, BUT AT NO TIME WHEN I LOOKED BACK DID I SEE EITHER HORSEMEN OR DISMOUNTED MEN ON EITHER THE NORTHERLY OR SOUTHERLY SIDE OF THE CREEK. NOTHING IN SIGHT IN OUR REAR BETWEEN US AND WHAT I AM SURE WAS THE PACK TRAIN.

[This completes the extracts from Goldin's letters to Albert W. Johnson covering a period of about seven years. My own correspondence with Goldin covers only a period of two or three years, ending at his decease. His mind remained clear to the last, and I have been struck by the clarity of his descriptions and very strongly impressed *with his unassuming and evident truthfulness*. I AM NOW *PERSONALLY SATIS-FIED* THAT HE CARRIED A MESSAGE FROM CUSTER TO RENO, but as it has been disputed, and no one living can either verify or disprove it, the statement in my book, *The Custer Tragedy*, must stand, although were I to rewrite it, I should make the statement just as it here appears.—FRED DUSTIN]

In the transcription by Dustin of the extracted letters from Goldin to Johnson, he also included what he called a CHECK LIST BY GOLDIN. That checklist is quoted here even though it has no immediate relationship to the Goldin-Johnson letters. It reads:

[49]

"In checking over the roster of "G" Troop, I find the names of the following men who, to the best of my knowledge, were not in the battle, but as most of them were dismounted recruits, they were left back at Powder River. Akers, Lauper (saddler), Barnet, Gray, Geist, Henderson, Katzenmaier, Laden (cannot recall this man either as Laden or Ladue), McKee, McKay, Rowland, McDonough, Smith, Sordon (probably Gordon) Tulo, Carter (trumpeter on furlough), Stephens, Stevenson. The name of McVey should appear as having been in the fight. He was badly wounded and sent down on the Far West."

THEODORE W. GOLDIN
TO
PHILLIP G. COLE

Dr. Phillip G. Cole
New York City

Dear Mr. Cole:

I want to thank you very much for your unique, very interesting and fully appreciated Christmas Greeting, supplemented by additional kindly words which come to me in a letter from our mutual friend Brininstool. I can assure you they made the sun shine a bit brighter at Christmas time.

Mrs. Goldin says she feels sure she must have passed your place on the Hudson on her trip down the river in September although of course unable to locate it.

I trust you will always feel that you made no mistake in your purchase of those Benteen letters. Frankly I hated to part with them as they were the one remaining link connecting me with a somewhat unusual friendship between an officer and an enlisted man of the Old Army, but at the same time I

was glad that they fell into such good hands and some day
may find a resting place where the contents may be available
to real searchers after the history of the Old West.

I have many times regretted that the talks I had with
Gen. Benteen on my two visits to him at Atlanta, Ga. could
not have been reduced to writing as they contained much important additional data in many cases supplementing or going
deeper into matters mentioned in those letters.

Those were wonderful days as we set there on the shaded
porch of his home, puffing at our Missouri cob pipes and
now and then sipping an undeniable mint julep prepared by
the old colored butler who had been in the family since childhood, and even today I can almost visualize the dear old man
as he leaned back in his arm chair, his snow white hair and
unwrinkled ruddy face, unwrinkled by time and touched on
matters having to do with the old Seventh, of which he had
been a member almost from its organization. I cannot depend
on a memory not as good as it was a half century ago to
repeat even the outlines of those talks.

Mrs. Goldin joins me in the best of wishes for an un-
usually Happy New Year for yourself and family with a full
measure of success in all your undertakings.

Sincerely yours,
Theo. W. Goldin

P. S. A persistent attack of neuritis makes the use of pen or
pencil almost an impossibility.

Dr. Philip G. Cole
New York City

Dear Doctor Cole

Your letter under date of Dec. 28th, 1932 reached me this morning and brought your many kindly words of greeting that I can assure you were deeply appreciated.

I will not attempt at this time to tell you all they mean to me and how much I appreciate the opportunity to found a closer relationship with you. As I pass down the western slope toward the land of eternal sunset such letters as yours are like added rays of sunshine through the rifts in the clouds of advancing years and failing sight and health and will long be cherished by me.

I note your request for a letter dealing with my experience in the campaign of 1876 and assure you that you are not asking too much and that at some time in the not distant future I will do my best to comply with your request hoping that I may be able to satisfy your desires.

My eyesight is very poor, so much so that I am unable to read a line of print, or a letter and while able to operate my machine by a self invented touch system I have to run the chances of making many errors and have to rely on Mrs. Goldin to correct them.

Unable to read I am dependent on a memory not as good as it was fifty six years ago when we were riding the Montana trails, but I still regard it as good enough to enable me to deal in my own personal experiences and recollections without reference to other stories or official documents, so in due season you may expect the letter you ask for.

[55]

I have always regarded my correspondence with Gen. then Captain Benteen and my visits with him at his home as among the most cherished experiences of my life.

Thanking you again for your many words of kindly greeting and good wishes and until able to comply with your request believe me

Sincerely, possibly Fraternally yours,
Theo. W. Goldin

Wisconsin Veterans Home
January 15, 1933

Dr. Philip G. Cole
551 Fifth Ave
New York City

Dear Doctor Cole:

In further reply to yours of Dec. 28, 1932 in which you ask for a letter in a way connecting up with the Benteen letters in your possession I have found myself a bit in doubt as to just what to write that would best comply with your request but have finally decided that the story of my acquantance with Gen. Benteen and what led up to the writing of the letters might best comply with your request. To do this will necessitate going back to a time long preceding the writing of the letters in question, but as it will give some explanation of the relations existing between a commissioned officer and an enlisted man of the Old Army I feel that it will on the whole best tell the story, but in doing it we will have to go back to a time long preceding the writing of the letters you have.

When I enlisted in the regular army after losing out in a competitive examination for West Point, I, at the suggestion of the recruiting office gave my occupation as that of a clerk and was assigned to duty with a squadron of the Seventh Cavalry then stationed in the south.

In the spring of 1876 the entire regiment was mobilized at Ft. Abraham Lincoln, D. T. preparatory to taking part in the expedition then organizing against the hostile Indians, I was detailed for clerical work at headquarters and it was while on this duty that I formed a slight acquantance with Capt. Benteen the senior captain of the regiment and later on during this expedition and in and following the fight on the Little Big Horn I saw more or less of him, an acquantance that continued during my service with the regiment, it was just an ordinary acquantance, mainly in the line of duty which for the time being ended when I left the service.

After my discharge in November 1877 I returned to my home in Wisconsin and many years later took up the study of law, was admitted to the bar, formed a partnership with my brother-in-law and continued in the practice for many years, part of that time connected with the political end of the legal department of a leading middle west railroad.

In the 90's Gen Godfrey published an article in the Century Magazine covering the fight on the Little Big Horn. I found in it many errors and misstatements and knowing through the Army Register that Gen. Benteen had been retired and was living on his home plantation at Atlanta, Ga., I procured and sent to him a copy of the article in question together with a letter giving my own recollection of the several incidents in which I felt that Gen. Godfrey was in

error, this brought me the first of the letters you now have
and later was followed by a more extended correspondence
making up the letters you now have. I later twice visited Gen.
Benteen at his home enjoying many interesting talks with
him which I have many times wished might have beeen
reduced to writing by him.

My professional duties and the failing health of the
general brought an-end to the very interesting correspondence,
but I considered the letters of importance enough to retain
them all through the years that followed until in connection
with some literary work we were planning I sent them to Mr.
Brininstool and with my approval they were transferred to you.

Gen. Benteen, like Major Reno, has been the victim of
much unfair criticism and much bitterness by those allied
with the Custer faction of the regiment. I regard most of these
criticisms as unfair and untrue as I always found Gen. Benteen
to be in every sense a soldier and a man of unquestioned honor
and I have often regretted that his untimely death prevented
him making the defense I am sure he would and could have
made.

These lines I believe will serve to explain the origin and
continuation of our correspondence. I have been led to understand that my letters to him were either lost or destroyed after
his death and the breaking up of the old home.

You also ask for some reminiscences of my connection
with and impressions of the Battle of the Little Big Horn. It
will be hard for me to give much in the compass of this letter,
partly for the reason that some years ago and after the celebration of the semi-centennial of the fight I prepared very full
notes which I placed in the hands of our friend Brininstool
and they were by him put in shape for publication, but owing
to the coming of the depression, which is still with us, we

were unable to publish the story owing to the fact that reputable publishers were trimming down their publications to meet conditions. This mss. is still in the hands of Mr. Brininstool and was carefully checked by him with orders, reports and other authentic sources and found to be accurate. What disposition he will make of the story I do not know, as it is in his hands to do with as he sees best.

Theodore W. Goldin
to Phillip G. Cole

I might say that just before we left the Rosebud and on June 21, 1876 I was called to headquarters to assist the sergeant major in preparing various orders and in compiling our records for the field desk we carried on a pack mule and when we left the Rosebud the following day I was, by order of Lieut. Cook, regimental adjutant, retained at headquarters as an orderly or messenger and when the command was divided on June 25th, while still some fifteen miles from the village of the enemy and so far as I have ever been able to learn, without any definite knowledge as to the exact location or strength of the village I remained with the column under Gen. Custer until we reached a point possibly a mile down stream from the point where we knew Reno was already engaged with the upper end of the huge village. In the meantime Gen. Custer had left this column and ridden to a point out of our sight, but which evidently overlooked the scene of Reno's engagement. I state this because we later learned that men in Reno's command saw and recognized him on the bluffs. In the mean time the rest of his command had continued down the stream but hidden from the Indians by a high ridge paralleling the course of the high bluffs above the river. When about a mile below Reno's position we slowed down to a walk and it was at this point that Custer rejoined us and a few moments later I was given a message to deliver to Major Reno. What this message contained I do not know, but my orders were to get it to Reno at once, remain with him until the two columns affected a junction when I was to report to Lieut. Cook. On my trip back I saw no Indians nor could I see the valley or the village because of the ridge until I sought a place to descend to the river and cross it to reach Reno, then I could plainly see the immense village and Reno's little squadron fighting in the bottoms apparently against heavy odds. While making the descent of the bluffs and fording the river a number of bullets whistled entirely too close for comfort about my ears, whether aimed at me, or whether they were shots fired high by the Indians I do not know. I do know I was might uncomfortable for a few moments. I reached Reno just about the time his Indian allies on the extreme left of his slender line broke and ran, some of them it was reported not stopping until they reached the supply camp on the Powder River, others not until they reached their reservation at Fort Berthold. I delivered my message, Reno glanced at it, asked where I left Custer and what he was doing, folded his message put it in his notebook and turned to watch the movement of the left of his line, which seemed to be forced back into the timber. When I reached Reno the only officers near him were Captain Moylan of A Troop and Lieut. Hodgson, squadron adjutant, killed a short time later. It was only a few moments after this that the retreat was ordered. I ran for my horse which had strayed away a short distance, mounted him and started for the river riding perhaps a hundred yards or less from the retreating column. I saw no Indians on the left of the retreating column, they seemed to be massed on the right flank aiming to prevent the column from retreating up stream and forcing them to make for the bluffs directly in their front. It was at the river crossing that our heaviest loss of life occurred as the horses had to be forced over a cut bank into the river and had to negotiate a cut

bank on the opposite side. When perhaps a hundred yards
from the river my horse fell I thought he was shot but learned
later that he had only stumbled. I did not waste much time
in trying to find out but got under cover of the brush and
driftwood along the bank, later making my way across the
river and up the bluffs and rejoining what was left of Reno's
command, arriving just a few moments before Benteen's
squadron came up.

The Indians in the meantime had left Reno and hur-
ried down the valley where it was now evident that Custer
was just coming into action some three miles down stream

Neither time nor space will permit me to continue the
details of what followed.

We continued the fighting the rest of the afternoon of
the 25th with no knowledge of what had become of Custer.
The fight was renewed at daybreak of the 26th and continued
until late in the afternoon, when the Indians broke camp
moved up the valley and were soon lost to sight, giving us a
chance to get food and water.

I might say that on the 26th a small party made the trip
down ravine to the river and obtained a supply of water which
was turned over to the wounded. Later in the day the same
party made a second trip, this time one of the party was so
severely wounded that his leg had to be amputated at the
knee. I understand other parties made the trip and that later
the members of the parties were awarded the Medal of Honor
or Valor, as it is now called. Many years later through the
active interest of Secretary of War, Daniel Lamont, I received
this medal which I cherish as an evidence of a duty well
performed.

I find my letter is reaching too great a length so will
bring it to a close.

If at any time in the future I can afford you any further desired information I hope you will not hesitate to call on me.

There is but little one can tell in an action where every man did his best, not much chance for personal distinction. We all realize that it was fight or die, possibly both, so we did the best we could.

With renewed thanks for your many kindly words in your recent letter believe me

Sincerely yours,
Theodore W. Goldin

January 16, 1933

Dear Doctor Cole:

I am enclosing herewith a letter written in reply to your request, I trust it will be what you wanted. It at least tells how the Benteen letters came to be written.

The reminiscent part of it does not go very far, but some way I just could not get the right kind of a start. I may be able to do better some day. Wish you might see the mss. Brininstool prepared from my notes, it covers the field quite thoroughly.

I received a letter from Brininstool on the 14th, enclosing a letter from Mr. Joseph Jackson of Madison, at the head of the Administration Department of the Jackson Clinic. I had the pleasure of meeting him as well as two of his brothers in 1927 while passing through the clinic and through an operation for the removal of an alkali stone as large as a good sized English Walnut from my bladder. It was while convalescing that I met Dr. Joseph and I think it was a Dr. Frank Jackson, both of whom had as I recall it done some ranching in North Dakota.

I wish Brininstool might find a place for what I believe is a mighty fine collection of curios, photos and valuable documents pertaining to the history of the Old West. It seems a shame to have it scattered to the four winds when properly located it might prove of real value in the days to come.

As you requested I did my best to sign that letter, but when I tell you I am so blind I cannot see what I am writing and have also a miserable attack of neuritis in my writing arm and shoulder that I made a poor job of it.

If you feel at any time that I can be of assistance to you in any way I will be glad to respond to the extent of my ability.

Mrs. Goldin says: "Tell Dr. Cole that in case he visits the Century of Progress Exhibition in Chicago we would be more than pleased to have them take a side trip and come up and see where we hibernate," I second the motion

Sincerely yours,
Theo. W. Goldin

February 1, 1933

Dear Doctor Cole:

In your letter of January 26th you suggested adding something of a reminiscent nature to my letter authenticating

[63]

the manuscript sent you by Mr. Brininstool, something connected with the battle of the Little Big Horn, but at the time I answered the letter I was unable to recall anything of that nature not covered by the manuscript in question; but since writing you there comes to me a bit of a story that had its origin at the time of the fight but with its culmination many months later, I cannot recall that I ever tried to reduce the story to writing but as it has something a bit amusing as well as interesting as connected with Montana Indians I am going to try to tell it as best I can, and possibly it may prove interesting to your youngsters if not to yourself so I'll dedicate it to them.

In the manuscript you have there is a reference to the fact that at the time I made my crossing of the river after Reno's retreat and the loss of my horse I was swept off my feet by the swiftness of the current, the smooth stones that filled the bottom of the stream preventing me from regaining my footing and that as I drifted down the stream one of our Crow Indians, Half Yellow Face, a young chief of that tribe, who was watering his pony on a gravel bar extending out into the stream saw me and throwing me the end of his lariat pulled me ashore and directed me to where the command had halted on the high bluffs above the river. At the time I asked him as best I could where he was going, he replied by making the sign of scalping an enemy so I inferred he was out to see if he could not add a scalp or two of his hated foes, the Sioux and the Cheyennes. That closed the incident for the time being and I left him, but later in the day, or possibly on the 25th, I saw him again, this time he was in the hospital wounded in one or both arms; I am uncertain now just what the wounds were but he was laying there bandaged and alone save for one young Indian who was sitting beside him. I

[64]

stopped and asked him if he got his scalps, he nodded, said something to his companion who reached under the blanket thrown over the wounded man and drew forth three fresh, bloody scalps, as the young warrior held them up to my view. Half Yellow Face ejaculated, "Sioux, Sioux." Later on when we came back with water I passed near him and seeing the wistful look in his eyes stopped and gave him a good drink from one of my canteens, and later in the day, after the Indians had left as we were trying to get some much needed food, I happened to think of him again and took him a large cup of hard tack soaked in water and liberally spiked with Bordens Condensed Milk. This I gave to his companion who was still with him and he fed it to the warrior. We had no fuel at that time with which to do any cooking, but the following morning I made him a cup of coffee, fried him some hardtack and so called bacon, gave it to his companion and the way he stowed it under his belt was ample evidence of his appreciation. I did not see him again for many months as he and others of his tribe left us and made their way back to their reservation then located on what is known as the Crow Mission, on and near the Little Rosebud and Stillwater rivers. The incident faded from my mind entirely with so many other things more exciting to occupy our minds.

In the early fall of 1877, during the Nez Perce campaign, our regiment struck this Crow Mission and went into camp there for several days awaiting information as to the movement of the enemy. One day while wandering through the camp I was suddenly surprised to have an Indian rush up to me frantically shake my hand and slap me on the back; seeing I did not recognize him he ejaculated: "Me Half Yellow, Me know you, you give Injun water and something to eat, Me no forget." We talked a little while, he in his

broken English, and then we parted. That evening he came
over to our camp with the interpreter at the agency and with
the latter's assistance I was able to make out that the Indian
felt I had done something unusual for him and the talk
wound up with the statement that he wanted to adopt me
as his white brother, offering me a trophe, ponies and even a
squaw if I would remain in the village, but learning I could
not do this he still insisted on the adoption and wanted to do
it the next night. I took the matter up with my troop commander and he laughingly told me to go ahead and they would
come over and see it done.

During the following day I spent some time talking with
the interpreter, the agent and other white men who had
lived among the Indians for many years, seeking to learn as
much as possible of what was likely to take place but without
getting much satisfaction. They all said it was not an uncom-
mon occurrence for the tribe as a whole to confer the rite of
adoption on a white man of more or less prominence; it was
quite unusual for a single Indian to take such a course and
they all agreed that while the ceremony was more than likely
to follow the lines of the larger ceremony all we could do was
wait and see.

That evening soon after darkness set in the interpreter
called for me and we made our way to the village, some
little distance from the agency buildings. Here in an open
space in front of the tepees a large fire was burning, the tom-
toms under the vigorous blows of several squaws were sending
forth their discordant music and the Indians were gathering in
a semi-circle facing the fire. In the front row seemed to be a
number of the chiefs and leading warriors, back to them
another row of warriors apparently of lesser prominence
while back of them were grouped many younger Indians and

the squaws, while off to one side, tended by two or three
squaws was a huge kettle from which ascended a really appe-
tizing aroma. We paused and remained standing at one end
of this semi-circle and a moment later Half Yellow Face,
stripped to the waist and his face and body painted with the
gaudy colors that gave him his name, one side of his face a
bright yellow, the other an equally bright red, while the same
colors appeared on his body. He moved to a place in front of
the fire facing the rows of spectators and began to talk. The
interpreter told me that as was usually the custom he was
telling in brief the story of his life, his prowess on the field
of battle, his success on the hunt. All this time the tom-toms
were beating a slow, weird music. The interpreter translated
for me his long harangue which really if properly translated
has in it strains of real oratory. He ceased at last, walked over
to where I was standing, took me by the arm and still
accompanied by the interpreter, led me in front of the
leading chief and then in language really fine he went
on to tell the story of our meeting of the previous year
on the battle field, following it with a really elaborate story
of the few little acts of kindness I had rendered him. I will
not attempt to give his story as it was interpreted to me. It
was almost fifty-six years ago, but as he talked it seemed to me
he was making much of a few small incidents. He closed by
announcing that it was his desire to adopt me as his white
brother as a slight token of his appreciation for my acts. He
offered me a place in his tepee until I had one of my own,
offered me robes and ponies and all the equipment of a
warrior, but having been previously advised refrained from
offering me a squaw. His language, if it was properly interpreted was at times almost poetic. He closed by taking me
in front of the chief, who, as I now recall it was Iron Hand,

the head chief of the tribe, introduced me by the Indian name they or he had chosen, "Little Soldier," and asked that I be known as his white brother. The chief nodded gravely and we moved away to a place at the end of the circle. Again the tom-toms gave forth their strident music, this time to a quicker rhythm, and led by Half Yellow Face and followed by most of the young warriors we formed a circle around the fire and to the now louder music of the tom-toms and the weird chant of those on the outside we began a shuffling dance around the fire, stirring up such a dust that the spectators were almost concealed from our view. How long this dance continued I will not pretend to say, long enough for me to become almost exhausted, but it ended at last and we returned to our places in the circle. Then some one, either the head chief, or the medicine man of the tribe, filled one of the Indian pipes, lit it, drew a whiff blowing the smoke from his nostrils east, west, north and south and passed the pipe to the next in line where the same ceremony was repeated, when the pipe became empty it was returned to the east, refilled and relighted and passed back to where it had stopped in the line and in that way passed down the front row of chiefs and warriors, always traveling from east to west. This seemed to complete the cere-monies as the lines were broken up, and forming in single file we moved toward the kettle I have referred to. I was tired and hungry and needed no urging to take one of the wooden trenchers and wooden spoon and dip it for myself. What the stew was made of I do not know save that there were many vegetables together with various roots and herbs and chunks of meat, I did not know then what it was but being hungry I did not refuse a second helping, but this venture proved my Waterloo as when the meat struck my trencher I saw that it still had hair on it and I was not long in deciding that it

[68]

had at one time formed part of the remains of a fat, succulent puppy, of which I knew the Indians to be very fond. All traces of hunger vanished, I lost all further interest in the proceedings, made my escape as soon as possible and returned to camp.

The next day our orders came and we marched away and I never saw Half Yellow Face but once again and that was some time later when he joined us at Canyon Creek with a party of young warriors after we had fought the Nez Perces. I only saw him for a moment then, but when I next visited the agency on the Little Big Horn I found that he had gone the long journey to the Happy Hunting ground of his people. Once in 1924 and again in 1925 I tried to find some Indian who remembered the incident, but only found one, White Man Tans Him, an old warrior who too has taken the trail from which there is no return.

I have tried as best I could to tell the story as it comes back to me after all these years. I send it to the youngsters with my kindest regards.

Theodore W. Goldin

FRED DUSTIN AND THEODORE W. GOLDIN CORRESPONDENCE

There is some question as to whom the following letter from Theodore Goldin was addressed, but Fred Dustin evidently thought enough of the fragmentation of it to add a footnote (undated) and remark of it when transcribing it: "AN IMPORTANT LETTER." It reads as follows:

Dec. 14, 1931

. . . regarding that quotation you mentioned . . . Reno in forming his lines facing the village brought "A" Troop on his right, French with "M" Troop in the center and McIntosh with "G" Troop on the left. As I learned later the Indians under Varnum were on the extreme left, across where the railway and highway now run. The Indians (Hostiles) seemed to have regarded this place as the weakest in the line and massed for an attack there.

The reference to the arrival of a messenger must have referred to my arrival, as no other messenger from Custer was sent back so far as I know. Just about the time of my arrival, or possibly a few minutes before, the attack on the left was so vigorous that our allies broke and ran. . . . This defection threw the brunt of the attack on "G" Troop, and they were forced back into the timber. This movement was on foot at the time I reached Reno and was the only thing left for McIntosh to do, otherwise he would have been cut off. Reno's command was already fighting on foot, and had he ever charged as some have intimated he was ordered to do by Custer, it would have meant the annihilation of the entire squadron and left only Benteen's squadron and the pack train, as it was not long after this that Custer's men went down.

WHEN I REACHED RENO he, Capt. Moylan and Lieut. Hodgson, acting squadron adjutant were together. [It is not known if the all caps were Goldin's or those of the man doing the transcribing—F.D.] I handed the message to Reno; he read it hastily, asked me where I left Custer, made no comment to the other officers, put the message in his note book, and soon after this the retreat was begun. So far as I ever knew, no orders were sent to French or McIntosh, they mounting up and joining the retreat as they saw the right of the line moving out. It was here that so many dismounted men were left behind, mostly from "G" and "M" Troops, fourteen or fifteen in all as I recall it. To have charged the village at any time after Reno began fighting would have been suicidal. [The above statement is of much value, although it contains some errors. When Reno deployed the three troops on foot, FRENCH was *on the left*; Moylan in the center, and McIntosh *on the right*. When the line wheeled to the cover of the edge of the timber, French and Moylan "about faced," so that French was then on the *right* of the line, Moylan still in the center, and McIntosh was THEN

[74]

on the left. Goldin locates the Indian Scouts exactly where I have placed them, and it is well to bear in mind that ALL of the white troops were on their right, and that ONLY THOSE ON THE LEFT could see the tepees at the upper end of the village, for those on the right were shut off from that view by the trees and brush along and in the old river bed. IT MUST NOT BE FORGOTTEN THAT THE RIVER'S COURSE CHANGED *AFTER* the fight, so that it again flowed in this old bed, and is now again cut off artificially at this point.—F. Dustin]

Saginaw, W. S. Mich., Feb. 24, 1932

Mr. Theo. W. Goldin,
Masonic Home,
Dousman, Wis.

Dear Sir and Brother:—

I am addressing you as "Brother" as you are an inmate of a masonic home, and I myself, am Past Master of my own lodge in this city.

For many years I have been a student of a historic event you took part in, and in fact have even tried to write the story of it.

If you have seen Mr. C. E. DeLand's fine history of that affair, you will note that he has quoted from my manuscript somewhat.

I have had a great deal of correspondence with him and

considerable with others regarding the battle and events leading up to it and subsequent.

Among my correspondents is a man named Ghent, W. J.
Ghent of Washington, D. C. In his second letter to me, he
announced himself as neither "pro-Custer or anti-Custer" but
in subsequent letters he has unmasked himself as a rabid anti-
Reno advocate.

My own investigations have not been along any "pro" or
"anti" lines, but purely an endeavor to picture facts as far as
ascertainable. In doing this, of course I have changed my
views in some things and been confirmed in others.

One of the things that has filled me with disgust is the
enterprise of some newspaper men who have manufactured
the most wonderful tales themselves and on the other hand,
have so garbled, distorted and changed the stories of others as
to render them almost unrecognizable.

I have had some experience in this myself. The only
"feature" or for that matter any other article that I ever
received pay for from a paper was so cut and re-wrote that a
portion conveyed exactly the opposite meaning that I intended
to convey, and it was not a historical paper either, but on a
subject "pseudo-scientific" and was typewritten.

This man Ghent states to me in a letter that you were
never separated from your troop in the battle: in short, you
were never away from Reno's command.

He has further attempted to show that no one was killed
in Reno's Command until the order to "MOUNT!" was given
in the woods.

There are, therefore, some matters that I would be glad
to receive your testimony on, and to that end, I am asking
certain questions which I hope you will kindly answer.

The fact that you were recommended for and received a

[76]

Medal of Honor carries much weight with me, and also that you were found worthy to be received among the Ancient Craft also is of consideration.

Fred Dustin and Theodore W. Goldin Correspondence

QUESTIONS

1. Were you detailed as orderly to Custer by McIntosh, and if so, where did you leave your troop to join Custer?

2. Where did you leave Custer?

3. Where did you cross the Little Big Horn to rejoin McIntosh?

4. Where did you rejoin MacIntosh?

5. What part of the fight was going on when you rejoined?

6. What men to your knowledge were killed: first: on the first skirmish line across the valley; second: in the second position in the woods before the command, "Mount!"?

7. Where was Bob Tail Bull killed?

8. Where was F. C. Mann (a civilian) killed and who was he?

9. After retiring to the bluff, did you hear an altercation between Weir and Reno and if so, what was the substance of it?

10. Give any other facts bearing on the above inquiries that you can.

I will much appreciate your kindness in answering the above as it will be of value in my last revision of my work.

I am now an old man, and my last revision of my paper,

[77]

"Custer's Last Campaign," was made over twenty years ago, and was about 300 type-written pages, so that the work I am now on will be my last, I suppose.

We have recently completed a fine Masonic home thirty miles west of here, to replace the old one which had grown too small.

Trusting that I am not imposing on you, I am,

Sincerely and Fraternally Yours,
Fred Dustin
705 S. Fayette St.,
Saginaw, W.S. Mich.

Wisconsin Veterans Home
Feb'y 29, 1932

Mr. Fred Dustin
Saginaw, Mich.

Dear Sir:

Yours of the 24th addressed to me at the Wisconsin Masonic Home at Dousman was forwarded to me from there as I have not been a resident of that home for over two years.

I have had the letter read to me most carefully, as I am no longer able to read a word, or read even what I write on the machine.

Having just returned a few days ago from a month in the hospital here I regret that I am not able to fully answer your questionnaire relative to matters pertaining to the Little

Big Horn affair. It would require some time and the examination of papers, which I am not now able to do.

I will say that I was enlisted as a clerk and from time to time was on duty as clerk at headquarters, *not* by detail of Lieut. McIntosh, but by orders from the adjutant's office and was serving in that capacity just before we left the Rosebud June 22d, and continued with headquarters on that march and until *sent* back to Reno with a message.

I have had some correspondence with this man Ghent, of whom I have of late heard considerable from various sources, but have neither had the time nor the inclination to write him at any length.

What you say relative to his statements regarding myself, to say the least, amuses me. Let it go at that.

As a Mason I think you will appreciate the fact that I was considered worthy to be advanced to the 33d degree in Masonry, by the recommendation of men who have known me all my life is a sufficient guaranty of my honorable career as man and Mason.

Were I disposed or able to go into the details mentioned in your letter I would hardly care to do so as in collaboration with Mr. E. A. Brininstool of Los Angeles, Calif. I have prepared a full record of my connection with the Battle of the Little Big Horn which is now in his possession so that I do not consider it wise or courteous to again open the subject.

Regretting my inability to comply with your request, believe me

Fraternally yours,
Theo. W. Goldin

Note—Owing to my failing sight and other troubles the use of pen or pencil is beyond me.

Saginaw, W.S. Mich.
Oct. 4, 1932

Mr. Theodore Goldin,
Wisconsin Soldiers' Home,
Waupaca, Wisc.

Dear Sir and Brother:—

At the request of Mr. E. A. Brininstool I am sending you an exerpt from "Adventure" and he suggests that you send in a reply to it, as you will note by his marginal words.

I have had much interesting correspondence with him, DeLand and Graham.

He had your story of the Water Party sent me in H.T.T. [Hunter-Trader-Trapper] Magazine, and I found it of the greatest interest. I hope to see more of the same kind.

I trust that you are in better health than when I had a letter from you some time since.

Sincerely and Fraternally Yours,
Fred Dustin

Wisconsin Veterans Home
October 29, 1932

Mr. Fred Dustin
Saginaw, Mich., W.S.

Dear Brother Dustin:

Yours of October 4th, with the enclosure from Brininstool was received during the absence of Mrs. Goldin on an

extended eastern trip, leaving me with no one to do my reading for me, and before her return, while on a trip to Milwaukee to attend the Conclave of the Grand Commandery I
was taken suddenly and seriously ill, an illness from which
recovery has been slow leaving me without strength or ambition for anything. I am now slowly climbing the grade again
and am trying to work my way through the pile of correspondence that accumulated during Mrs. Goldin's absence and
my subsequent illness.

The enclosure you sent me was a mass of flaring misstatements and false assumptions and were I in shape to do
so I would have been glad to have answered it, but being unable to read a line it would have been a hard undertaking to
have done the matter justice. I regret to say that in some way
in clearing up my table the article has been lost or I would
have returned it to you. I find I am no longer in physical
condition or blessed with mental energy enough to tackle a
thing of this nature as I would have to do it depending on
memory alone as I cannot read notes, reports or matters of
that nature. I regret the loss of the article annotated as it
was by Brininstool.

The writer seems to be of the Godfrey school giving
every credence in the world to any statement of Godfrey's.

Benteen's squadron was miles away from both Reno and
Custer when he turned back, being well over in the vicinity
of where Lodge Grass is now located, and if Godfrey was
able to see and recognize Custer's command by the white
horse troop it must have been before they passed the point
where Reno later made his final stand and where Custer rode
over to the bluffs overlooking the valley and saw Reno engaged with the enemy, as a hundred yards beyond that point
the command was out of sight of either Benteen or McDougall
and the pack train. I recall looking back as we passed this

[81]

point and seeing both Benteen's squadron and the packs then
some distance back on the trail, and later when I went to
Reno with that dispatch I again caught a glimpse of them,
Benteen then having turned back and was moving down the
valley, but still to the southwest of the packs. When Reno
retreated my horse fell and supposing he was shot I lit out
for the brush along the river, and later as I started to cross
Benteen was just coming up to join Reno, arriving just about
the time I joined the command.

After Custer passed the point I mentioned above his
column could not be seen by Benteen or any troops up the
river.

While in the brush along with Herendeen the scout,
we heard the three volleys fired by Custer's men and later
after Herendeen came out with his dismounted and wounded
men these volleys were mentioned and officers said they had
not been heard on the bluffs. This claim was later given possible confirmation by an experiment tried by a detachment
from old Ft. Custer, when a detail was sent to Custer Hill
while a party of officers proceeded to Reno Hill after com-
paring watches and setting a time when the volleys were to be
fired. The report was that these volleys were not heard on
Reno Hill. This statement was made to me in 1926 at Crow
Agency by a retired officer who was with the party.

In these later years I find I have to think harder and
longer to recall the more minute details of those two days,
but in the end I am generally able to bring them back.

Mighty sorry that clipping was lost or destroyed as with
Brininstool's notations. It might have been worth something
to some one.

In a recent letter from Brininstool he wrote me that our
dear friend Major Ostrander had a severe setback and was

again confined to his bed. I wrote the old hero but as yet have heard nothing from him, did not really expect to but I wanted him to know I was thinking of him. He is one of the kind that gets mighty close to your heart and a man whose friendship I cherish very highly.

I am living very much in the past these days owing to the fact that I cannot read and keep abreast of the times and have to depend on Mrs. Goldin and the radio for the little I do get, but as she is unable to read for any length of time and our power here is not of the best I just keep a bit of a touch of elbows with the things of today.

I shall be glad to hear from you at any time and if there is any way in which I can be of service to you do not hesitate to call on me.

Sincerely & Fraternally yours,
Theo. W. Goldin

Neuritis prevents the use of pen or pencil.

Saginaw W.S. Mich.
Nov. 3, 1932

Mr. Theodore W. Goldin
Wisconsin Veterans' Home
Waupaca, Wisc.

Dear Brother Goldin:—

Your welcome letter came a couple of days ago, and I am surely glad to hear that you are recovering from your

recent illness. I note your attendance at the Grand Commandery from which I infer that you are a past commander.
I do not myself belong to the Commandery but do belong to
all the other Masonic bodies including the Consistory, and it
is evident to me that your services to the craft have been
eminent, as your honorary 33 degree means just that.

My own Masonic work has included Master, High Priest
and Illustrious Master of the York Rite bodies, and I have
spent near a generation in the work, and it is a matter of
satisfaction that two of the four honorary 33 degree masons
in this city are past masters of my own Lodge. We have five
blue lodges, three chapters, a council and a commandery here,
and at Bay City, fifteen miles north, is the consistory.

I have corresponded for years with good old Brother
Ostrander, and for twenty or twenty-five with Mr. DeLand
and during the past year or so have had an extensive correspondence with Mr. Brininstool, all of whom I have found
were natives of my home state, New York.

I think in a former letter that I told you that I had been
for years (thirty or more) collecting material on Custer's last
campaign, and twenty-two years ago had written a manuscript of near three hundred pages on that matter. If you have
read Mr. DeLand's book, you will note the he refers to my
manuscript and quotes from it.

In the last twenty years I have gathered a great deal of
authentic source-material, in fact a surprising amount of it,
and have annotated it for the purpose of writing it over, correcting some of my former errors and conclusions and adding
the new material.

Some months ago, I wrote you, propounding several questions, nine of them in fact. You courteously replied, stating
that your statement was in the hands of Mr. Brininstool, and
that you would not care under the circumstances to give to any

one else the same. I thought that your reasons were very just, and later Mr. B. sent me your story of the water party in Hunter, Trader, Trapper with which I was delighted.

I have found all my questions answered by correspondence with other parties except 6-7-9.

You will remember of course, that those who have tried to bolster up the Custer side have asserted that not a man was killed on Reno's skirmish line, either in its first position across the bottom or in its second in the woods until the retreat to the bluffs began.

I know that is not true, for Morris positively states that several men were killed on the first line, and it is equally certain that Reynolds, Bloody Knife, the negro Dorman and a soldier or two were killed before the charge from the woods. I had also understood that Bob Tail Bull was killed far out on the left of the line in the bottom, but the "Arikara Narrative" leaves me in doubt, as it would seem that he was killed near the river in the charge, but the matter is still indefinite to me.

In Brady's book you are made to say that you heard an altercation between Reno and Weir on the bluff, and I quoted this in my original manuscript, but am I correct? Or rather was Brady correct?

I got a story probably thirty years ago, that Weir, who was a bitter critic of Reno, was threatened with a killing by one of the Ree scouts after you were back on the Yellowstone for assertions of cowardice of Reno and the Rees, and I have also heard the story of a first sergeant who was with Reno who so far forgot his rank in his indignation as to call Weir a liar to his face. I do not know as to the exact truth of the stories, but the one regarding the Ree scout is somewhat corroberated in the little book, "William Jackson, Indian Scout," by James Willard Schultz.

You will remember that the two half-breed Blackfeet,

the Jacksons, were among the Indian scouts, and Jackson's story somewhat confirms the threat mentioned, but in an indirect and rather mild way, but does not mention Weir by name.

If you can give me any information not incompatible with your collaboration with Mr. Brininstool, it will be gratefully received.

If you find the clipping I sent you for Mr. B. I know that you will forward it to him.

I trust that this will find you feeling much better, and thanking you for your good letter, I am,

Sincerely and Fraternally Yours,
Fred Dustin
705 S. Fayette St.
Saginaw, W.S., Mich.

Wisconsin Veterans Home
Nov. 7, 1932

Mr. Fred Dustin
Saginaw W.S. Mich.

Dear Brother Dustin:

Your very interesting and welcome letter of the 3d reached me Saturday and as this is one of the days when I feel like writing I will try and answer it the best I can. With your letter came one from our good friend Ostrander who is again confined to his bed but who refuses to quit but keeps on writing and fighting like the real soldier he was.

As soon as I heard of his illness I wrote him a note of condolence with no expectation of receiving an answer, at least for some time to come, but along it came. Not a word of complaint, just a statement that he was a bit out of commission. Wish I had his pluck, but we were not all cast in a heroic mould.

I was in attendance at the Conclave of our Grand Commandery by virtue of the fact that in 1898 I was Grand Commander of Wisconsin and today am the oldest living Past Grand Commander, so you can see I am always glad to attend these gatherings when possible. Following my term as Grand Commander and in 1900 I was appointed Inspector General for the State, a position I held until 1903 when other business made is necessary for me to drop out, I received my 32d, in 1896, and the Hon. 33d, in September 1902, and for some time took an active part in the degree work of my Consistory, but failing sight has forced me to the side lines and based on the advice of my doctors at the time of my recent illness to live as quietly as I could and avoid excitement I guess I am in for a seat in the bleachers.

I may overlook something to which you desire an answer; if I do fire it at me again and I'll do the best I can.

There is no question but that there were several killed during Reno's fight in the bottoms, among them Charley Reynolds, Bloody Knife the Ree guide and Isaiah Dorman the half breed interpreter and I think one or two others but I cannot now definitely recollect as to this. Of course the heavy loss was on the retreat, mostly at the crossing, although Lieut. McIntosh was killed before he reached the crossing and Lieut. Hodgson after he had gotten across the river. G Troop suffered the heaviest loss at the crossing as it was the rear troop having been stationed on the extreme left of our line.

I remember the Jackson boys very well. Did some scouting with them after I left the service. They were brave, capable fellows and always did good work.

That chapter in Brady's book has been the cause of a lot of annoyance to me and left me in a wrong light so far as many of its statements were concerned. At Brady's request in 1904, while acting as Chairman of the Stalwart Republican State Central Committee of Wisconsin, I dictated a chapter to my stenographer and sent it to him. I never saw a proof of it and while Brady promised to send me a copy of the book, I never received it and in fact did not see the book until many years later when, to my surprise and indignation I found that he had written the chapter over changing it to fit his views of the fight and so altering it that I was hardly able to recognize any part of it as my work. I at once sought to get in touch with Brady in order to get at his reasons for so changing the article, but on inquiry learned that he had recently died, leaving me helpless so far as securing a correction or explanation was concerned.

I believe I did state in the article that there was some sort of an altercation between Weir and Reno, relative to a forward movement to locate and aid Custer. I DID NOT hear it as it was just about over when I climbed the hill after leaving Herendeen the scout and crossing the river while Herendeen went back to guide a larger party of the dismounted men with one or more wounded across at the ford where I made my crossing. I heard some loud talking as I approached where the officers were gathered to report my escape, but what it was I cannot say, all I know was that just as I came up Weir separated himself from the group, evidently laboring under considerable excitement and I heard him say to Lieut. Edgerly, his field Lieut: "Edgerly, mount D Troop and we will try and find Custer," or words to that effect. I was told later by Lieut. Wallace that Weir and Reno had some hot words because Reno refused to advance until the packs came up and that Weir's action in mounting his troop and moving out was really an act of insubordination and that it was suggested to Reno that he place Weir under arrest, but Reno did not seem disposed to do it. Weir's action caused considerable comment both at the time and later during the summer.

Fred Dustin and Theodore W. Goldin Correspondence

Guess there is no question but that the most of the Rees had a bad attack of cold feet and some of the tougher ones did not stop until they were back at the agency at Ft. Berthold. That isn't so strange when we recall the fact that the brunt of the attack in the effort to break our line and get in Reno's rear preventing his retreat along the way he came in was directed against the extreme left flank which was held by our Indians, and they, after their many defeats at the hands of the Sioux and Cheyennes in years past, when confronted by such an overwhelming force soon broke thus forcing McIntosh with G Troop to swing back into the timber from which point they retreated a short time later. Much of this is hearsay on my part as I had only just reached Reno with that dispatch when the break occurred followed a few moments later by the retreat, in which I, riding some distance on the left flank of the retreating column, was thrown from my horse when he stumbled and fell and in some miraculous way was able to reach the underbrush some distance below the real crossing. There were no Indians so far as I saw on that left flank. All of them were on the right flank seeking to prevent Reno from retreating up the valley in the direction from whence he came, forcing him to turn sharply to the left and forced him over a cut bank and out at a similar bank on the east side of the river. From where I lay I could see that many of the men were

[89]

having a hard time to force their horses over the bank and an even harder time making the landing on the other side. The last of the column was barely across the river and lost to sight in one of several ravines leading to the bluffs when Herendeen and I heard the three volleys fired by Custer's command and the most of the Indians left Reno and disappeared down the valley in the direction of the firing. It was to this movement on their part that I always felt I owed my life, for had they remained in that vicinity the chances are I would have been discovered and sent to join those who had already fallen. Shortly after this, when I crossed the river and made my way to the command on the cliffs I did not encounter any Indians but I did pass the body of Dr. De Wolf and the soldier to whom he had dismounted to give first aid on that retreat; both were dead.

As to Weir's conduct during the remainder of the time we were in the field I know little or nothing, save that the relations between Weir and Reno and some of the other officers seemed strained. Weir never went to headquarters save when summoned.

Guess I had better get off the air or I'll be writing a book. If I have overlooked anything you really wanted answered, tell me so specifically and I will answer it the best I can.

I have a fine letter from Brininstool who will have an article in WINNERS OF THE WEST, the official publication of the National Indian War Veterans on the Ft. Fetterman affair which I am sure will be well worth reading. He had an article in the October number telling of how Buffalo Bill was drawn off from his intention of arresting Sitting Bull at the time the Ghost Dance craze was at its height. I had heard the story substantially as he tells it many years ago. Possibly he may send you a copy. If so I am sure you will enjoy it.

I also have a splendid letter from Johnson of Minn. covering many interesting matters and showing much personal research work in years past.

With best wishes and kindest regards, believe me

Sincerely & Fraternally yours,
Theo. W. Goldin

Saginaw W.S. Mich.
Nov. 17, 1932

Mr. Theo. W. Goldin
Wisconsin Veterans Home
Wis.

Dear Brother Goldin:—

Your fine and interesting letter to hand, and I was sure glad to know that you felt like writing. Your Masonic service certainly has been one to commend you to the Ancient Craft and your 33rd degree means a great deal.

I thank you for the information as to the Custer affair, and am again asking for more. I hope I will not tire you with my queries, but I am hoping to complete the revision and rewriting of my manuscript this winter.

You have undoubtedly heard the story circulated by General Godfrey about 1926 that Major Reno had out and out proposed to Benteen to abandon the wounded and retreat to the Yellowstone. This cruel and unpardonable story was to me preposterous, but it did not come to me until soon before

Godfrey died, or I should have had something to say to him about it.

In a certain sense, this story was old, very old indeed, for Colonel Gibbon, in a published article in 1877, stated that "the wounded had in some way got the idea that they were to be abandoned." Long, long ago, I think that I learned of certain matters which at the time did not impress me, but have come back to me with great force. It appears that Reno and Benteen were talking the night of the 25th about the possible contingency of being forced to leave the wounded if help did not come as there was a possibility of the same conditions being forced on the command that caused Reno to leave the bottom for the hills. This conversation was overheard by a sergeant, I think, and some other enlisted men. This was all the foundation for Godfrey's story, given out nearly fifty years after the event and after neither Reno or Benteen were living to affirm or deny.

I cannot understand *WHY* an officer of Godfrey's standing should have given out this tale unless afflicted by senile dementia.

Now, I ask, if you have any version of this story? Had there been anything to it, it is not difficult to see that it would have been used at the Court of Inquiry against Reno, for Godfrey claimed to have obtained the information *from Benteen* June 28, 1876, the day you were burying the dead, but did not get the details from Benteen until 1881. On the 28th, according to Godfrey, he simply had *intimations* from Benteen. I am inclined to think that Godfrey, like Weir, was so prejudiced against Reno, a prejudice which in his old age became almost rabid. I simply feel that in the efforts to damn Reno, some of his detractors have hardly stopped at anything. Reno's character was against him, but unless it could be shown that *his character* adversely affected his conduct at the battle, it would have no more bearing on the events of those days than Custer's immorality (both Custers) or Keogh's sodden drunkenness.

A very sad feature to me has been the holding up of Custer as an immaculate hero and his officers (those of the regiment except Reno and Benteen) as model Christian gentlemen. I think you will get my idea of this matter. Reno has been represented as a coward, a drunkard, poltroon and a liar by the supporters of Custer while the latter has been pictured as a demi-god, sacrificed by the former.

HISTORY neither makes gods or devils out of men, but pictures them as they were, but history is not partisan: it is impersonal and the value of any historical work lies not in the *opinions* of he who write it, but in the facts recorded, not in part, not on one side, not colored by prejudice or dislike, but by impartial setting down ALL THE FACTS as far as obtainable, which bear upon the subject.

Another matter on which I would like further light, is whether the "Crow's Nest" where Varnum and the scouts went, and where Custer also went, was on the RIGHT HAND or LEFT HAND of the Creek. Also, were you with Cooke when he accompanied Reno toward his upper crossing some distance before he returned and joined Custer?

I trust that you are improving. I had a letter from good old Brother Ostrander since receiving yours. He is still full of fire, and I only wish that his bodily strength was equal to his mental.

> I am, my worthy brother and commander,
> Fraternally yours,
> Fred Dustin

Wisconsin Veterans Home
Nov. 19, 1932

Mr. Fred Dustin
Saginaw, Mich.

Dear Brother Dustin:

Your very welcome and interesting letter is before me, and as this is one of the days when writing comes easy I thought I had better answer it as best I could.

I am slowly plodding along the trail, not making any speed or accomplishing very much of anything, nor do I look forward to any particular come back in the near future if at all. My doctors, or rather the one in whom I have the most confidence tells me that while my general health is not so bad I might as well make up my mind that somewhere in my anatomy there are bits of worn out machinery that as yet medical science has discovered no pills or potions capable of rebuilding the worn out parts and that my best bet is to take things quietly, avoid over exertion and excitment and just let Mother Nature have her way. Good advice I guess, but hard for a man who has lived the active life I have to follow, but I guess I will make it in time.

I too had a letter from Ostrander telling me that he was as full of fight as ever, but handicapped by lack of health and strength. I sympathize with him from the depths of my heart. He is sure no quitter even under the most adverse conditions.

I was glad I was able to answer some of your queries to your satisfaction.

I often look back over the years of my Masonic activities with many pleasant memories, realizing as I now do that those activities are ended as owing to ill health and to a certain

[94]

extent limited financial resources. I am unable to keep the close touch I would like to keep and am trying to content myself with sitting by the side of the trail and watching the parade pass by.

Not until quite recently did I ever hear that story of Reno's proposition to Benteen to abandon the wounded and seek to turn back to the Yellowstone. I cannot believe it; the suggestion was not like anything I ever knew of Reno.

To me it sounds like other impossible statements made by Godfrey. In the first place I have reason to know that at the time of the fight, nor at any other time, did Benteen have a very high opinion of Godfrey. This I gather from an extensive correspondence with Benteen after his retirement as well as from impressions gained by a visit of several days at his home in Atlanta, in both the correspondence and our many conversations we spent most of the time in discussing the '76 campaign and this naturally brought out many remarks regarding officers of the regiment, often taking us into very close study of officers and their actions, and from these things I feel warranted in saying that Godfrey was the last officer in the regiment to whom Benteen would have told such a story even had it been true. Further than this, had there been anything to the story isn't it a safe bet that Godfrey or some other friend of Custer and an enemy of Reno would have brought that out in that court of inquiry?

The fact that it never was breathed until after Reno and Benteen were both dead in my judgment but adds to its falsity. We all know much about Reno that was not to his credit, the same can be said of Custer with equal truth. Godfrey and men of his kind taking advantage of the fact that officers who might and could have talked held back because of a desire to save Mrs. Custer an added pain, continued to push their defamatory statements to the front, and toward the end Godfrey

[95]

must have been a mental derelict if we are to credit him with all the statements attributed to him.

To me it has been more than passing strange that as one by one the officers who were in that engagement passed over the divide Godfrey showed up in some new and theretofore unheard of bit of heroic service.

Some day, as men dig deep for facts, many of these things are going to be exploded. I do not, of course, expect to live to see it, but come it will.

I was not with Lieut. Cooke while he rode with Reno's column. I have an indistinct recollection that Tom Custer was with him but it is not entirely clear in my mind. I think the names of those of Custer's command who left Reno before he crossed the river came out in the testimony at the court of inquiry.

With only one officer—Varnum—now living who was with us in the fight, and his health so poor that the chances are he will never write anything of his recollections of those days it looks as though the source of first hand information was about exhausted.

As I now recall it the Crow's Nest was on the right of the trail as we came up out of the Rosebud Valley, and some little distance from it, just how far I am unable to recall as I never back trailed over our march that morning and the night before.

Have not heard from Brininstool in some time but think he is working on some other matters of a historical nature.

If I can be of any further assistance to you at any time do not hesitate to call on me.

Sincerely yours,
Theo. W. Goldin

[96]

Mr. Theo. W. Goldin
Wiscon. Veterans Home, Wis.

My Dear Brother Goldin:—

I have your letter of November 19 answering some of
my queries and telling me about yourself.

Like yourself I have been active in Masonry for many
years, but now with the snows of sixty-six winters, I am content to see the work go on by others, occasionally advising
and sometimes taking an honorable part in something special,
but I do not regard the years gone, for like every other person
who really tries to do his part, I have the satisfaction of having
lived to as good purpose as my limited ability, education and
means have permitted, making mistakes of judgment perhaps,
but not those mistakes or rather crimes of intemperance, dis-
honesty and wickedness that leave scars which never heal.

Regarding the story of Reno's proposed desertion of the
wounded, I considered it preposterous, for to me it seemed
almost a crime to put forward such a story or to circulate it,
and I am sorry that General Godfrey in his old age permitted
himself to be made a tool in the matter. I have never realized
until the last year or two, that his animosity and dislike for
Reno was as pronounced as it was, but frank readings of his
story in the Century surely indicates that his prejudice was of
long standing.

I myself realize that Reno was far from what might be
wished, but I have also learned that the most of his detractors
owed their spite to a Custer-worship that blinded them to
all else.

In his story, Godfrey says: "Reno emptied his revolvers and then threw them away." I have never seen the statement elsewhere but have seen it disputed. I have never seen any evidence that he carried more than one revolver. I think that I remember seeing this statement flatly contradicted, and perhaps you can give me some information. I am not sure but it was yourself or Morris that said that Reno DID NOT throw away his revolvers, but I have not time to look over my material, and will ask if you can help me out.

I thank you again for the information you have so kindly given me, and wish you the good things that you so deserve.

With best wishes and kindest greetings, I am

Fraternally yours,
Fred Dustin

Wisconsin Veterans Home
January 12, 1933

Mr. Fred Dustin
Saginaw, W.S. Mich.

Dear Brother Dustin:

Your most welcome letter of the 9th lies on my table asking for an answer and as this happens to be one of the days when writing seems a bit easy I'll tackle it.

Like yourself I look back over the years when it was possible for me to be active in Masonry with a great deal of pleasure. I often find myself recalling old faces, old friendships, many of them broken by the passing of men I learned

[98]

to know and love. I am still interested in the welfare of the Order although unable to take an active part in any of the work, and yet, do you know when I visit a Lodge and look in vain for faces once familiar to me there comes to me a feeling of lonesomeness. The greetings of the Brothers present is as hearty as ever, but the faces are new, most of them younger, and I feel like a stranger.

Glad I was able to answer some of your queries at least in a way.

The story that Reno advocated abandoning the wounded is one I never took any stock in, but it gained more or less publicity owing perhaps to the fact that toward the last Gen. Godfrey let his animosity lead him a bit too far afield.

You ask what, if anything, I know relative to the story that on the retreat Reno emptied his revolvers and threw them in the faces of the charging foe. I never believed it and my disbelief was later strengthened either by one of Benteen's letters to me or by a statement made at one of my visits to him. The story had been mentioned and Benteen denied its truth ending by saying that so far as he knew Reno, like most officers, carried only one revolver and then said: "I have the gun Reno carried on that day. Later on in the campaign I traded guns with him I guess because I had heard the story and wanted proof in my hands that it was not so." After that I had no hesitation in denying the story whenever it was mentioned to me.

Godfrey had many good traits but his blind devotion to Custer led him into the camp of men like Ghent and Col. Bates and he either learned to draw the long bow, or it was done for him. It is true there was more or less of a division of sentiment in the regiment as to Custer, whose life did not partake of the angelic, but this was largely owing to doubts as to his ability as an Indian fighter. Even his enemies had nothing but good to say of his record in the civil war, but felt that his recklessness in Indian fighting was a dangerous thing. Then too, among some of the older officers there was always a feeling that he was in error in attacking Black Kettle's band on the Washita after the warning he received from Gen. Hazen that the Indians were there by his orders and worst of all his conduct in abandoning Major Elliott and his men to their fate without even a shadow of an effort to save or find them.

Brininstool recently sent me the clippings of a story published in a Washington, Pa. paper and written by one Forrest and purporting to be the stories told him by a man named Pigford and another fellow named Roberts. Pigford was in the fight all right as his name appears signed to that petition circulated in July '76. Some of his story, considering the lapse of years is all right and fairly believable, but like so many of the fellows he proceeded to spill the beans in one case by telling of killing an Indian who was firing arrows into our lines from a SHOT GUN while hiding in a tree, but his most glaring act in the bean spilling episode came when he stated that under orders from Capt. French, his troop commander, he with two other men were sent out to find traces of Custer and that they reached a point within 300 yards of that last stand and witnessed the final scenes of the tragedy and that after it was over and before they had a chance to make their escape, the Indians swarmed down on them headed for Reno's command and that both his companions were killed, but he is unable to remember their names and that the fleetness of his horse was all that saved him. Giving the rest of his story full credit he spoiled it by this one claim which every one familiar with the terrain knows was impossible and that no one, two or three white men could have gotten within that distance of Custer Hill without being discovered and wiped out.

Brininstool wrote Forrest calling attention to many inaccuracies and impossibilities but like a lot of would-be historians, Forrest still insisted that all these things were possible and we dropped the matter not replying to the latter which I believe is now in DeLand's hands.

I learned years ago how futile it was to try and make these embryo historians see the error of their ways so let them ramble.

If I can be of any assistance in trying to clear up points for you do not hesitate to call on me.

With the best of wishes for a happy, successful and prosperous New Year, in which Mrs. Goldin, who is my censor of all correspondence, joins me, believe me

Sincerely and Fraternally yours,
GOLDIN

Jan. 21, 1934

Mr. Theodore Goldin
Waupaca, Wis.

My Dear Brother Goldin:—

It is a long time since I heard from you except indirectly and I trust that you are well.

Since our last correspondence I have had much with others concerning the Little Big Horn and related subjects. I have just read Peter Thompson's story in "Black Hills Trails," but I cannot believe that he wrote it himself. It is too much like a newspaper man's work who has taken a few leading facts and garbled them to suit his own purposes just as Ralph Meeker did in 1876, also Whittaker and plenty of others. You knew Thompson I understand, and I have gathered from other accounts that his horse gave out between Reno's Creek and Reno's final position, and that he with another private in the same fix later joined Reno.

In the "Arikara Narrative," several of the Ree scouts relate that they saw a soldier with his horse down at the point mentioned, and later another, so I am sure that Thompson was one of them, but his alleged "story" is very much confused in details while the story I have compiled as a small part of the events of that day in which Thompson was concerned, was very simple and to the point. His record was a very honorable one in the fight, like your own, and it is regrettable that falsehood should cast doubts and shadows on it.

I have read Mr. Brininstool's account of your experiences in going for water, and they are in such contrast to those described in the Thompson tale that there can be no comparison. The Medal of Honor records of that fight which I have copies of were authentic and are of great credit to men like yourself who took part.

Were you on that scout with Reno in which he found the great trail? You will likely remember that the officer who kept the itinerary of that march was killed in the fight, and his papers lost, so I have only very fragmentary accounts, and things which happened on his (Reno's) return make it of considerable interest. If you can give me any facts I will be grateful.

Masonically, there is little work in any of the bodies, and we have been weeding out some of the poor timber that we unfortunately acquired in "boom" days after and during the war, and the lull in petitions is one of the best things that has happened to the Blue Lodges in a generation. and has not hurt the other bodies. Financially, all the bodies to which I belong, Blue, Chapter, Order of High Priesthood, Council and Consistory, are in fair condition, although a closed bank is holding up our funds in the first two. Personally, this bank situation (very largely political), for both of our banks are solvent, is making it hard but if this inflation bubble does not burst too quick, I being an old man, will likely pull through all right, but—I am sorry for the young generation who will be called on to foot the bills the States and general government are piling up.

Trusting that I will hear from you soon and with best wishes, I am,

Sincerely and Fraternally Yours,
Fred Dustin

Wisconsin Veterans Home
January 24, 1934

Mr. Fred Dustin
Saginaw Mich, W.S.

Dear Brother Dustin:

Your letter of the 21st reached me this morning and as this is one of the days when I am able to write and as I am also writing some other letters in connection with the same subject matter I will try and answer it.

I never took full stock in Pete Thompson's story either as I have read it or heard him relate it as I did at the semi-centennial in 1926. For a long time I was very much inclined to be skeptical as to the manner of his joining Reno's command, but was rather inclined to think he was one of the "C" Troop men who was detailed with the pack train, but the story of the Rees as to seeing the two men back there on the bottoms when they were slipping out after Reno's retreat gives the story a little more foundation. If they joined Reno on the bluffs after his retreat it must have been before I was able to cross the stream and rejoin him after my horse fell and threw me on the retreat. Of one thing I am sure, no stragglers joined us after I crossed the river which, in fact, was just as Benteen's squadron came up, as they were just dismounting when I climbed the bluffs and I had been able to see them for some distance up the river as they came on. There are details of Pete's story later in the fight that so far as we were ever able to learn were not borne out by the facts, particularly his story about the water parties of which I believe there were several who went down after our second trip in which Madden was wounded. We never heard of any heavy fighting by any of the parties, and so far as I ever recall, the volley that was fired from across the river and got Madden was the only firing done.

I have just finished reading an article by Sergt. Windolph of "H" Troop in which among other things he tells of being sent out by Benteen to protect the water parties and of firing into Indians on the west side of the river. So far as I can recall there were no Indians on the west side of the river, all of them surrounding us on the east side. Brininstool has this article which was published in the SUNRISE magazine, but which adds but little authentic data.

My troop was not with Reno on that scout that led to the finding of the trail, but remained with Custer at the mouth of Powder River, later moving up to Tongue River and then out until we met Reno on his return so that I am unable to give you anything worth while as to that scout. I do not recall the name of the officer who kept the itinerary of that scout, but understood he was killed with Custer later and his report was never written up but was given Custer and I believe Terry verbally at the mouth of the Rosebud.

A recent letter from Brininstool tells me that some of his material has been filmed by one of the movie outfits at Hollywood and that another one is being prepared for a prominent movie star who has taken a fancy to them. I was glad to hear of this as Brinny's recent severe illness had taken all the pep out of him and he was doing but little, save mark time since he got out that Benteen story. This new venture will give him something to think about and work on and I am sure will do him good. He seems to be in better health and I am hoping will not be open to another attack of his intestinal trouble which came near making him a candidate for the promised land.

In a letter received from him a day or two ago he wrote of hearing briefly from dear old Major Ostrander and that he was in bad shape confined to his bed and suffering intensly. It may be that the dear old man is nearing the entrance to the long, long trail. His age and his long continued poor health do not offer much encouragement for a come back. We will miss the old man. I know that all through his long illness he has kept at work trying to get as much history done as possible.

Mr. Goldin, who has to do all my reading for me is now reading F. F. Van de Water's book, THUNDER SHIELD which we have found quite interesting as far as we have gotten and as he deals with the Custer incident I expect to find it even more interesting.

I have been in correspondence with him and find he is

now engaged in writing a life of Custer and I infer from what he says that it will not be of the same style as those of Godfrey, Col. Bates and others. He has a mass of facts that will if used not prove very pleasant reading to the Custer hero worshippers. He tells me he is trying to make it a story of facts rather than fiction. I am glad both it and his book were not published until after the death of Mrs. Custer.

If at any time you think I can be of any help to you, draw on me.

My health is none too good although Mrs. Goldin and myself are able to carry on after a style.

With kindest regards and best wishes believe me

Sincerely and Fraternally yours,
Theo. Goldin

Feb. 17, 1934

Mr. Theo. Goldin
Wapaca, Wis.

Dear Brother Goldin:—

Your letter of Jan. 24 was duly received and I was glad to hear from you. Your information is enlightening and I sure thank you for your courtesy.

I did not amplify my statement about the Rees seeing two soldiers whose worn-out horses had caused them to be left behind by Custer's command, and I will explain further.

There has been so much fiction, so much guess-work, so

much taken for granted, so many view points that the story as a whole is involved in obscurity, and in my historical work which I am trying to produce, I am aiming at telling the story AS A WHOLE as accurately as it is possible for me to do. To do this has required not only a great deal of study and research, but a considerable fund of patience. Now as to the Rees, their story AS A WHOLE has never been told. I have picked it out piecemeal from the "Arikara Narrative," the stories of the six Crow Scouts, of the officers and men, of Girard, of William Jackson and of others.

So many statements are misleading: for instance, Godfrey states that "40 Ree scouts accompanied Terry's force from Lincoln," and leaves the inference that forty Rees went into battle with Reno. As a matter of fact, a number of these scouts were not Rees at all, but there were the two Jacksons and two Crows, and of this number, three were killed (Rees) and one Ree and one Crow badly wounded. There were about twenty-five of the so-called Ree scouts with Reno just after you separated from him, and some of these had been left behind, one or two scouting to the left, and one or two more on account of poor horses, and one was with the packs so that there were about a dozen that either did not cross the Little Big Horn at all, or parted from Reno just *after* his first crossing at the upper ford, and gathered up some Dakota ponies at the right, driving them across the river where later they joined those left behind, some of whom saw the two dismounted soldiers. ALL OF THESE REE SCOUTS of this particular group JOINED RENO AFTER HE HAD RETREATED TO THE HILL, but on the easterly or rather southerly side of where he made his last stand. Most of them shortly after retreated, driving a small herd of Dakota ponies, and headed back toward the supply camp at the Powder. This in brief is

Fred Dustin and Theodore W. Goldin Correspondence

the Ree story, but SOME of them remained with Reno until he was relieved by Terry.

I note you have been reading an article by Windolph. This I have never seen and it would oblige me greatly if you can tell me where I can get a copy. A book which came out a year or two ago, "A Warrior Who Fought Custer," is one of the most revealing things in connection with that fight that I have ever read. For the first time a warrior who fought Custer speaks out without reserve, and it astonishingly corroborates many facts heretofore either very hazy or disputed. I have found it invaluable.

I have not yet seen the book "Thunder Shield," but hope to be able to get a copy soon. My finances have been very low for several months, and one of our closed banks holds a small sum I had laid aside for taxes so that I have been hard pressed and not able to buy several books needed at this time.

I think that the lips of many a man has been sealed except in private, by the fact that Mrs. Custer lived. Her fine personality, and her worship of her husband were factors in suppressing the truth. I am quite sure that if Varnum had spoken his mind he would have made some statements that might not have been palatable to Custer-worshippers, to put it mildly, and certainly Benteen would have had some scorching remarks had he been willing to talk. We know what Hughes *did* say in print, and what Brisbin and Gibbon privately said, to say nothing of many other officers of the command.

Since Mr. Brininstool's serious illness I have not heard from him more than two or three times where before he wrote often twice a month, but I had a letter from him dated Jan. 24, in which he says he has been under the weather much of the time since Xmas.

He says that when Van de Water gets out his book,

"there will be weeping, wailing and gnashing of teeth," by several parties, "willie ghent" as he calls him, among them. He does not like "willie" and I do not wonder at it, although it seems to me that he is too trifling a creature to bother with.

As to our dear old friend and brother, Ostrander, I have not had a letter from him for some time, but he sent me a copy of an interesting paper a short time ago. I expect to write to him to-morrow.

He surely is a grand old man, and it is pitiful that he has to suffer so. His historical work, while not of great volume, is of great value, and he has inspired others with his own truth, fidelity and interest.

As for myself, I must say that my correspondents have been more than kind with only one exception, and that one exception has not improved his own position by his actions.

I again thank you, and if you can give me the information asked for it will be duly appreciated by

Your "Friend and Brother,"
Fred Dustin

Fred Dustin and
Theodore W. Goldin
Correspondence

Wisconsin Veterans Home
February 22, 1934

Mr. Fred Dustin
W.S. Saginaw, Mich.

Dear Brother Dustin:

Yours of recent date at hand. Mighty glad to get it as it brings me some new bits of information.

I am sorry I cannot give you the information you ask

[109]

regarding the published story of Sergt. Windolph. The copy I saw was one sent me by Brininstool and was a reprint of an article published in the SUNRISE Magazine, but I cannot recall the date. I returned it to Brinny after reading it. I am sure he can give you the information you ask. There was really not much in the story save that he stated that he overheard a conversation between Custer and Benteen in which Benteen suggested the idea of keeping the regiment together. He also stated that he overheard Charlie Reynolds say that there was the biggest Indian village down in the valley that he had ever seen. This must have been after Custer returned from Crows Nest on the morning of the 25th. My impression was that Reynolds was not with that party, but in a letter written by Varnum he gave the names of those who were with him and Reynolds was among them.

In another letter written by Varnum he stated that he commanded "H" Troop in 1889 and that Windolph was his first sergeant, and a good one, level headed and not apt to speak untruthfully of any events he tried to relate.

I heard a new story about Peter Thompson. It seems that in some way Pete was sent to Washington to represent the Medal of Honor men of the Little Big Horn battle. Just how this came about I do not know, but in any event he was there and was the guest at a dinner at the Army & Navy Club. He was grilled in regard to his story and the questioning was so sharp and he got tangled up and left the banquet table.

The original plan for the funeral of the Unknown Soldier included plans for mobilizing all Medal men as a special escort. The plan went so far that we were advised as to the route we were to take and were advised where we were to be quartered, but soon after this Congress bucked on the appropriation and we were notified that it had been called off.

Strange to say in all these years I have never seen a copy of Thompson's story and know of it only in the few fragments I gathered from listening to him at Crow Agency in '26 and in hearing others repeat it. It has always been strange to me that he never brought his partner into the story to back him up. That was what came near bringing on a fight between Pete and Bill Slaper in '26. Slaper and the man Pete says was with him enlisted together in Cincinnati, Slaper going to "M" Troop and his partner to "C." They were both discharged on the same day by reason of expiration of term of service and both returned to Cincinnati together and Bill claimed that the story was never mentioned by his friend, but Graham fell for it as did the people near where he lived and the editor of the Belle Fourche Bee.

I received in the same mail with your letter one from Brinny, and I am taking the liberty of enclosing it herewith as there may be something in it that may interest you. Hope there is.

It appears from this letter as well as letters I have had from Van de Water that he is working hard to get his material whipped into shape, and from what I can gather he has a lot of mighty good stuff. No doubt in my mind but that his book will stir up fellows like Ghent, Bates, Whitaker, if he is still alive, and others who have sought and are still seeking to hold Custer up to the world as a perfect man, while Van will paint him as a man of clay and hold the proofs to back his statements.

I am very anxious that he get a slant at letters Benteen wrote me about the time of the first publication of Godfrey's Century article, and which are now owned by Dr. Philip G. Cole of New York to whom Brinny sold them with my consent. There is good stuff in them if Van can get at them.

Of course they are Cole's property, but both Brinny and myself have suggested that Cole let Van see them.

I have not heard from Major Ostrander for some time,
his last now was written in bed and I begged him not to over
exert himself by trying to reply to my letter to him.

I fear the dear old man is looking over the wall into
the promised land. It is too bad that he has to suffer as he does.

I know that much of his work has been done under hard
physical conditions and that only his nerve and pluck have
carried him through. He tells me that he thinks his trip to
the G.A.R. reunion at St. Paul last fall was too much for him
as he never fully recovered from it. He is fortunate in having
a really wonderful nurse. She has pulled him through several
bad spells, but I fear that continued suffering and illness have
sapped his strength so that there is not much left to draw on.
We will miss him sadly. I agree with all Brinny says in his
letter.

Just recently I have discovered a bit of difficulty with
my memory. For instance, Mrs. Goldin will read my letters
carefully and sometimes when I sit down to answer them I
find difficulty in recalling all that was in them. If I could
see to read the letters I am sure I could overcome this difficulty.
My memory of things of things past seems as good as ever, it
is just things of a few hours that get confused as often after
a letter has been answered and mailed I recall something I
overlooked. I write you this so that in case I fail to answer
any question of yours I want you to come back at me for an
answer. I am hoping my memory of days of old will not fail
me although it might not be strange if it did as I am now
nearly 76 and so far I notice no fault in it and am hoping I
will be able to render my friends some little service during
my time here. My general health is good; my real trouble is

with sight and hearing and impaired circulation that makes getting about at times something of an undertaking.

I want you to feel at liberty to call on me any time you think I can help.

Fred Dustin and Theodore W. Goldin Correspondence

Sincerely and Fraternally yours,
Theo. W. Goldin

Feb. 26, 1934

Mr. Theodore Goldin
Waupaca, Wis.

Dear Brother Goldin:—

Your letter of the 22nd received and I was very glad to hear from you. Regarding Windolph's story I will write Mr. B. about it.

If what you say about Thompson's being grilled at a dinner in Washington is correct, he surely was in a "bad way," as his story as printed in the book, "Black Hills Trails," is not only preposterous but under the circumstances impossible. From beginning to end it is vague, hazy and uncertain, and although I have never been on the ground, my long study of the terrain through maps, descriptions and photographs has so familiarized me with it that the story *as a whole* is ridiculous although *parts* of it might easily be authenticated.

The Ree scouts whose relations are found in "The Arikara Narrative," gave a clue to Thompson's story which proves that his "wanderings" over the field, following Custer nearly to his *battlefield*, were figments of *somebody's* imagination.

Your letter from Mr. Brininstool which you enclosed I am returning. Like all his letters it is interesting. He is death on fakirs but I have found that we must discriminate somewhat, for there are two kinds of fakirs; those who themselves deliberately falsify, and those who are the victims of such writers as Joe De Barthe whose life of Frank Grouard was about the most impudent piece of invention ever put out as a "life" of anyone.

Whittaker's life of Custer was not so much a fake as an intense partisan propaganda, for his leading facts were good but were nullified by his "sins of omission" and false inferences, just like the one you cite concerning a drunken officer's having him courtmartialed in '67. It was his superior officer that preferred charges against him as well. But Whittaker was a dime novel writer and could not stick to fact in minor matters, for while his *leading* statements were in general correct, his errors in detail were so numerous that his work is worse than worthless to the student of Custer's life who cannot discriminate. One short chapter of 25 pages contains in a not too careful analysis seventy-five errors and misstatements.

Regarding your memory, that is a trick it plays on most of us after we reach sixty. I am sixty-seven and have the same difficulty, so that you at seventy-five are as good as I who am eight years younger.

When a young man down in New York State where I was born and grew up, I was foreman in a lumber yard. Working under me was a man named CHARLES PRIOR, who had a friend in the same town who he called "Buddy," but whose real name I do not remember. They had both been in Keogh's troop, "Wild I," and I got some very interesting things from Prior who had served in the Civil War and had a fine discharge from that service which I have seen, and afterwards

[114]

enlisted in the regular cavalry, being with Buddy assigned to the Seventh, Troop I.

From his description, Keogh was one of those drunken brutes that were relics of the war, a soldier of fortune merely like many Irishmen of his type. He is referred to by Mrs. Custer in one or more of her books, but not by name. From Prior's account Keogh's sergeants were usually "tough," and judging from "Buddy" especially. Perhaps they needed to be for he, Buddy, got into trouble with one and knocked him down for which he was chased around by Keogh who was just drunk enough to be ugly, and the upshot of the matter was that Prior and Buddy deserted and I am under the impression that Prior said that it was sometime previous to the time Terry's column left Ft. Lincoln on its march to the Little Big Horn. Buddy was later apprehended and served a year at some eastern penitentiary, but Prior claimed that he got off easier. Just how much truth there was in Prior's story I cannot say, but it is sure that his characterization of Keogh was correct, for it has been more than once corroborated by others. From Prior's account it would seem that Tom Custer was a drunken sot who kept his commission only through his brother's protection in his own immediate command. Be that as it may, his habits were a long way from being those of a good officer, for he too, was a relic of the Civil War, a type of those whose records are largely found in the office of the Judge-Advocate General in the form of court-martial papers. For five or six years following that war, the history of the Seventh Cavalry was one of continually changing official personnel, with dismissals, cashierings and "resignations" all too prominent.

I have your story of the "Water Party" written by Mr. Brininstool, and it is of deep interest. It is these individual relations that are of value, for an officer like Godfrey for

[115]

instance, honorable and honest in intention, could not, even if unbiased, give a true picture of more than a general view of the whole fight, while giving details of his own participation. I have been able to harmonize many discrepancies by studying the accounts of different participants, and even a man like Ghent unwittingly gave me certain very valuable "leads" which have been of great use to me.

In sifting the wheat from the chaff, it is necessary to exercise patience, discrimination and toleration. A story as a whole may be unreliable, but it may furnish a few corroborative facts that might not otherwise be obtained. Thompson's alleged story is an instance in the matter of his horse giving out between where Custer's battalion left Reno's Creek and Reno's Hill. Even that incident might have been discredited had not the Rees seen such an event; *they*, of course, did not know Thompson, *but saw a soldier* as described.

I thank you for your good letter, and if you can give me any "further light" I shall be much pleased. I attended the Consistory last week for two days, and as usual enjoyed the work; also conducted a school of instruction in my Chapter, attended a M.M.M. degree in a sister Chapter here, and participated in a Blue Lodge communication in the E. A. degree where two life memberships were conferred on two friends, one a post office inspector, the other a sexton of our Methodist church here on the West Side. We have three Masonic temples, and a Shrine temple here, 5 Blue Lodges, 3 Chapters, a Council, a Commandery and Shrine.

Fraternally Yours,
Fred Dustin

Dear Brother Dustin:

Yours of Feb. 26th has remained on my desk unanswered for a longer time than usual. I have no valid excuse for the delay save that I simply slowed up on most everything owing to lack of energy and ambition proceeding no doubt from an increase in some of my permanent disabilities. This trouble is at times a mighty annoying one but cannot be overcome. I am waiting for spring to appear around the corner hoping it will bring with it a bit more strength and ambition. My really serious trouble is with my badly impaired circulation and hardening of the arteries for which there seems little hope of relief as the months pass by.

Mrs. Goldin and myself have had a recent attack of California fever, even going so far as to secure rates and to write the San Diego Chamber of Commerce for information, but I guess a drastic dose of looking things square in the face, considering health conditions and the size of the bank roll and the uncertainty of pension legislation, which is practically our main source of income has abated the fever materially and left us with the idea that we had better hold to a good thing where we have a house, eats, medical attendance with also light, heat and my own clothing allowance, all of which would have to be met from our moderate income if we went west to die on the coast. I will admit that we hated to abandon our plans but some good will come from not making the change.

I understand that Thompson got a grilling at that dinner in Washington that finally drove him from the table. I have been unfortunate in that I never had a chance to read his story or even hear him, but the fragments that have come to me from time to time from one source or another have left the story so confused and in most instances contradictory that I have given up trying to straighten it out. For instance, if the story of the Rees is worth anything his horse must have played out even before Custer crossed Reno Creek as the Rees in their retreat after they broke in the bottoms carried them back in the direction from which they entered the bottoms as it is certain they were never any nearer Custer than that. Godfrey has stated that when Benteen's squadron was moving down the valley to join Reno he saw nothing in their front save one lone horse to the north of Reno Creek apparently unsaddled and grazing.

We know the Rees picked up some cavalry horses most likely horses that had escaped from Reno's outfit when the horseholders were killed.

I was not with Reno on the bluffs until just about the time Benteen joined him as I did not dare try to cross the river until the Indians left Reno and moved down to join the attack on Custer, but I do know that we never saw or heard of any one joining us from the direction Custer had taken.

Ellison writes me that in the Camp material they found a notation of a trip Camp made over the field with Thompson and some others some years after the fight but from what he writes me the story Thompson told Camp differs from any others I have heard and only serves to confuse matters more than ever. I have but little doubt that Pete was with some one of the water parties, but not with ours, and the story he tells about almost hand-to-hand fighting is something we never heard of at the time.

I believe in 1914 his story was published in the Belle Fourche Bee, written, I understand, by himself. Ellison has been trying to get a copy of that story to compare it with the one in "The Black Hills Trails" but so far has failed.

Your statement relative to Keogh and Tom Custer is in line with what I knew of them in the service and what I heard of them at different times. My troop was in the south from the end of the Black Hills Expedition in '74 until the spring of '76 when we came north to join the Terry column so that I never saw much of either Keogh or Tom Custer save at scattered intervals and while in the field, but knew by hearsay that the reputation you gave them was that generally understood in the regiment.

I can realize all you say as to winnowing the wheat from the chaff in an attempt to get as nearly as possible to the facts. I used to try to combat a lot of these fake stories but gave it up when I found that both magazines and newspapers preferred them to plain, truthful facts.

Godfrey, a fine old fellow in a general way, was so biased in everything he wrote regarding Custer that his stories were not to be depended on. Whitaker's story was as full of holes as an old kitchen skimmer.

Some years ago Gen. Hazen wrote an article very severely criticizing Custer's book, "Life On The Plains." I recall reading the article when it appeared but it was so long ago I cannot even pretend to recall it.

I understand Frederick F. Van de Water, the author of "Thunder Shield," is at work on a Life of Custer and that his material is supposed to be in the hands of the Dodd Mead Co. by September 1st. I know a little of some of the material he has and am led to think that the story will be a whole lot different from any yet published and will be made up largely of provable facts and reliable material. I am hoping it will be out before I cross the divide as I believe it will make interest-

[119]

ing reading and cause writers of the Godfrey, Ghent, Bates type to sit up and take notice.

A note received this morning from Brininstool tells me that our dear old friend Major Ostrander is still confined to his bed and suffering much from his bladder trouble and Brinny intimates that he fears the old man is looking over the fence into the Promised Land. We will miss him sadly as he was a real man, square, honest and truthful and one it was a pleasure to know.

I have not visited my Consistory for several years, nor the Grand Commandery and not even Grand Lodge for at least two years. My own Blue Lodge and Commandery are too far away for me to think of visiting them.

I really cannot think of anything I can write you that will be of value to you with the mass of material I am sure you have, but if, at any time you think of anything on which I might be able to throw a bit of light, do not hesitate to ask for it.

I often find myself mighty thankful that my memory of those old days still remains good even though there are times when I have to scratch my gray head a bit to get things in chronological order. When the time comes, as it may, that this memory fails me I will feel that it is time for me to pass on as those days and the correspondence I have regarding them go far to make up my life.

Speaking of that article of Gen. Hazen's, I believe Dr. Philip G. Cole of New York City has a copy of it which he purchased from Brininstool and Brinny tells me he omitted to retain a copy of it as he should have done.

Mrs. Goldin tells me that in the early part of this letter there are several lines which cannot be read. I do not know what is the matter with my machine. It is out of adjustment in some way and I may have to send it to Milwaukee to be overhauled. Inasmuch as I cannot see what I write, this trouble is mighty annoying and always leaves me uncertain as to my work.

We will try and see how important the omission is and may have to rewrite the first page.

With kindest regards and best wishes believe me

Sincerely and Fraternally yours,
Theo. W. Goldin

May 10, 1934

Mr. Theodore Goldin
Soldiers' Home, Wis.

Dear Brother Goldin:—

I have another question for you which is one that so far as I know has never been asked or answered, at least in print.

On the Custer Battle monument are the names of over 260 soldiers who fell in the fight. On the field surrounding the stone are individual markers where bodies were found and "buried." In your fight on the hill and in the bottom you had about fifty men killed, but my question is, *where and when were those on the hill buried?* As far as I have learned, there is not a single marker to an enlisted man either on the hill or in the bottom, and in fact, I think I have a record of only four, McIntosh, De Wolfe, Hodgson and Chas. Reynolds thus indicated by stones. I understand that when Gibbon's command arrived and went into camp in the bottom below your location on the hill, they dragged away some of the dead horses and covered some of the men's bodies. Can you give me something definite, especially as to when and where the men on the hill were buried?

[121]

Another question that has given me some trouble is this:
The night of the 26th, after the Indians left, Reno changed
the position of the troops somewhat, and had them again
entrench, moving nearer the river as I understand. Now the
question is: How far did you move, and has not this last
position been somewhat confused by writers with the first one?
I am not of course referring to the *first* rally on the hill but
first to the position you occupied during the fight, and second
the position to which the Major moved you *after* the fight as
noted in his report.

I had a letter from Major Ostrander a few days ago. The
dear old brother tells me that he is practically bed-ridden, and
can only sit up a few minutes at a time. He is such a fine
soul! I grieve at his disability. I have not heard from Brin.
in a long time, and begin to wonder if he is again ill. Must
write to him. Have been very busy this spring, and my own
years tell on me. We cannot expect to last forever, but while
we *do* hold out there is much to do and much to live for in
many ways, but nine years ago when I had that calamitous
illness that cost me my best eye and nearly my life, my grip
on the latter relaxed considerably.

I have bought several of T. B. Marquis' little pamphlets
lately, and find them useful, as well as his other two books.
Just got Gen. Hugh Scott's book, and had not finished reading
it when the paper had the notice of his decease.

Well, Brother Goldin, I may attend the Grand Chapter
next week, but am not yet fully decided; however, *will* attend
the Consistory the week after. With best wishes for your health
and welfare, believe me,

Sincerely and Fraternally Yours,
Fred Dustin

[Letter of Goldin to Dustin dated May 12, 1934, is missing from the Battlefield Collection and is therefore lost to this published collection.]

May 15, 1934

Dear Brother Goldin:—

Your letter of the 12th received, and I surely thank you for the information so freely given. As I think I said in my last letter, I have never seen in print or heard where Reno's dead on the hill were buried. I have been pleased and surprised at various items of quite important information that I have been able to "scare up" in my study and correspondence about this fight.

There is one thing that has developed, and that is that Godfrey's and other maps are wrong in giving Reno's second line across a neck of land formed by the river. A careful reading of the testimony at the Court of Inquiry, and other sources of information, indicated that French was on the left of the line, Moylan in the center, and McIntosh on the right, and that when the skirmish line changed positions, it simply pivoted on the right flank of McIntosh's troop, and occupied the edge of the woods and brush, and facing about, French was on the *right* and McIntosh on the left at or near the edge of a depression, probably the old stream bed of the river, which is plainly shown on the Maguire map made on the spot after Terry arrived. Again, the skirmish line shown by Godfrey's map is two or three times too long, and there are a number of other palpable errors on it.

In regard to the McIntosh marker, I do not know that

anything more than the cross you mention marks it. I have seen in pictures that it is enclosed by a fence. The collating of all the information has been a very pleasant task, but I have *so much* material that my manuscript has grown to around 500 pages, and more coming.

About the burial of Hodgson, here is what Capt. Mc-Dougall said at the Court of Inquiry: "The body was lying near where Maj. Reno crossed the river . . . On the night of the 26th I took Privates Ryan and Moon and got Lieut. Hodgson's body and carried it to my breastworks, and on the 27th buried it after sewing it up in blankets and a poncho."

I have understood that a monument now marks Reno's position on the heights, but am not positive as to the fact.

It would be a great satisfaction to me to spend several days on that historic ground, take pictures and verify locations and clear up some obscurities in my own mind. I may go, but it is somewhat doubtful at present.

Gibbon in his magazine article states that when his command arrived at Reno's position in the valley, the bodies were highly offensive and men were set at work burying them and hauling away the carcasses of horses, which tallies with what you say about those in the bottom being buried by the 7th Infantry.

As it is near mail time, I must close, and again thanking you, with kind regards to Mrs. Goldin and yourself, I am,

Sincerely and Fraternally Yours,
Fred Dustin

Dear Brother Dustin:

Yours of recent date at hand. It contained a bit of information which, if I ever heard of it I had long since forgotten it and that was as to the recovery and burial of the body of Lieut. Hodgson by Capt. McDougal. I talked with Gen. Godfrey regarding Hodgson in 1926, and he was of the same opinion I was that the body was buried where he fell. I no doubt read McDougal's testimony at the Reno Court, in fact had a complete copy of it for years but in my much moving around it was lost. If McDougal testified that he aided in recovering and intering the body it was no doubt true. I did hear that men of our command visited the body and found his watch and money and all else in his pockets gone. However, the present location of the Hodgson marker is NOT near where he was buried if on the hill, but is at or near the point where Reno made his first halt after the retreat and where he was later joined by Benteen.

There is, or was a white picket fence surrounding the grave of Lieut. McIntosh, inside this fence is a stone erected I understood by his wife. The stone when I last saw it was almost hidden by wild rose bushes planted inside the fence.

After we were there in '26, Brininstool paid for a white enameled wooden cross which Major Asbury of the Crow Agency was to have erected at the grave of Charlie Reynolds. I understand this was done. Albert Johnson wrote me that it was in place the last time he visited the field.

I sure wish you might be able some day to visit the fields; it would give you a bit better understanding than you

can get from maps or even photos. I never regarded the Godfrey map as very reliable. It was prepared to back his views.
I regarded the Maguire map as about the best one I ran across.

I notice that a bill appropriating $75,000 for the erec-
tion of a suitable fireproof building to house the relics willed
by Mrs. Custer has been introduced in Congress so that this
collection may ultimately find its home near the battlefield.

I have understood that an effort was made to get water
on the National cemetery as well as make some other needed
improvements there. Hope they can do it as it is a barren,
lonesome looking place now.

I was sorry to learn of the death of Gen. Hugh L. Scott,
whom I knew first as a Lieutenant in the 7th Cav. in '76, and
later as a brigadier and major general on the Mexican border.

If at any time I can afford you any information draw
on me.

Guess my Lodge days are about over. Too hard to get
about, but my interest still remains

Sincerely and Fraternally,
Theo. W. Goldin

May 25, 1934

Dear Brother Goldin:—

Your interesting letter received and noted, and I find
there were some questions I wanted to ask, but on account
of closing my letter in a hurry, failed to do.

There are also one or two points of interest that I would
like a little light on if you can give them.

Moylan, in his testimony before the Court, stated that Calhoun was his brother-in-law. Can you tell me the correct relationship? I know that Calhoun married Custer's sister, and during the Winan's administration in Michigan (Democratic), she was appointed State Librarian, so I have presumed that Moylan married Calhoun's sister. Is that right?

Also, when Gibbon came up, McIntosh was recognized by a sleeve or cuff-button, by an officer of Gibbon's command (or by a staff officer of Terry's) as *his* brother-in-law. Can you tell me who he was and the proper relationship?

About Hodgson, Reno and Sergeant Culbertson testified that after the Major found that Hodgson had been shot and left, he, Reno, took Culbertson and several others and went down the gully you ascended later, the same command went up, and found him dead some fifty yards from the river, his watch and chain gone, but Reno took off his class ring from his finger. Reno stated that he was a particular friend and favorite. His burial later by McDougal was noted in my last letter. I presume that what you related about the contractor for the headstone concerning that of Hodgson was correct. It has always seemed to me that as nearly as possible the markers for those in Reno's command should have been set up where they fell, or at least we know that the dead marked the line from where the dismount was made, then in the edge of the woods, and from these to the river and up and on the bluff above, as well as your last position where eighteen or twenty or more fell.

The prejudice created against Reno seemed to extend to his command as far as their heroic defense went, but on Monument Hill and about those white stones, marking the spots where soldiers fell, are very much in evidence. I feel that the hill (Reno's) and the bottom land should be a part of the reservation. I certainly hope to visit the field, as it seems to me that that alone is all that is necessary to round out my work, and it is not at all improbable that I will visit it.

Yesterday afternoon I attended the closing sessions of the Consistory, witnessing the Twenty-First, Patriarch Noachite, and the Thirtieth Knight Kadosh. After supper, the Thirty-Second was exemplified with W. A. Penney, a brother 75 years taking the part of Constans, and taking like a man of twenty-five. He is a 33rd and just a few days ago was elected Commander-in-Chief for the ensuing three years, and will thus round out a most useful and masonic life. At supper we had brief but fine talks by the U. S. Circuit Judge, the Grand Chaplain and Grand J. W. of the Blue Lodge. We have a fine cathedral at Bay City, dedicated eight years ago. Hope this finds you well, and believe me,

Sincerely and Fraternally Yours,
Fred Dustin

Wisconsin Veterans Home
June 2, 1934

Dear Brother Dustin:

Yours of the 25th of May duly received but with the mercury circulating around 100 and above I was only able to muster energy enough to hobble over to the band stand and listen in on the loudspeaker to the ball game, but as today is much better I will try and answer your letter.

I do not know that I can afford you much in the way of information in answer to your questions but will do the best I can. I never knew Moylan's wife but according to his testimony she must have been a sister of Calhoun's as the latter married a sister of Custer's. We were never stationed at the same post with Moylan so I knew but little about him save what I saw in the field and heard through camp rumors. He was not a popular officer, either with his men or his brother officers and in the fight at the Little Big Horn earned the reputation of having a streak of yellow in him that made him all the more unpopular.

Fred Dustin and Theodore W. Goldin Correspondence

As to McIntosh, the only brother-in-law of his that I ever heard of was Lieut. Gibson of "H" Troop. They married sisters. The story as to his body being identified by a cuff link is to me a bit far fetched. I never knew "Tosh," as we called him, to wear anything requiring cuff links save in garrison and as he was stripped when we saw his body on the morning of the 27th, also scalped and otherwise mutilated that part of the story is a bit like a fairy tale. On the morning of the 27th, Lieut. Wallace, Lieut. Hare and a number of enlisted men forded the river a short distance below where Reno crossed it on his retreat, moved up to the point of the crossing, identifying most of the men who fell at that point and then turned back following substantially the line of the retreat. I pointed out to Wallace the point or near the point where I saw McIntosh's horse fall with him and near there we found the body which Wallace and Hare recognized—scalped, stripped and mutilated as I stated above. I do not know who, if anyone in Gibbon's command, later recognized the body but never knew of his having any other brother-in-law save Gibson. We continued back along the line of the retreat finally reaching the point of Reno's stand in the bottoms and on that ride identified the bodies of Bloody Knife, Isaiah Dorman and Charley Reynolds. From the body of the latter we moved down into the upper edge of the village continuing down along the lines perhaps a mile when we heard recall sounding from the bluffs and hiked back in a hurry to our position on the bluffs. We saw the remains of a huge fire just about at the point where we turned back but had no time to make much of an investigation.

We heard that a party had gone down to the point where Hodgson fell, found him partially stripped and his watch and any money he might have had gone, but your letter telling me of the bringing of the body to the hill and its final burial was new to me although I must have read it in the proceedings of the Court of Inquiry of which I had for years a complete copy, but read it so many years ago it had gone out of my mind.

I knew that Hodgson was a favorite of Reno's and at the time of the fight was acting as *de facto* squadron adjutant.

I have no information as to where he was finally buried by McDougal but imagine it was, like many of the others, under the picket line where the ground was trampled down by the horses after the shallow graves were filled in. This may account for the placing of the Hodgson marker where it is, although it was at some distance from where any of the dead were buried. The marker at the grave of Dr. DeWolf is located at the point where he fell, but aside from McIntosh and Reynolds there were no markers placed in the bottoms near the scene of Reno's stand or at the river where so many of our men fell, nor on Reno Hill.

I first visited the fields in 1924 and again in 1926 and found quite a heavy growth of scrub timber and brush at the point where the crossing was made. So far as I have known no real effort has ever been made to locate those bodies at the crossing, but I believe it would be possible even at this late date to discover traces of them if the effort was carefully made.

I have a letter on my desk just received from Brininstool

telling me that a long projected eastern trip to his old New York State home had been abandoned owing to the ill health of his brother. I had hoped the trip would be made as we were planning to meet in Chicago for what would more than likely have been our last pow wow.

Looks as though my days of attending the sessions of any of the Bodies Subordinate or Grand are over. It is too difficult for me to get about to undertake it. I had a pressing invitation to make the trip to Frisco to the Grand Encampment on the special train of my dear and valued friend Andrew D. Agnew, Acting Grand Master, but it had to be turned down as all others will have to be from now on.

Just before the depression hit us Wisconsin Consistory purchased a fine property on the lake fronting Milwaukee and were maturing plans for a million dollar cathedral, but along came Old Man Depression and all plans were abandoned although in order to save taxes they fixed up the building and hold all meetings there save those for conferring the degrees.

If at any time you think of anything else where I can be of help, just call on me.

Hope you will be able to visit the battlefields. It would help in rounding out your work, especially if you could have some one with you familiar with the ground, but there are not many of that class left. Possibly the custodian of the National Cemetery, an old veteran, but who was not in the fight, might afford you some assistance.

I had a friend—an old 7th Cav. trooper—living at Hardin, Mont., 12 miles from the field, who was exceptionally well posted but he is now in the California National Home.

With best wishes and kindest regards believe me

Sincerely and Fraternally yours,
Theo. W. Goldin

[131]

Saginaw W.S. Mich.
June 5, 1934

Dear Brother Goldin:—

Your very welcome letter was received a few days ago, and the information you give me is of much value. I can only regret that I have not been able years ago to get in touch with you as well as others who have now traveled to the "undiscovered country," for there were many things that might have been brought out that would have had a high historical value as well as clearing up more or less events that have been puzzling.

About Moylan, like a number of officers who came into the Seventh Cavalry at its formation and soon thereafter, he had a somewhat peculiar experience as well as record, a fact attested by the Army Register and Mrs. Custer's book in which she tells about him, but with her "reserve" whereby most any officer might have been supposed to be the one in question, from the fact of her giving no names. The same thing occurs many times in her writings, as for instance, Keogh was described by her as a drunken sot, which was of course, not a bad description, but owing to the lack of name might have fitted seven or eight of the officers very aptly. The history of the officers of the Seventh Cavalry as a whole, from the time of its organization to 1876, was not a really creditable one. I have found one desertion, cashierings, forced resignations and court-martials "too numerous to mention," in the records of that ten years and did not speak well of the quality of the commissioned force.

About McIntosh, perhaps I was unfortunate in using the term, "cuff-link" in the matter of his identification, so I will quote from Charles F. Roe, then a lieutenant commanding one of Major Brisbin's troops of the Second Cavalry, who relates as follows in his account of Custer's last fight published in 1927. He had arrived with his troop at the place where you had your fight in the bottom and says: "In front of my troop a dead body was lying; it was naked, badly mutilated, which was often the case, and the features hammered to a jelly. As our sergeant-major picked up a gutta percha sleeve button, he said, 'This may lead to its identification.' Some one remarked, 'Here comes an officer.' It was Lieutenant Gibson, of the Seventh Cavalry, who was shown the stud as a possible means of identifying the body. He said, 'Yes, I think it will—it is my brother-in-law.' Before leaving Fort Abraham Lincoln his wife gave him those sleeve buttons."

When I said "cuff-link," I was speaking from memory, but have looked it up as above.

In my study of the individuals holding commissions in the Seventh at the time of that fight, I have come to the conclusion that there were several "queer specimens" among them, such as De Rudio, Keogh, Tom Custer and others with more or less "checkered careers."

I have long wished to obtain a complete copy of the proceedings of Reno's court of inquiry, but have never seen it complete. Reno's critics were silenced by it as far as further persecution was concerned, but the poison had spread too deeply to be corrected in the minds of the great body of the people whose silly hero-worship of Custer has not ceased to this day with many.

I certainly hope that Reno's position in the bottom, his line of retreat to the bluffs and his stand there will be included in a reservation, and proper markers placed before it is too late. The maps published are faulty. For instance, Reno's line across the bottom is made to appear about three times too long; his second line is far from where it actually was; his line of retreat across the valley too long, and Custer's advance is away too far east of what it actually was. I am referring now particularly to the map made under the direction of Godfrey, and copied by others. After Gibbon came up, the engineer officer Maguire, went over Custer's route, and mapped it on the spot, and Lieut. Woodruff of the Seventh Infantry rode over it the day you were relieved, and after Terry came on the hill.

Godfrey has seemed to me to be very opinionated, a man of integrity and courage, but becoming so warped in his judgments by his prejudices that his relations have had their value much impaired by his bias, and his several accounts contain so many misstatements, that with Major Brisbin, I would emphatically say: "Godfrey, why don't you tell ALL THE TRUTH?"

In 1926, when DeLand visited the Custer Field, he secured some of the shells you used on that day, and sent me one which I treasure as a relic, and in my care (but not my own) are two Indian arrows, one which was sticking in the body of a soldier, the other picked up on the field. I also have a valuable manuscript account giving in detail the burial of Custer which was written out carefully by First Sergeant John Ryan, whose troop buried the Custers.

I have read and also heard from several sources, that when Terry came up to you on the hill, the tears were streaming down his face, and that officers and men received his coming with delirious joy, but Godfrey says: "The men were awed into silence by the grave face of the General."

I can appreciate your feelings when you were relieved. In regard to Terry, I have a question to ask. Some of the writers say that he was named by the Crow scouts "No Hip-

Bone," on account of being lame. One or two other writers say that it was Gibbon, and still others have said that either Gibbon or Brisbin was called "The Gray-Beard." As both were elderly, and as I know that Gibbon wore a beard, but DO NOT know about Brisbin, can you straighten out this confusion of names for me? I know that Brisbin was lame from rheumatism, but the looseness of writers is almost maddening in their crazy statements which would confuse a smart lawyer to untangle, so the question is WHO was "No Hip-Bone," and who was "Gray-Beard?" I have even seen the account of one of those newspaper historians in which he calls Terry "Bear Coat," a designation which I understood was applied to Miles the following winter.

I am sorry Brininstool is not coming east as I had hoped to get him to swing north a little from his route and call on me here as DeLand did. It is getting late, Brother Goldin, and I have a Chapter meeting to attend, so must close with kindest regards and say,

> Sincerely and Fraternally Yours,
> Fred Dustin

Wisconsin Veterans Home
June 12, 1934

Dear Brother Dustin:

I have your letter of the 5th before me. It has been unanswered longer than usual owing in part to the extreme heat and in part to not feeling in the mood for writing.

[135]

I found much of interest in the letter, some new things to me.

The identification of McIntosh's body by Lieut. Gibson, his brother-in-law, clears that matter up as so far as I knew he was the only brother-in-law "Tosh" had.

In the early days of the regiment it had its full quota of addicts to the use of nose paint, a condition that continued down until 1876 among certain of the older ones, but the 7th was not alone in this; it was pretty general in the old army.

The regiment did have its full share of cashiering, courts martials, etc. The only case of desertion I knew of was of 2d Lieut. John Aspinwall. He was a boyhood friend of mine; beat me in a competitive examination for West Point and was in the regiment when I joined it some years later.

The primary cause of his desertion can be traced back to Custer and his habit of playing poker with the young officers of the regiment, something few of the older officers would do. I saw Aspinwall the night before he deserted, learned the story from him and some years later at the request of his father, a Methodist minister, went to Toronto, Canada, to see him while he was down with typhoid fever, arriving only to find him dead.

As to the various nicknames you mention I can only say that so far as I know Terry had none. The lame man was most likely Brisbin who suffered much from rheumatism and exposure that summer. Most likely the whiskered man was Gen. Gibbon who all the time I knew him wore a heavy beard. The appelation "Beat Coat" I never heard applied to anyone save Miles.

Godfrey had many good traits but his worship for Custer led him to color his stories a bit fancifully—often leading him into making contrary statements that in some cases were decidedly conflicting.

I imagine it would be difficult to secure a copy of the proceedings of the Reno court. Did you ever know that soon after the trial started the court found that the proceedings as published by the CHICAGO TRIBUNE were more complete and accurate than those of the official reports and that from this discovery to the end of the trial the report of the TRIBUNE was made the official record of the court? The copy I had was that made by the TRIBUNE reporters. Sorry it was lost or you might have had it.

I note in your letter a statement made by Brisbin asking Godfrey why he did not tell all the truth. I infer from that you must have seen a copy of the letter written by Brisbin to Godfrey shortly after the publication of Godfrey's original Century article, but marked not to be used during the life of Mrs. Custer. Brisbin told a lot of true facts in that letter and I have always imagined the copies that got out came from Brisbin as I do not imagine Godfrey would ever have let it get away from him. It was too scathing to be pleasant for its recipient.

In most cases as near as I can figure it out, men like Whitaker, Col. Bates, Ghent and others who have kept on trying to inject the poison in Reno's record were all pupils of Godfrey's or imitation defenders of Mrs. Custer who needed no defenders but who had the regard and respect of all who knew her and whose devotion to the memory of her husband was respected even though it was known the army over that her hero was a man of straw.

I am looking forward with much interest to the appearance of Fred. Van de Water's life of Custer, which, if I mistake not is going to create something of a sensation. I understand the Mss. has to be in the hands of the publishers by Sept. 1st.

Just now after the siege of extreme hot weather we are

[137]

having a run of cloudy, really cold weather with now and then a dash of much needed rain.

We find the change from the cottage to the dormitory a good move for us. I was finding it more and more difficult to get about and find the change much to my advantage.

Glad if I am able to clear up any points for you. If you think I can do more draw on me.

Sincerely and Fraternally yours,
Theo. W. Goldin

Dec. 6, 1934

Mr. Theodore Goldin
Wisconsin Veterans Home, Wis.

Dear Brother Goldin:—

It is a long time since I have either written you or heard from you, but I presume you long ago heard of the sad death of our good old "friend and brother" Ostrander. It was painfully sad to me to learn of his passing. I know he has suffered excrutiating pains for some years back, and at his advanced age we could not look for much come-back: we can only say, "Soft and safe to you, our brother."

I am getting ready to again take up my Custer manuscript, and again asking you for information.

You will recollect that in a former letter I asked you if you could tell me who it was that the Indian scouts called "No-Hip-Bone," and you thought it possibly was Brisbin. I see that Van de Water mentions the fact that Gibbon was per-

manently lame, and that brought to my mind that as I remembered it, he (Gibbon) had received a severe wound in
the Civil War. *This* would identify him as "No-Hip-Bone"
probably. The writers have not only been very careless; they
have been worse. I saw that one called Terry "Bear Coat," and
to another he was "No-Hip-Bone." It was Miles that was
Bear-Coat of course, not Terry at all. Do you remember the
kind of beard that old Major Brisbin wore? That old officer
had grit, surely, for Gibbon stated that he insisted on marching out with his cavalry battalion although he had to hobble
around his post on crutches.

Another matter, that it is possible you have already given
me information on, was not "the gray horse troop" the one
commanded by Lieut. Smith, Troop "E" I believe it was?

And still another thing that possibly you can give light
on: As far as I have been able to trace the matter, Mark
Kellogg, the newspaper man, did not accompany the column
from Fort Lincoln to the Powder, but came up on one of the
boats to the depot at the Powder, and there joined your
command. Am I right in this?

I have attended two annuals already this week, Council
and Chapter, installing the officers for each body, and this
evening I expect to be at my Blue Lodge Annual, but instal-
lation is not until next week, and after a session of the
Finance Committee of the Chapter also next week, I presume I
will "rest up" from any Masonic meetings for a few weeks.
I trust that this will find you and Mrs. Goldin in good health
and spirits, and believe me,

Fraternally Yours,
Fred Dustin

Wisconsin Veterans Home
December 18, 1934

Dear Brother Dustin:

Your good letter of the 6th has been for some time unanswered owing to the fact that since its receipt I have not been and even now am not in shape for intelligent letter writing owing to a run down condition that leaves me without ambition or energy.

I was glad to hear from you and am sorry I will have to admit my inability to satisfactorily answer your several questions owing both to lack of memory and lack of familiarity with the Indian names bestowed on officers of the frontier army. Miles' appelation of "Bear Coat" is the only one I recall definitely.

I saw but little of Brisbin but my memory is that like many of the officers on campaigns he wore a full beard but even of this I am not positive.

The passing of dear Major Ostrander was a sad blow to his many friends. I do not know whether you are aware of the real way he passed on. Loyal to the last his old and faithful nurse wrote merely telling of his passing on a certain date. Nothing more. The facts were that after his long fight the load got too heavy and one day when his nurse was out doing some marketing the old man loaded up his old civil war pistol and went out that way. I learned this through a press clipping sent my old friend Bill Hooker from a Seattle paper. The old man made a splendid fight but the load was too heavy.

My health has forced me to give up all Masonic activities, have not attended one for nearly or quite two years. My interest is still there but I can't make the grade.

Try me again some time. I may be able to do a better job of letter writing.

Sincerely and Fraternally yours,
Theo. W. Goldin

FREDERICK BENTEEN'S
LETTERS TO HIS WIFE

Frederick Benteen proved to be an officer very much aware of the historic event he had survived. This is best demonstrated through the "July 4th, 1876, Letter," and the famous "Installment Letters" to his wife.

The two letters mentioned above were found by Major Benteen, the captain's son. Major Benteen had salvaged several letters from a destructive fire in which much family property was lost; these letters turned out to be those to Captain Benteen's wife which were written just after the Battle of the Little Big Horn. Major Benteen made these letters available to Mr. Brininstool who, in turn, made copies available to Dr. Cole with the expressed hope he would ". . . enjoy them and appreciate their value as much as I have." Believed by some to be forgeries, much effort was expended in an official effort to verify the handwriting in the letters. This was done by a comparison of them with some official correspondence on file with the Adjutant General's Office in Washington. The intermediary was Representative Phil D. Swing of California's Eleventh District. Representative Swing made contact with Major-General C. H. Bridges, the Adjutant General. After a short delay, General Bridges forwarded to Mr. Brininstool, through Representative Swing, photostat copies of Captain Benteen's handwriting and signature. This was done under cover of a letter of transmittal dated June 7, 1929. Two letters, written almost thirty years apart, were deliberately selected. The long period between them would allow for any changes in script to become fixed and noticeable.

The first letter, addressed to the Honorable Edwin M. Stanton, Secretary of War, was dated 24 November 1866 and acknowledged receipt of Benteen's appointment as captain in the Seventh Regiment United States Cavalry. The second letter, addressed to the Adjutant General, United States Army, was dated 28 May 1894, and in it Benteen accepted the commission of brigadier general by brevet. From the handwriting samples provided by these two letters it was proved beyond a doubt that the two disputed letters had indeed been written by Captain Benteen after the Battle of the Little Big Horn.

Benteen had begun the famous "Installment Letters" on July 2, 1876, and then after a long pause, he began again on July 23, 1876, and continued through the 25th. There was another hiatus at that date and the next and final letter was dated July 30, 1876.

A letter dated July 4th, 1876, could be considered, chronologically, as part of this series, but Colonel Graham in his book, *The Custer Myth*, separated it from the "Installment Letters" and described it as ". . . the most significant of all the papers found by his son." Colonel Graham showed the letter to General Godfrey and said that he believed the letter to be of historical importance. General Godfrey replied: "It is far more than that. It was written long before any controversy had arisen over the way the battle was conducted, and under circumstances that give it special credit. It is history itself." This letter is included here after the "Installment Letters." All grammatical errors in the originals have been retained.

Str. "Far West"
Mouth of Big Horn & Yellowstone
July 2, 1876

My darling Wife—

We have just arrived at this point, marching from the indian village. On the 25th of June, last Sunday, week, Genl.

[146]

Custer divided the 7th Cav. into 3 Battn's.—about 15 miles from an indian village, the whereabouts of which he did not know exactly. I was ordered with 3 Co's., D, H, & K, to go to the left for the purpose of hunting for the valley of the river—indian camp—or anything I could find. I found nothing, and after marching 10 miles or so in pursuit of the same, determined to return to Custer's trail. Reno had 3 Co's. (A, G, M.)

When Custer arrived in sight of indians, he ordered Reno to charge—and promised to support him. R. did so—but Custer went a long way off to the right, behind the bluffs—intending to attack the village at the opposite end to R. the result of which was—that Custer, Keogh, Yates, Tom Custer, Cook, Porter, Calhoun, Sturgis, Harrington, Riley, J. J. Crittenden, & A. E. Smith & Dr. Lord were killed—& with them every man of the 5 Co's. who were along. Reno with his 3 Co's. was driven to the bluffs, & I with mine arrived just in time to save them & mine. Tom McDougall, who was back with his Co., in charge of the pack train, got up with us, all right. We endeavored to go where Custer had gone, not seeing or hearing from him however, but we could not do it—and had to fall back to a ravine—or series of depressions in ground—where we corralled our packs, and kept them off nicely—the next day they came at us more fiercely—but could do nothing with us—save shoot the animals—and kill a few men—the 3rd day Genls. Terry & Gibbon came up—but the indians struck their village & left the night before. There was 5000 of them—So Genl. Sheridan telegraphs Genl. Terry.

Str. "Far West" July 23d 1876
Mouth of Yellowstone & Rosebud

My Darling Wife:

The Steamer is now taking on wood, at the camp, where one month ago, yesterday, Genl. Custer cut loose from Genl. Terry—and started up the Rosebud. We started out in "Grand Galore," Gens. Terry, Gibbon & Brisbin (Maj. 2nd Cav.) and their staffs, witnessing the Review which passed them in column of fours, guidons flying, trumpets sounding the March &c. Custer remained until the column passed. Little did he think, that in 3 more days five full companies of that gallant command—along with himself—would be totally annihilated —not one of them left to tell the story! But! 'twas so ordained. It was at this point he issued the order breaking up Wings & Battalions. We are now bound up the river to the command— which is below the mouth of the Big Horn, Gibbon, Comdg. Our trip up has been thus far pleasant and uneventful. I have fully recovered—and feel first rate—tho' I think should feel much better were this Str. heading for Rice.

July 24, 76

We cached (i.e. hid) 65 tons of freight on the bank today—on account of fearing that there wasn't water enough in the river, but I think they are of the opinion, now, that the proceeding wasn't at all necessary. Met two companies of 2d Cav. with 2 Gatling guns under Lieut. Low, the Dtchmt under command of Capt. Wheelan, of 2d (crossed sabers) who thought they were about 50 miles from command: they were simply scouting around. Wheelan informed us that Capt. Thompson, of his Regt. had blown his brains out in camp,— cause, sickness, whiskey etc. Wheelan, by the by, told me some time ago soon after our fight—that he met my father in St. Louis at the Cav. Barracks, was introduced to him by Genl. Sturgis; Queer, isn't it? In one month more—today—I shall be XLII ("Five & Forty cts")! "The Bulk"! I hope you have thought to have the newspapers of the post which contained references to our Expedition preserved for me—as we will not see many of those articles. I have Winsburg & the mare & "Cuff" aboard the Str. Thought it best to bring them up so: "Cuff" would like to have gone down—but I thought probably 'twould be better to keep the horses up here.

Lieut. Walker of 17th showed me a portion of a letter from his wife—in which she stated that they had a rumor down there that Moylan, Gibson & DeRudio showed the white feather in fight of 25th: the same rumor prevailed thro' the camp on Powder River: Moylan heard of it and threatened vengeance dire on the perpetrator of the rumor. I think had DeR. made as good use of his eyes as 15 or 20 of the men did—he would have gotten out as they did—and neither M. or G. exhibited any great degree of activity—according to my light, probably others—the men, may have so seen it—and such things fly fast. Long ere this you will have gotten my long letter, by "Josephine," and I suppose you have answered as lengthily by the boats coming up with 5th and 22d Infty. Tell Fred I shall expect to have him read me some nice little stories by the time I get back: he must learn to ride his pony, but that must be kept for amusement after his studying is done. I have told you how the pay accts. left with you could be used—one being made out for July—the other can be used for any number of months on one. I will quit this now—as I have nothing I can think of to say—So—until then, will leave other page.

July 25—1876. Str. "Far West"
12:30 P.M.

My Trabbie Darling,

Just one month ago—today—at just about this time of day, Genl. Custer and his command commenced the attack on the indian village—one short half hour finished—I think—that five Co's. One would think that but a short space of time to dispatch so large a number of men, but when the immense number of indians attacked is taken into consideration, and the fact that the cavalry was probably thrown into a panic at the 1st check received—and gotten in just the condition that indians would get a herd of buffalo, suiting their peculiar mode exactly, it is not so very surprising.

I had a queer dream of Col. Keogh the night before last, 'twas, that he would insist upon undressing in the room in which you were. I had to give him a "dressing" to cure him of the fancy. I rarely ever thought of the man—and 'tis queer I should have dreamt of him. We are steaming along very slowly—and 'twill probably take us until tomorrow about this time, to reach camp at Big Horn. I don't think 'tis at all settled that the site of the depot will be at that point—as it cannot—perhaps—be supplied by boats.

My Darling Wife,

We arrived at this point today—marching from the Big Horn. The weather has been hot enough to cook eggs without other fire than the sun furnished. I can tell you it has been terrific.

Grant Marsh has just told me that the boat was going down to Powder River for the grain that was left there by us—and he wants me to go down with him. I should like very much do so, but there are so many things to do around the company that I can illy afford to be absent at this time.

My last letter was sent via Fort Ellis—it will take sometime to get around by that route—if it gets at all—which is exceedingly doubtful. It is a matter of speculation whether we shall (find) the indians on other side of Yellowstone. I believe Genl. Crook is impressed with the belief that they are being reinforced from the Agencies—and other officers think we shall find them. I am of the opinion that as soon as we cross to the South side—they will come to the N. side, for on this side is all the game,—i.e. buffalo. I cannot think that such an immense body of indians can have been kept together for so long a period—and can be held in a country where small game, such as Elk, deer & Antelope—is about all they can find.

Sergt. McLaughlin's time is out tomorrow. I don't suppose he will care to re-enlist. Were I in his place I should not. He will have to remain until a boat goes down. There isn't the slightest thing new going on—I am well. I haven't had an opportunity of answering Dr. Taylor's letter as yet, but shall do so. Remember me kindly to everybody. Oceans of kisses & love to you & Fred.

Devotedly—Your husband
Fred Benteen

[The more important letter—the one dated July 4th— printed here for the first time in its entirety, follows.]

July 4th 1876. Montana
Camp 7th Cavalry, Yellowstone River,
Opposite mouth of Big Horn River

My Trabbie Darling,

I wrote you hastily yesterday, to get it off on steamer "Far West", which boat steamed off at 11 o'clock A.M. as intended by her. I acknowledge the receipt of your 4 letters, the 5th one hasn't come as yet, but, perhaps you meant that five had been written in all. I had just commenced this one to have it in readiness for an opportunity to read,—when a courier or orderly comes around with a Circular, announcing that a mail leaves at 6 P.M. to-day, so, I shall be in readiness this time and have an opportunity of collecting my thoughts. I will commence this letter by sending a copy of the last lines Cooke ever wrote, which was an order to me to this effect.

Benteen, Come on, Big Village, Be Quick, bring packs, W. W. Cooke.

(P. S. Bring pacs) He left out the K in last packs. I have the original, but it is badly torn—and it should be

[152]

preserved—so keep this letter—as the matter may be of interest hereafter, likewise for use. This note was brought back to me by Trumpeter Martin, of my Co. (which fact saved his life). When I received it, I was five or six miles from the village, perhaps more, and the Packs at least that distance in my rear. I did not go back for the packs, but kept on a stiff trot for the village,—when getting at top of hill so that the valley could be seen—I saw an immense number of indians on the plain,—mounted of course and charging down on some dismounted men of Reno's command; the balance of R's command was mounted, and flying for dear life to the bluffs on the same side of river that I was. I then marched my 3 Co's to them—and a more delighted lot of folks you never saw. To commence—on the 22d of June—Custer with the 7th Cav. left the Steamer "Far West", Genl. Terry and Genl. Gibbon's command, (which latter was then in on the side of river and in same camp in which we now are). And moved up the Rosebud, marching 2 miles—the next day we marched 35 miles up the same stream. The next day we marched 35 more miles up same stream, and went into bivouac, remaining until 12 o'clock P.M. We then marched until about daylight, making about 10 miles; about half past five we started again, —and after going 6 or 7 miles we halted and officers' call was sounded. We were asked how many men of the companies were with the Co. Packs & instructed that only six could remain with them—& the discourse wound up with—that we should see that the men were supplied with the quantity of ammunition as had been specified in orders, and that the 1st Co. was in the desired condition and it being near the point of Assembly I went to it, assured myself of same, then announced to Genl. Custer that "H" Co. was ready; he replied, the advance is yours, Col. Benteen. We then moved four or

[153]

five miles and halted between the slopes of two hills—and
the Regt. was divided into Battalions—Reno getting Co's "A.
G. & M." I getting "D. H. & K.". From that point I was
ordered with my battalions to go over the immense hills to
the left, in search of the valley, which was supposed to be very
nearby—and to pitch into anything I came across,—and to
inform Custer at once if I found anything worthy of same.
Well, I suppose I went up and down those hills for 10 miles—
and still no valley anywhere in sight, the horses were fast
giving out—from such climbing—and as my orders had been
fulfilled, I struck diagonally for the trail, the command had
marched on, getting to its feet before the Pack train got there—
or on the trail just ahead of it. I then marched rapidly, and
after about 6 or 7 miles came upon a burning tepee—in which
was the body of an indian on a scaffold, arrayed gorgeously—
none of the command was in sight at this time. The ground
from this to the valley was descending—but very rough—I
kept up my trot—and when I reached a point very near the
ford which was crossed by Reno's battn. I got my first sight
of the valley and river—and Reno's command in full flight
for the bluffs—to the side I was then on—Of course I joined
them at once. The ground where Reno charged on was a plain
5 or 6 miles long, and about one mile or more wide; Custer
sent him in there—and promised to support him—after Reno
started in, Custer with his five Co's instead of crossing the
ford went to the right—around some high bluffs—with the
intention—as is supposed—of striking the rear of the village;
from the bluff on which he got he had his first glimpse of the
whole of it—and I can tell you 'twas an immense one. From
that point, Cooke sent the note to me by Martin, which I have
quoted on 1st page. I suppose after the five Co's had closed
up somewhat Custer started down for the village, all throats

[154]

bursting themselves with cheering; (so says Martin). He had
3 or 4 miles to go before he got to a ford as the village was
on the plain opposite side to Custer's Column—so, when he
got over those 4 miles of rough country and reached the ford,
the indians had availed themselves of the timely information
given by the cheering—as to the whereabouts and intentions
of that column, and had arrangements completed to receive
it—whether the indians allowed Custer's column to cross at
all, is a mooted question, but I am of the opinion that nearly,
if not all of the five companies got into the village but were
driven out immediately—flying in great disorder and crossing
by two instead of one ford by which they entered, "E" Company going by the left—& "J. I. & L." by the same one they
crossed. What became of "C" Co. no one knows—they must
have charged there below the village, gotten away or have
been killed in the bluffs on the village side of stream—as very
few of "C" Co. horses are found. Jack Sturgis' and Porter's
clothes were found in the village. After the indians had driven
them across it was a regular buffalo hunt for them—and not
a man escaped. We buried 203 of the bodies of Custer's command the 2d day after fight. The bodies were as recognizable
as if they were in life. With Custer—was Keogh—Yates and
Tom Custer (3 captains), 1st Lieut's Cooke, A. E. Smith,
Porter, Calhoun, 4 2nd Lieuts. Harrington, Sturgis, Riley and
Crittenden, (P. I. of 20th Inf.) Asst. Surgeon Lord was along
—but his body was not recognized; neither was Porter's nor
Sturgis' nor Harrington. McIntosh & Hodgson were killed at
Reno's end of line, in attempting to get back to Bluffs. De-
Rudio was supposed to have been lost—but the same night
the Indians left their village, he came sauntering in dis-
mounted, accompanied by McIntosh's cook. They had laid
hidden away in the woods. He has a thrilling romantic story

[155]

made out already—embellished, you bet! The stories of O'Neil, (the man who was with him) & DeR's of course couldn't be expected to agree, but—far more of truth, I am inclined to think will be found in the narrative of O'Neil—at any rate it is not at all colored—as he is a cool, level headed fellow, and tells it plainly and the same way all the time—which is a big thing towards convincing one of the truth of a story.

I must now tell you what we did. When I joined Reno's command, we halted for the Packs to come up, & then moved along the line to bluffs towards the direction Custer was supposed to have gone in—Weir's company was sent out to communicate with Custer, but it was driven back,—we then showed our full force on the hills with guidons flying, that Custer might see us—but we could see nothing of him, couldn't hear much firing, but could see an immense body of indians coming to attack us, from both sides of the river,— We withdrew to a saucer like hill, putting our horses & Packs in the bottom of saucer and threw all of our force dismounted—around this corral;—the animals could be riddled from only one point—but we had not time enough to extend our line to that—so, we could not get it. Therefore the indians amused themselves by shooting at our stock, ditto men—but the men could cover themselves. Both of my horses (U. S. horses) were wounded. Well they pounded at us all of what was left of the 1st day and the whole of the 2nd day—withdrawing their lines with the withdrawal of their village— which was at dusk the 2nd day—Corporal Lee, Meadow & Jones were killed; Sergt. Pahl, both of the Bishops, Phillips, Windolph, Black, Severs, Cooper &c (21 wounded altogether). I got a slight scratch on my right thumb, which, dash, as you see, doesn't prevent me from writing you this long scrawl. As this goes by Fort Ellis, it will be a long time in reaching you. Genl. Terry with Genl. Gibbon's command, came up the morning of the 3rd day about 10 o'clock. Indians had all gone the night before. Had Custer carried out order he got from Genl. Terry the command would have formed a junction exactly at the village—and have captured the whole outfit of tepees, etc. and probably any quantity of squaws, pappooses, &c. &c. but Custer disobeyed orders from the fact of not wanting any other command—or body to have a finger in the pie, and thereby lost his life. (3,000 warriors were there.)

I told you in my letter of yesterday that I had sent a pony, a nice little boy pony on the "Far West", by Grant Marsh, for Fred. Grant Marsh wanted to bring you and Fred up here this trip but, on the whole, I guess you had better not come—'tis too dangerous a business for you. The name of the lodge to which I belong is St. Louis Lodge, No. 5 I.O.O.F. and the encampment is Wildey Encampment, both of St. Louis. I am anxious to hear from both of them.

My communication addressed to the secretary of St. Louis Lodge I.O.O.F. or to the scribe of Wildey Encampment I.O.O.F. both of St. Louise, will be gotten all right. If you have an opportunity of sending my papers by some boat that is coming directly to us, send them. Otherwise, do not. Boston Custer & young Mr. Reid a nephew of Genl. Custer were killed; also Kellogg the reporter. I am very much obliged for the remembrances of Dr. and Mrs. Taylor. Return mine to them with interest; also to tell all the other good people of the garrison. I am glad to know that Humbert did not send Janie off, there was nothing about our game that night at the store that I owed Humbert $20 which I gave him next morning.

This is a long scrawl—but not so much in it after all— and I am about getting to the end of my tether. Reno has assumed command—and Wallace as Adjutant, Edgerly Qr. M. By the death of our Captains Nowlan, Bell & Jackson, 3 coffee-coolers are made captains—and Godfrey is Senior, 1st Lieut. Mathey 2d, Gibson, 3d. Quick promotion. I am inclined to think that had McIntosh divested himself of that slow poking way which was his peculiar characteristic he might have been still in the land of the living. A Crow Indian, one of our scouts who got in the village reported that our men killed a great many of them, quite as many, if not more than were killed of ours. The indians during the night got to fighting among themselves and killed each other, so the Crow says —he also said as soon as he got possession of a Sioux blanket he felt all right—as there was such a collection of indians many of them wholly unacquainted, that not the slightest attention was paid to him. There was among them Cheyennes, Araphores [Arapahoes?], Kiowa, and representatives probably from every Agency on the Mo. River. A host of them there, sure. The latest and probably the correct account of the battle is that none of Custer's commands got into the village at all. We may not be back before winter—think so very strongly. Well, Wifey, Darling—I think this will do for a letter so with oceans of love to you & Fred & kisses enumerable, I am devotedly, your husband—Fred Benteen

LITTLE BIG HORN
NARRATIVES

In 1898, Major Benteen found among his father's effects, along with the packet of letters, two manuscript narratives concerning the Little Big Horn battle. They both were loaned to General Godfrey, who retained possession of them until his death. At that time, Mrs. Godfrey returned one of the manuscripts, presumably the earlier one which was believed to have been written in 1890 sometime after the Battle of Wounded Knee. An unknown number of final pages were missing and have never been discovered. They apparently disappeared together with the second manuscript. Despite the lost pages, Colonel Graham considered it the more important of the two, which seems purely speculative since the second manuscript has never been located. But it is important, and a transcript is faithfully reproduced here.

On June 22d, 1876, the 7th United States Cavalry, then on the Yellowstone River, Montana Territory, passed in review, guidons fluttering, horses prancing, before Brevet Major General A. H. Terry, commanding then the Department of Dakota, Headquarters in the Field; the 7th was en route, where? none knew of the Regt. but General G. A. Custer. However, I have since been informed by Brevet Major General John Gibbon, who was of the reviewing party, that his last salutation to General Custer was "Now, don't be greedy Custer, as there are Indians enough for all of us"!

On that day we moved up the "Rosebud," marching twelve (12) miles, and bivouacked: in the evening the orderly trumpeter was sent to notify the officers of the regiment that Genl. Custer wished to see them at his headquarters, and after arrival of the last officer, General Custer commenced his talk, which was to the effect, that it had come to his knowledge that his official actions had been criticised by some of the officers of the regiment at headquarters of the Department, and, that while he was willing to accept recommendations from the junior second lieutenant of the regiment, he wished the same to come in a proper manner, calling our attention to the paragraph of Army Regulations referring to the criticism of actions of commanding officers; and said he would take the necessary steps to punish, should there be reoccurence of the offence.

I said to General Custer, it seems to me you are lashing the shoulders of *all*, to get at some; now, as we are all present, would it not do to specify the officers whom you accuse? He said, Colonel Benteen, I am not here to be catechised by you, but for your own information, will state that none of my remarks have been directed towards you. Then, after giving a few excellent general orders as to what should be done by each troop of the regiment in case of an attack on our bivouac at any time, the meeting of the officers was over, and each adjourned to his palatial "Pup tent." On the next day, owing to the report of the lieutenant having control of the marching of the pack-train, the mules or packers of my troop having been reported with two other troops as being the most unmanageable in the regiment, I was directed to assume command of those three troops, and to march the battalion in rear of the last mule of the train. I saluted the General, and

awaited the opportunity of crossing the Rosebud in rear of the
regiment: it took exactly one hour and thirty minutes to get
that pack-train across the creek, and get it started on other
side:—The country through which we were marching was
very broken, and over ravines that would have concealed
thousands of Indians, so, after marching, say seven or eight
miles, and the train being scattered for perhaps two miles, it
occurred to me that perhaps the Casabianca business might be
over construed, and that the pack train had better be "Rounded
up," or I might have a knotty explanation to grind out should
it be lost, which was one of the easiest of things to have
happen, as I was marching. So, a trumpeter quickly galloped
ahead with orders to halt the train, and on arrival of the battalion at the train, one troop of battalion was put in advance
of it, one troop on the right flank of centre of train, nearest the
hills, and the remaining troop in the rear of train. The march
that day was 35 miles. Some little while before reaching
bivouac of regiment, I missed Dr. Lord from my side, he
having accompanied me on the march for the two days. However, on arrival at bivouac, the Adjutant of Regt. 1st Lieut.
W. W. Cooke, came out to indicate place of bivouac for each
troop, to have it in its proper order for marching on next day:
after learning which, I said, See here, "Cookey," "G. A. C."
ordered me to march the 3 troops of the battalion composing
guard for "packs," in rear of the last mule of train; now as
the C.O. of Regt. told us last night that he was open for
recommendations, &c., I tell you as adjutant of regiment, that
the first thing we know, some Casabianca will be getting such
orders about the train, and if the roughness of the country
holds out, and the Indian signs continue to thicken, why, the
train will go up, then, the circus adjourns.

I am willing to admit this was getting close upon in-

fracting the paragraph of Army Regulations to which our
attention had been invited on the evening previous; but I was
telling it to the adjutant that it might be sandwiched in as it
were in conversation with the commanding officer of the regiment, and I knew if he did that I would not be put in the
light of a fault-finder, but that in more elegant language the
spirit of my talk would be given, and perhaps might call the
attention of the General to a matter that might mar the success
of the campaign. However, the Adjt. refused, point blank, to
say anything about it to Custer, saying, I might tell him myself
if I chose. So, the next morning as General Custer was passing,
I chose to do so; telling him, that I could not, without en-
dangering the safety of the packs, carry out the orders he had
given me concerning the marching of the battalion composing
the "Packs" guard. I then told the arrangement I had made
of the battalion; and this from the fact that from the time
he left me at the bivouac of the night before, not one sight
of his command had been gotten. The General said, I am
much obliged to you Colonel, and I will turn over the same
order of march for the rear guard to the officer who relieves
you.

Well, after the 2d day's march, and I had seen to the
bivouacking of my troop, I got out my seine for purpose of
seeing the kinds of fish the Rosebud could set up for supper.
The attempt however resulted mostly in "water-hauls," and
being ravenously hungry, "S.O.B. and trimmings," had to serve
for bill of fare. Dr. Lord not putting in an appearance at the
meal, however, after I had crawled under a bullberry bush
for sweet repose, the Dr. came into camp, telling me that he
had halted alone some miles back, being completely tired out,
broken down, so much so that he had given up all hopes of
getting to camp. He declined tea, and wanted nothing to eat

or drink. I state this to show what must have been the physical condition of the Doctor on June 25th, on going into the fight, after an almost continuous march of 84 miles.

The repose I found under the bullberry bush alluded to, can be classed with the goose egg of the cricketer, for there were myriads of mosquitoes under that bush when I got there, and I don't think that any of them got away.

1st night's loss of sleep.

3rd day we marched to, strange to say, a creek called "Muddy Creek," where, on coming into camp I heard the voice of my old friend Col. Myles W. Keogh hailing me, saying, come here "old man," I've kept the nicest spot in the whole camp next to me, for your troop, & I've had to bluff the balance to hold it, but here it is, skip off," so I "skipped," putting my troop in the vale the gallant Irishman had held for me.

It wasn't far from twilight then, so, after getting supper Keogh came over to my bullberry bush, (he was more luxurious than I was, having a tent fly for shelter) and the crowd was listening to one of the Italian patriot, De Rudio's recitals, of his hair breadth scapes with Mazzini, or some other man, in some other country, all of which I rudely interrupted by saying. See here, fellows, you want to be collecting all the sleep you can, and be doing it soon, for I have a "Pre." that we are not going to stay in this camp tonight, but we are going to march all night, so, good-night. I had scarcely gotten the words from my lips before the orderly trumpeter notified us that we would meet at the commanding officer's headquarters at once: my preparations for sleep consisted in putting off my cavalry boots, so little time was consumed in robing: However, that was sufficient, and other officers rapidly went to their summons, it being quite dark there, and the "Pre." telling me

'twas a move. I called up my 1st Sergeant, and had him see
that the aparejos were "O.K." ropes, bridles, &c., all right, and
have everything ready about the troop for a speedy move.

I then commenced a search for the Head Quarters; however, before getting far, I met an officer returning from the
"Call," saying, 'tis no use going, *You* were right—we move at
11 o'clock, P.M. Sharp, tonight: all right, then, there's no
sleep for your humble again tonight.

2d night's loss of sleep.

If it took a minute to cross that pack train over the
"Muddy," it took two hours; other side of creek Colonel Keogh
hunted me up, he being the officer in charge of rear guard;—
he was making the very air sulphurous with blue oaths, telling
me of the situation; however, from having been there very
many times myself, I knew it better than he did; so I consoled
him with, "Never mind old man, do the best you can, and it
will all come out right."

I don't begin to believe that Job ever had much to do
with shaved tailed pack mules.

Well, my advice seemed to brace Col. Keogh a bit, and
I kept the ding-donging of the tin cup, frying pan—or something, that was my guide as to direction, the pounding of that
on the saddle of the horse on the left of the troop preceding
mine, being all I had to go by, the night being pitch dark, and
the gait was a trot, so I hadn't much time to swap words with
Col. Keogh, or, my guide would be gone.

This trot was kept up for perhaps eight or ten miles;
then, came a halt, no orders for same being received, and no
orders for anything received by me. So, the Packs remained
on mules; saddles & bridles on horses. I crouched down by a
sage bush until daylight, and there spied Colonel Reno and
little Benny Hodgson going for coffee, hardtack & Trimmings.

I invited myself to assist in disposing of that repast; and met
with a "1st Class' welcome at suggesting it.

In a few moments, it seemed, the column moved forward,
no orders however, for same were gotten, but my troop & I
followed the procession: then came almost as sudden a halt!
no orders for that. The rear of column knew of none, however,
a few moments brought us a summons thro' an orderly, to
"Officers' Call," at Head Quarters: when there, General Custer
notified us that he had been on the mountain to the left, where
our Scouts (Crows) were all the night; that they had told
him thro. the interpreter, that they could see dust, indians and
ponies, & all that. He could see nothing through the old telescopic glass they had and didn't believe there was anything to
be seen; now, strange perhaps to say, I did believe it:—another
"Pre." I knew it, because, why, I'd sooner trust the sharp eye
of an indian than to trust a pretty good binocular that I always
carried; and I'd gotten that from experience. However, 'twasn't
my "chip in," so I said nothing. At this halt General Custer
notified us that the first troop commander who notified him
that the requirements of an order issued a few days before
were being carried out strictly in the troop, that officer and
troop should have the post of honor, the advance. I notified
him at once that in my troop the requirements were being
strictly adhered to. I feel quite sure it wasn't expected from
me; but he stammered out, Well, Col. Benteen, Your troop
has the advance.

When all had reported, I was ordered to move in advance with my troop, which I did, but had gone but a short
distance when General Custer rode up, saying, I was setting
the pace too fast. He then rode in advance; and after going a
few miles the command was halted between hills on every
side, and Genl. Custer and his adjutant stepped aside, and

were figuring on paper for quite awhile, at what, we knew not. However, when thro, I was called up and notified that my command was 3 Troops, and that I would move to the left to a line of bluffs about 2 miles away. Sending out an officer and a few men as advance guard, to "pitch in" to anything I came across, and to notify him at once; I started on my mission immediately:—this was just about 15 miles from where I found the dead body of Genl. Custer 3 days afterwards.

I omitted stating, that while en route obeying Custer's last order, I received two other orders from him, and these through the Chief Trumpeter and the Sergeant Major of the regiment; the first to the effect, that, should I not find anything at the first line of bluffs, then, to go on to the second line of bluffs, to pitch in, and notify him at once, being included: the order through Sergt. Major received 15 or 20 minutes later, was, if nothing could be seen from second line of bluffs, then, to go on until I came to a valley, to "pitch in," and to notify him at once, being also included: now, all of this time the balance of the regiment was on the march, and the last glimpse I had of them was the grayhorse troop in rapid motion. I thought of course they had struck something. However, I had that valley to find, and away we went for it, myself and orderly being in advance of the advance guard. The 2d line of bluffs showed no valley,—only bluffs & bluffs:—so, another of my "Prees." came; and said, old man, that crowd ahead is going to strike a snag: indians have too much sense to travel over such country as you have been going unless they are terribly pushed; so, you'd better get back to that trail, and you will find work; then "Right Oblique" was the word until we got out of the hills to the trail; my command getting to it just ahead of the train of Packs, the horses not having been watered since evening before, and this being along about one o'clock P. M. of a hot June day, they were needing it badly. So, on the trail

I halted at a morass for a few moments for the purpose of giving the men and animals a chance at it. I attended to the watering of the horse I was riding, for the brute was tricky, and unless you took the precaution to lariat him to something, after the bit was taken from his mouth, and he thro' drinking, you could not hold him by the strap of halter: no one could: and away he would go; and when he got good and ready, he would rejoin the troop. Well, at this watering, I lariated old Dick to a stump of iron wood before removing the bit; and after drinking he pulled up taut on the stump, and looked as if to say, "Well, I didn't much care to go off this time anyway": but that was the time of times, old fellow, for you would have been saved two wounds, and two days where water was worth its weight in green backs, though beautiful and blue, within a stone's throw from our stand.

After leaving the watering place, a few miles brought us to a beautifully decorated tepee of buffalo hide, just on trail.

I dismounted, after riding around the lodge, peeped in, and saw the body of an indian on a scaffold or cot of rude poles. By this time the battalion was up—and away we went again. A mile or two brought orders through a Sergeant to the officer in charge of pack-train. I told him where I had last seen it—another couple of miles brought an order for me thro' the orderly trumpeter of day, from the adjutant of regiment, to the effect: Benteen, Big Village, Be quick; Bring Packs.

P.S. Bring Packs,

W. W. Cooke,

Adjt.

Well, the Packs were safe behind. I knew *that—better than anybody*. I couldn't waste time in going back, nor in halting where I was for them. So, we went—V.V.V.

I resume with the last order received from the Adjutant

of the 7th Cavalry; the last lines penciled by him, viz: "Benteen, Come on, Big Village, Be Quick, Bring Packs. P. S. Bring Packs, John Martini, the trumpeter, bringing this dispatch was a thick headed, dull witted Italian, just about as much cut out for a cavalryman as he was for a King: he informed me that the Indians were "skidaddling"; hence, less the necessity for retracing our steps to get the Packs, and the same would ge gained by awaiting the arrival of them where we then were. We did neither; but took the Trot! and, from the ford where Reno first crossed the beautifully blue Little Big Horn we saw going on what evidently was not "skedaddling" on the part of the indians, as there were 12 or 14 dismounted men on the river bottom, and they were being ridden down and shot by 800 or 900 indian warriors.

We concluded that the lay of the land had better be investigated a bit, as so much of the Italian trumpeter's story hadn't "Panned out." So—off to left I went, seeing a group of 3 or 4 Absaraka or Crow indians; from them I learned this; Otoe Sioux, Otoe Sioux, the "Otoe" meaning, innumerable, or—Heaps of them;—and we soon found that there were enough of them.

From the point I saw the Crows. I got the first sight of the men of Reno's battalion who had retreated from the river bottom, recrossed the river a couple of miles below, and were showing up on the bluffs on the side of the river that my battalion had kept and was then on: the battalion being in line, Reno, knowing of course we were soldiers, came riding to meet me as I moved towards him. My first query of Reno was—where is Custer? Showing him the last order received from the Adjutant of Regt., Reno replied that he did not know, that Custer had ordered him across the river to charge the indians, informing him that he would support him with the whole "Outfit," but he had neither seen nor heard from him since:—Well, our battalion got just in the nick of time to save Reno's.

After a few words with Col. Reno I inquired as to the whereabouts of "D" Troop of my Battn.—and was informed that Capt. Weir had, without orders, gone down the river. This being the case, I sallied after Weir, and about ¾ths of a mile lower down, from the top of the highest point in vicinity, saw Weir's troop returning; hordes of indians hurrying them somewhat. Reno came to same point after I had thrown Captain French's troop in line at right angle with river, to hold that point, dismounted, till Weir's troop got thro, and to then retreat slowly, and I would have that part of command looked after. This didn't finish as well as I had hoped and expected it would. However, from fact of the indians not making the most of the opportunity, and Lieut. Ed. S. Godfrey carrying out his instructions more faithfully and in a more soldierly manner, we had time sufficient to get some kind of a line formed: the first officer I saw when establishing a line, was Lieutenant Geo. D. Wallace, recently killed by some of the same Sioux, at the "Wounded Knee" fight in Dak. I said, Wallace, put the right of your troop here. His answer was, "I have no troop, only three men." Well, said I, stay here with your three men, and don't let them get away, I will have you looked out for:—and Wallace and the three men stayed, and they were looked out for. Col. Reno was on the left—forming the same line—which wasn't a line but an arc of a circle, rather irregularly described too. And when we met about centre, my own Troop remained to be disposed of, so I put it over much ground, almost as much as the other six companies occupied, protecting left flank, and well to the rear, just on the edge of line of bluffs, near river.

The formation as described, was dismounted; like the horses of command, being placed in a saucer like depression of prairie, the lower rim of the saucer, instead of a rim was a gentle slope. The hospital was established at the upper rim, and was about as safe a place as there was around the vicinity, the blue canopy of heaven being the covering: the sage brushes, sand being the operating board: but the stout heart and nervy skilful hand of Dr. Porter (the only surgeon of the three of command that hadn't been killed), was equal to the occasion.

I state but the facts when I say that we had a fairly warm time with those red men as long as sufficient light was left for them to draw a bead on us, and the same I'm free to maintain, in the language of Harte.

I don't know how many of the miscreants there were;—probably we shall never know,—but there were enough.

Now, be it remembered, this wasn't a fight instituted by the army for glory going purposes, or anything of that kind; but rather, was a little gentle discipling which the Department of the Interior (the Department of U. S. Government having charge of the Indian Bureau), had promised would be given the indians if they, the nomads of the tribe, declined to come in to agencies in the Spring; be good, and draw their pay; runners having been sent out to the self supporters; i.e. those, who gave the Agencies the grand go by, as it were, to the effect, that if they didn't report, Soldiers would be sent out to bring them in. About the only answer that they returned as far as I wot, was "We will be here when you come for us"! and sure enough, they were there! but little thought anyone that they would be in such hordes.

I judged of the condition of the men of my troop somewhat by my own condition; though that is one of almost physical never tire; but not having had sleep for the two nights previous to this one, was getting just a trifle weary myself; so, up and down the line of "H" Troop 1st Lieut. Gibson and myself tramped, the night of June 25th & 26th, doing our very best to keep the sentinels awake, but we just could not do it. Kicking them; well, they didn't care anything about that. However, we two kept awake on our end of line, and at early daybreak ascertained that few, if any of our red friends had given up hope of doing us up. The clatter they made stirred our little bivouac out pretty effectually, then *all* being on the qui vive; thinking the situation was O.K. that I'd try and "Round Up" a few lines of sleep, to make up somewhat for the three night's sleep that I was short of. So, down I dropped on the hill-side, determined to gather what I could, in; but some wakeful red skin had pretty nearly my exact range, plumping me in the heel of extended boot; another bullet scattered the dry dust under my arm pit; however, I hadn't the remotest idea of letting little things like that disturb me, and think that I at least had gotten forty winks, when a Sergeant of my troop informed me that Lieut. Gibson of my troop was having a regular monkey & parrot time of it: to say that I felt like saying something naughty to that Sergeant, was putting it mildly, but down I ran and thro and thro' the pack train, getting together some 15 or 16 soldiers & packers, making them carry up sacks of bacon, boxes of hard bread, pack-saddles, and materials of that kind;—quite a sufficiency to build a respectable little breast work—which, after propping up as well as we could, I turned over with the Falstaffian crowd, to "Gib." my 1st lieutenant, telling him to hold the fort, notwithstanding what might become of us. Then I walked along the front of my troop and told them that I was getting mad, and I wanted them to charge down the

ravines with me when I gave the yell: then, each to yell as if
provided with a thousand throats. The Chinese act was sufficiently good enough for me if it would work; but I hadn't so
much real trust in its efficacy. However, when the throttles of
the "H sters" were given full play, and we dashed into the
unsuspecting savages who were amusing themselves by throwing clods of dirt, arrows by hand, and otherwise, for simply
pure cussedness among us, to say that 'twas a surprise to them,
is mild form, for they somersaulted and vaulted as so many
trained acrobats, having no order in getting down those
ravines, but quickly getting; de'il take the hindmost!

Then, then, I had the key to the beautiful blue water
that had been flowing so rippling at our very feet for two days
—and which wounded and well longed so much for,—there
it was, ours, for the getting. Well, 'twasn't the simplest of
matters to get a camp-kettle of it, even then, but as we were
on the brink of it, to none did it occur to picture or think of
how it had to be gotten; we proceeded to get it, but at the
expense of many wounded, and this for the sake of the already
wounded as well as the dry as dust living. Speaking for myself,
I am quite sure that I would gladly and cheerfully have given
the very prettiest and newest twenty dollar silver certificate
that I might have persuaded my first lieutenant to have lent
me, for just one Oz. of Spiritus Frumenti to have dashed into
just about same quantity of that pure Little Big Horn water,
if for no other purpose than to just brace me a bit, for to a
certainty I was "Plumb" tired out and sleepy too. However,
the business for the day had only fairly opened: and I got no
chance to steal off and sleep, or bless me if I would not have
done it.

To say that I ever had more serene satisfaction at killing
a Black tailed buck deer, on the bound, with a carbine, than

[174]

I had in putting one of Uncle Sam's 45s thro' as noble a speci-
men of the Dakotas as ever fluttered an eagle feather in his
scalp lock, was every word true at that time; though I'm rather
fond of indians than otherwise, but to plump him thro' his
spinal, as he was cavorting thro the ravines, there being so
many of them around, that one wouldn't be missed, and being
so confoundedly mad and sleepy, must say that I looked on that
dead red with exquisite satisfaction and not because he was
maiden hair either, for he wasn't—but I was so tired, and they
wouldn't let me sleep. Now, Strong man, I, a bit out of luck
in losing the 1st night's sleep in the category of three, still,
how tired must my good friend Dr. Lord have been, when he
galloped in with Custer before getting his quietus, and *he*,
A.H.L., was of weak physique.

It is known that Captain Benteen intended to write what he
considered to be the definitive story of the Little Big Horn affair,
but it is not known if he ever began or finished such a manuscript.
The ill-health he suffered in his last years probably prevented a
full undertaking of such a responsible task, yet his constant en-
thusiasm to set the record straight-as he saw it-could very well
have propelled him into such action.

This makes the following narrative very unusual. Is it his
effort to "set the record straight" or is it his second manuscript
recorded as missing from General Godfrey's effects? It is impossible not to notice its resemblance to the first version of his
narrative, and it also appears to be a more polished version of it.
There is absolutely no way of knowing, which adds more interest
to the Custer Mystery, the missing pages notwithstanding.

LITTLE BIG HORN, M. T.

June 25–26—1876

Trumpets sounding, horses prancing, guidons waving, proudly the twelve troops of the Seventh U. S. Cavalry passed in review before Brigadier General Alfred Terry, commanding the Department of Dakota, at noon, on the 22d day of June 1876.

The scene of the review was on Montana territory, on the banks of the Yellowstone River, in close proximity to the junction of Rosebud Creek with said river.

After passing the reviewing officer, the regiment ployed into column, and the line of march was taken for Rosebud Creek,—the distance marched that afternoon being twelve (12) miles.

On the night of that day, the officers of the 7th Cavalry were summoned to appear at the bivouac of Lieut. Col. Custer, commanding the regiment, and upon the assembling of the officers, Lieut. Col. Custer gave some directions about what formation of the troops should be made in case of an attack upon the camp by the indians.

Evidently, this meeting of the officers was not "called" for the promulgation of the directions which were given out by Lieut. Col. Custer, as these directions were wholly rudimentary and as the regiment had been campaigning for the past nine years with nearly the same officers, during which term of years, Col. Custer had never before seen fit to counsel or direct us as to the A, B, C of our profession; at this, however, no one felt injured, and Col. Custer drifted into saying, "That, while *he* was willing to accept recommendations from the junior Second Lieutenant of the regiment, that such recommendations must come to him in proper form; and—more-

[176]

over that he, Custer, was aware that his official action had
been talked of and criticized by officers of the regiment to
officers of the Department Staff—during the march from Fort
A. Lincoln, D. T. and that he now notified all such officers,
that such criticism must cease—or that the officers offending
would be proceeded against as the Regulations of the Army
provided".

It was then patent to us for what purpose the "Call" had
been sent forth, and as my relations with Lieut. Col. Custer
were not of the warmest personal nature, I was anxious to
learn the names of the officers whom he evidently mistrusted;
So, I said, "General will you not be kind enough to inform
us of the names of those officers whom have so offended"?
Custer stammered slightly, and said, "Colonel Benteen, while
I am not here to be catachised by you, I take pleasure in informing you for your own gratification, that you are not among
those officers whom I have alluded to".

The meeting then dispersed—each proceeding in the
direction of his own bivouac.

On the morning of the 23d of June I reported to Lieut.
Colonel Custer for orders as new officer of the day.

Lieut. Colonel Custer told me the letters of the three
troops of the battalion I was to take charge of as guard to the
pack-train for the day, and ordered, that, I was to march the
battalion in rear of the last pack-mule of the train. Soon,
thereafter, Lieut. Col. Custer marched at the head of the
column of the other nine troops.

It took exactly one and a half hours to get the pack-train
across Rosebud Creek, so, by that time Custer's column was all
of six miles ahead of my train,—and out of sight. For some
time I marched the train and the battalion as I had been
ordered to by Lieut. Col. Custer, but as the train was much

[177]

scattered, so much so that I could exercise no control of it from my position in rear of the whole of it, and as I would be held responsible for safety of same in case of an attack by indians, I determined to put the troops in such positions along flank of train that in case of attack the command was prepared to defend it; for such purpose, I placed one troop on flank at head of train, second troop, at center of train, while I remained with the third troop, on flank, and at rear of train. Our march that 2nd day was about 35 miles, and up the Rosebud Creek.

On arrival with the train and Battalion at the place of bivouac for the night, I found the regimental adjutant, Lieut. W. W. Cooke, awaiting my arrival for purpose of designating the place each troop of my train-guard was to occupy in the camp.

I said to Cooke, "that Gen. Custer had ordered me to march the whole battalion in rear of the last mule of the train, and, that I had carried out his orders until I feared to longer do so, as I might have lost a great portion of the train, in case it had been attacked;—telling Lieut. Cooke the manner in which I had marched the guard to protect train, and re-quested that he would communicate the same to Gen. Custer, so, that, the next officer in charge, should not receive such order as had been given to me regarding the marching of the train. Lieut. Cooke replied, no, I will not tell Gen. Custer any-thing about it, if you want him to know it, you must tell him of it yourself.

On the morning of the 24th June, General Custer rode by my bivouac of the night before; I approached him, and reported, that—on account of fearing for safety of train the day before, I had placed the battalion on guard differently from the manner he had ordered. Custer stammered slightly, and said, "I am much obliged to you Col. Benteen, I will direct the officer who relieves you to guard the train in the manner you have done". As my duties ended on delivering the train at camp on the 23d, I did not have to report to the commanding officer with the new Officer of the Day.

The march of June 24th was interrupted by frequent and sometimes quite lengthy halts of the column, but on what account, I was not aware, but on arriving at "Mud Creek", which was to be our place of bivouac, I was loudly called by Col. Keogh, to come where he was, that he had been saving for me a snug nook with beautiful grass in it for me, that I might camp next to him.

The reply to this was characteristic of the plains, something like, bully for you Keogh! I'm your man.

After our frugal repasts, which went for dinner, Col. Keogh and his Lieut. Porter, came over to my bivouac, where, sitting around, were four or five officers, engaged in listening to Lieut. De Rudio's yarns; however, I placed my saddle in position for a pillow, spread my saddle-blanket for a bed, and notified the geltlemen, "That I was going in for what sleep I could pick up as I was impressed with belief that we would not remain in that camp all night",—the officers, however, went on with their conversation, and before I had caught a wink of sleep, an orderly from regimental head-quarters, came with information to us to meet at once at head-quarters. It was then "pitch dark", so I called up my first Sergeant and directed him to see that everything was in order for an immediate move, as I didn't think we would be allowed to remain in that camp all of the night. The Sergeant assured me that everything was in good shape,—so I then started to find Custer's headquarters. I had not gotten far on the way thereto, when I stumbled across Lieut. Edgerly, who informed me that it was not necessary to go any further, as the only orders, were,

[179]

that we were to move at 11 o'clock that night; at which hour we did move;—however, there was an hour and a half consumed in getting the pack-train across Mud Creek, Colonel Keogh had charge of the Pack on that move, and the column remained impatiently on other bank of creek while Keogh was superintending crossing of Pack-Train.

Some little time after the column started on the march, the only guide of direction I had for my troop was the pounding of the cups on the saddle of men in rear of the troop preceding us in the column.

About this time, Col. Keogh rode up to me, complaining that he couldn't tell head or tail of the pack-train, didn't know where the sheol they were and what was he going to do about it? I told him to take it easier, that nothing but an indian could run one of those mules off—some of the packs of course might slip off and be left behind, but we could recover the same at daylight;—and the tin-cup pounding on saddles of troop ahead of me went on, all of which suddenly ceased, the column was at a halt; pack-train and all, spread out together. I should think an hour and a half after this, daylight began to peer through, and I noticed Gen. Custer passed me on horseback. Custer went on, saying nothing to me. Just then, I noticed Major Reno and Lieut. Hodgson on the other side of a ravine, about to sit down to breakfast; I went over and assisted them in disposing of what they had. In course of half an hour, without orders or bugle sound, the column in advance commenced moving forward, which movement was of course followed by the troops and pack-train in the rear. I should think that we went about a mile and a half, when the column again halted. I am of the belief that an orderly was sent to notify the officers that Gen. Custer wished to see us. At all events, the officers gathered where he was. Gen. Custer then told us that he had just come down from the Mountain where our Crow indian scouts had been during the night, and that they had told him they could see tepee-tops, lots of indian ponies, dust, etc., etc., but that he had looked through their telescopic glass, and that he could not see a thing, and he did not believe that they could see anything of the kind either. Now, in 1875, I had a very similar experience with indians in Dakota, and as the statements of the indians then, were absolutely confirmed by what was afterwards proved, I was strong in the belief that the Crow indians only reported what was shown them by their superior keenness of vision, and that the hostile village was where they located it, but as no opinions were asked for, none were given.

The column then advanced, I should think a mile or so, and the officers were summoned to Gen. Custer—on arrival of all, Gen. Custer desired to know whether the requirements of a regimental order which was issued on the Yellowstone River was being carried out; which order, was to the effect that every troop of the regiment should have a non-commissioned officer and six men on duty with the pack-train, in immediate charge of the pack-mules of each troop, and the 100 pounds of carbine ammunition and twenty four rounds of pistol ammunition should be issued to each trooper; that the officer who first notified him that the requirements were being observed, should have the advance of the regiment for his troop. I am really of the opinion that Gen. Custer neither expected or desired that I should have the advance of the regiment,—nor do I think that he was of the opinion that I would volunteer to be the first to assure him that all orders were carried out to the letter in my troop; however, my troop being right on top of us,—as it were,—I saw no way of evading the question as to whether we were a dutiful lot of officers in "H" troop but—by notifying him—that to my certain knowledge the requirements of the order he had alluded to were being carried out as a matter of course.

With a slight stammer, Gen. Custer said, then, Col. Benteen, you have the advance, Sir. The last officer to report, was to catch the pack-train to guard,—as the penalty for not being more rapid in reporting,—and this, I opine, few cared for,

After all had reported, I was notified by Gen. Custer to move my troop to right of the regiment, which was then in columns of fours.

The regiment had moved but a short distance, when Custer rode to right of the column and remarked that I was setting the pace too fast; he then remained in front, halting the column after a mile or so had been passed over.

Gen. Custer and the regimental adjutant—Lieut. Cooke went a few yards in advance of the column, just out of "earshot", and were diligently engaged in talking and making notes on a scratch pad; after fifteen or so minutes or so of this work I was called by the adjutant and was informed by Gen. Custer that I was to mount D. H. & K. troops, which were there in column, dismounted, and proceed to a line of bluffs about 2 miles off, at about an angle of $45°$: to send a well mounted officer and ten men in advance,—to pitch into any indians I could see, and in such case, to notify him at once. I at once "mounted" my battalion and set out,—sending Lieut, Gibson and ten men in advance. To say the country "Terrain" goes now—was "rough", that would be more truly descriptive —and by no means exaggerative of the lay of the land. But on we went, with high intent, from embankment—to embankment.

Perhaps, a mile or so had been covered, when the chief trumpeter of regiment overtook us, with the "Compliments of

Gen. Custer to Colonel Benteen. That, if I came across or could see nothing from the first line of bluffs, to go on to the second line of bluffs, pitch into anything I came across, and to notify Gen. Custer of same at once."

Again, we went on, from the "second line of bluffs" nothing, but more and more bluffs, still further on; but by this time we had been overtaken by another messenger from Gen. Custer, this time in the person of the Sergeant Major of regiment, bearing the "Compliments of Gen. Custer, that, if Colonel Benteen saw nothing from the second line of bluffs, then, to proceed to the valley, to pitch into anything I came across, notifying Gen. Custer of same at once."

Forward, again, once more, but no valley, nor sign of valley was to be seen.

The last glimpse we had gotten of Gen. Custer's column was the sight of the gray-horse troop at a gallop,—well, one couldn't tell much about the simple fact of seeing that much of a column at an increased pace, as owing to roughness of country, the troop might have lost distance, and had only increased the pace to recover its distance.

But through the whole oblique to left, the impression went with me, that all of that hard detour was for naught,— as the ground was too awfully rugged for sane indians to choose to go that way to hunt a camp—or for that matter, to hunt anything else but game.

I knew that I had to come to some decision speedily, when I had given up the idea of further hunting for a valley, and being thoroughly impregnated with the belief that the trail Custer was on would yield quite a sufficiency of indians, that, for the present, any little undiscovered band might be safely left for future garnering, and none of us too desired to be left out of the fight,—which all were absolutely sure

[183]

could be found at the other end of the trail that Custer was following,—so, with me the question was, shall I valley hunt any more or shall I hasten with these three troops to where I feel sure of getting all of the fighting they can want—and, may be help someone out of a hole there. My real Simon-pure straight orders, were, to hunt that valley, but I didn't know where the valley was, and thought that perhaps an opportunity might happen later to search for it, but just then I believed I hadn't time to do it, so, shouldering the responsibility of not having found the valley I pitched off with the battalion at a right oblique to reach the trail Custer's column had followed, endeavoring by speed to make up for the precious time that had been lost in our futile hunt for the valley. My battalion reached the trail Custer had followed just in advance of the right of the pack-train, and pretty close to a boggy place where ·I thought water for the animals could be gotten. So, perhaps 15 minutes were consumed in so watering them.

Just as my battalion pulled out on trail from the watering place, the advance mules of the pack-train floundered into the bog, going up to the packs in mud, however, I couldn't spare the time to assist in extricating them, as this is wholly one of the perquisites of the owner of that duty, i.e. guard to pack-train, and is by no means a labor of love.

About two miles from this bog, we passed a burning tepee, the tepee being quite handsomely decorated in colors, in indian art style.

Dismounting from my horse, I peered into the tepee, and on a bed of forks of and small limbs of trees was stretched the body of an indian warrior; as I hadn't time to investigate as to the causes of his having been made a good indian, I remounted my horse and kept the battalion pushing on a stiff walk; a mile or so further on I met a sergeant, Knipe, coming from adjutant of the regiment with orders—written—for the commander of pack train. I told the sergeant the train was some distance in the rear,—after reading his orders—and he kept on back to it; further on a couple of miles, I met my own troop trumpeter, "John Martin", bearing orders from the adjutant of regiment to me, which were, as follows, "Benteen, come on, big village, be quick. bring Packs, P.S. Bring Pacs". Cooke.

Well, by this time, I had acquired a tolerably fair "lay of the land"; if I went back for packs, I feared much valuable time would be lost,—if I halted where I was, waiting for "Packs" to come up, the condition wasn't being at all bettered, and this site of the "lay of the land" was sufficiently convincing to me that no indians could hope to get between my battalion and the pack-train, so on I kept the battalion moving, now quickening the pace to a trot; willing to assume an added responsibility as regarding safety of packs. A couple of miles or so brought me to where Major Reno's battalion crossed the Little Big Horn.

On the hillside I saw a group of Crow Indians, riding to them, they explained, heaps of Sioux; and just then I saw the advance of Reno's battalion appear on bluffs on the side of river I was then on—I formed my battalion in line and moved up the bluff, then, Reno, hatless, came riding down to meet me; I inquired where Custer was, showing the order I had gotten. Reno read the order—replying, that, about an hour ago, Custer had sent him across the river, with orders to charge a body of Indians in the valley, promising, that he would support Reno with whole outfit, that since that time he, Reno, had seen nothing of Custer and knew nothing of his whereabouts, but had heard some firing down the river, and supposed he was in that direction. Now, it had become

[185]

imperative that I should speedily connect with the pack-train, and Reno despatched Lieut. Hare, 7th Cavalry, to go to train and hasten it along. In an hour or less the train came up; some carbine ammunition was then unpacked from it—and it was issued to some of Reno's men.

About this time I saw one of the troops of my battalion proceeding to the front, mounted, without order from me; upon this, I followed with the other two troops; Major Reno having his trumpeter sound the "Halt" continuously and assiduously, but I had to get in sight then, of what I had left my valley hunting mission for. On reaching the highest bluff in the vicinity, I saw what I estimated to be about 900 indians in the valley from which Reno had just been driven; the officer who had preceded me on his "own hook" with his troop had gone down a gorge with it; indians were riding around the bluff on either side of this troop signalling; I then formed a troop dismounted at right angles with the river, and one on bluff parallel with river, so, that if Custer's forces were near, that our position would be defined. Just then, up the gorge, pell mell, came the troops which the commander had so fearlessly sallied forth with, and the preparation I had made, allowed he and his troops to come down to a less frantic style of going; then came the necessity of getting into as good shape—and on as good ground for defense as was possible, as 'twas clearly apparent that we were in for a good long fight.

Slowly, we fell back to about just the very point where Reno reached the bluffs from his retreat from valley; and with the little time allowed us, we formed a line, which stemmed the tide of indian fury while the fight lasted, which was till dark on the 25th—and until the retreat of the indians on the 26th of June.

Now, not a soul knew on that hill with Reno, where

Custer was,—supposition and regard thereto was that he had found more indians than he could conveniently handle with his battalion of five (5) troops, and that he had fallen back to connect with Generals Terry & Gibbon.

My battalion got to the point in time to save Reno's force; but from not knowing the position or needs of Custer, it was without the bounds of possibility to render him any assistance—that my battalion made such an attempt is clear enough; it is also clear enough to me after the occurrence that the whole combined seven companies of regiment could have rendered no assistance to Custer after Reno had been defeated, —even had there been time and we had known the whole lay of the land, and the reason for this is, that there were a great deal too many indians, who were "powerful" good shots, on the other side. We were at their hearths and homes—they had gotten the "bulge" on Reno, their medicine was working well, and they were fighting for all the good God gives anyone to fight for; we were not cognizant of the "wiping out" of Custer's command, but it seemed to me that the indians developed very much more adhesiveness in their attention to us than I had ever noticed among their characteristics; had I known of the defeat of Custer's force at this time, my only surprise would have been, why they didn't get us too?

End of existing manuscript. Final pages lost.

THE BENTEEN-GOLDIN
LETTERS

The famous Benteen-Goldin letters have been the object of much interest and desire by many collectors, as well as being the subject of many dissertations over the years. For the first time they are reproduced in their entirety. Colonel Graham, in his *The Custer Myth*, edited these letters and, as a result, much of historic value was deleted as unimportant material not related to Custer or significant events. Today, all information contained in these letters is of great importance—not only because of the Custer revelations but because descriptive narratives of this nature reveal a great deal about daily life on the military frontier. Moreover, they reveal more of the basic character of the writer than was generally believed. Colonel Graham also eliminated some of these letters altogether; those excluded by him are included in this chronological presentation.

In the very few copies of these letters that were made by Colonel Graham for distribution to friends and for sale he enclosed a letter of confirmation relating to the history of the typed sets that had been made. It reads as follows:

COL. W. A. GRAHAM, U.S.A., RET'D
555 Radcliffe Avenue
Pacific Palisades, California

Author:

The Story of the Little Big Horn

Come On, Be Quick, Bring Packs

The Lost Is Found, Etc. . . . .   (date)

Dear Sir:

I have lately compared the reproduction of the Benteen-Goldin Letters, a copy of which you acquired from me some months ago, with the photostat of a typed copy produced in 1934 by Dr. Philip Cole of New York, to whom the original letters were sold by E. A. Brininstool of Los Angeles. Before sale to Dr. Cole, Mr. Brininstool made a copy of the originals, and your copy is an accurate and correct reproduction thereof.

Comparison of the Brininstool copy with the Cole copy, *also made from the originals*, discloses certain differences. These are, (1) the presence in Cole's copy of an important *addendum* to the letter of January 6, 1892; (2) transposition of notations from the top margins of two letters to the lower margins of immediately preceding letters; and (3) extension of words abbreviated in Cole's copy, and addition of the definite article "the" frequently omitted in the originals.

Differences indicated by (2) and (3) above, are negligible, and do not affect the text. Examples of original abbreviations are "Battn" (battalion), "ex" or "exped" (expedition), "11worth" (Leavenworth), "N.P." (Nez Perces), etc. Cole reproduced them: Brininstool extended them. As to transpositions, please note that the words "I underscore to show you that after 19 years etc." belong at the top of the July 6, 1894 letter; and "My son won two first prizes etc.," at the top of the May 26 (1896) letter.

I enclose a sheet which supplied the *addendum* to the January 6, 1892, letter. Please insert it as page 13½. *It is historically important.* I suggest also that you file this letter with your copy.

Very truly yours,

W. A. GRAHAM.

Of course, all these corrections and the addendum are incorporated into these reproductions as they were made directly from the Graham copies. Colonel Graham also had an Introduction enclosed in the few sets which reads:

Colonel Frederick W. Benteen, writer of the within letters, was a Virginian, born at Petersburg in August 1834. At the outbreak of the war between the States— the Civil War of 1861-65, he alone of his family, remained loyal to the national government. Throughout the war he was a Volunteer officer of cavalry, and made a distinguished record, frequently having commands far exceeding those appropriate to his rank. At the close of the war he accepted a regular commission in the Seventh Cavalry, organized in 1866, of which Lieut. Col. George A. Custer, who led a cavalry division as a Brevet Major General in the Army of the Potomac, was normally second in command, though usually in control of the regiment due to the absence of its Colonel.

Benteen, who became senior captain of the Seventh soon after joining, never got along with Custer. There was a clash of personalities from the very start of their relationship, as the Goldin letters prove. Their differences did not begin at the Washita, as has usually been assumed.

Long before I saw or even heard of the Goldin letters, I had written of Benteen that he "was Custer's bitter and outspoken enemy. Not even death served to change his attitude: to the day of his own passing he never abated his hatred. But his known character and the habit of his entire life refutes the imputation that at any time or in any circumstances he failed in his duty as an officer and a soldier. He fought as he had lived, fearless, uncompromising, and grimly stern. Benteen was one of the best soldiers the United States Army has ever possessed." (*The Story Of The Little Big Horn*, pp. 105-6) The Goldin letters go far to demonstrate the accuracy of that characterization; but they establish even more, for they prove that Benteen not only disliked Custer but despised him, for reasons that he sets forth in plain, unvarnished terms.

In reading the Benteen-Goldin letters, however, it should not be forgotten that Benteen wrote them during the sunset of his life, for he died shortly after the last of the series was penned. He, together with Major Reno, had been attacked and charged by Custer's partisans with responsibility for the disaster of June 25, 1876. He had resented and brooded over the injustice of that charge for many years. From his viewpoint, the man who rashly led five companies of his regiment to destruction and unnecessarily imperilled the rest, because he met death in a heroic setting, had been glorified by propaganda; while he, the man to whom more than to any other, belonged the credit of saving what was left of the regiment, had been slandered and reviled because he had not rescued that man and those who perished with him. He was bitter: and these letters plainly reveal his feeling. Moreover, Benteen was the product of an era of bitterness and strife; of a time when passions ran high; when father and son were arrayed against each other, and brother against brother. All this must be taken into consideration when reading these letters; and the mantle of charitable understanding cast about this stalwart soldier of a bygone day, who saw so little of good and so much of evil in too many of his fellows; and indeed, about his fellows also.

Theodore W. Goldin (born John Stilwell), to whom the letters were written, was a runaway youth of 17 when he enlisted in the Army during April 1876 and was assigned to Company (Troop) "G" of the Seventh Cavalry. At the Battle of the Little Big Horn he was a recruit of less than three months service; and he was discharged without honor in November 1877 upon application of his adoptive parents, because of concealed minority enlistment without their knowledge or consent. After discharge he studied law, and was in practice at Janesville, Wisconsin, when his correspondence with Benteen began. He was then active in politics and an honorary Colonel upon the Governor's staff. Throughout the letters it plainly appears that Benteen believed that Goldin had served in the Seventh throughout at least a full five year enlistment; and it is equally obvious that Goldin did not undeceive him, though much of what Benteen wrote must have come to him as strange news from a stranger land. Goldin's Benteen-inspired articles published in the "Army Magazine" to which frequent references are made, I have been unable to discover. Evidently that magazine long since gave up the Ghost.

Recently, in discussing the faults and foibles, and the virtues of our fighting men of former generations, a retired Major General remarked to me that we of the present generation are too prone to judge them by present day standards, and, in consequence, to misjudge them. A century from now we ourselves will probably fare no better. If therefore we must judge at all, let us appraise the worth of Custer, of Reno and Benteen, and all the others of that "Old Army" which had so great a part in the winning of the West, by their achievements, which were godlike, rather than by their frailties, which were human.

W. A. GRAHAM

It would be difficult to add anything to what Colonel Graham has written in his Introduction to help the reader digest the contents of the letters which follow. It would be prudent, therefore, to read them all and then make a judgment rather than being influenced by each letter in turn.

P. O. Box 118,
Atlanta, Ga.
Oct. 20, 1891

Dear Mr. Goldin:—

Your favor of the 17th inst. received today.

It is very gratifying to know that my efforts while belonging to the 7th Cavalry were appreciated by the rank and file—i.e., the enlisted men—and your letter of today tells me that they were.

I was with the regiment from its organization to December, 1882, and of course can look far behind the date you came to me, and the backward glance is as full of memories— many of them glorious, and all pleasant, as from the point where you first drew saber.

Capt. Owen Hale was the last of our old "mess" of seven, to bite the dust, and I alone remain to think of them; I mean the mess association, and cherish their memories in that regard.

In 1866 I could have gone into the 10th U.S. Cavalry as a Major but I preferred a Captaincy in the Seventh. Fate, however, after being a Captain 17 years, threw me into a negro organization of cavalry anyhow; and being well off in this world's goods, and feeling that it was not proper to remain with a race of troops that I could take no interest in—and this on account of their "low-down" rascally character—and having served my 30 years—there seemed nothing to do but to commence looking after my property interests.

It cost me $10,000 more than my pay came to, to follow the trumpet calls of the United States, and this amount was not thrown away, or wasted, either.

Now, as a retired Major, I am getting along comfortably,

and am looking after my flocks and herds—city blocks in
prospective—and the interests of Fred, my only child. I lost
four children in following that brazen trumpet around.

I am pleased, my dear sir, at having heard from you, and
I wish you an un-interrupted run of everything that is good.

Very truly your friend,
F. W. BENTEEN, Bvt. Col. U.S. Army.

T. W. Goldin

P.O. Box 118,
Atlanta Ga.,
Nov. 10, '91

Dear Col. Goldin:—

Yours of the 3d inst. rec'd.

It pleases me to know that you knew and liked Lieut.
Aspinwall of the 7th Cavalry—for he was a good fellow.

I was commanding the post of Fort Rice, D.T., and appointed Aspinwall Assistant Commissary of Subsistence, which
office having funds, ready cash, monthly, completed, what was
begun in Custer's coterie in 1869, and ended the army career
of poor John.

Perhaps I can inform you of his end. He was at work
for a street car company in Montreal, being "starter", and was
in great favor with the company. He had been presented a
fine gold watch a short time before his murder, as is supposed;
he being found drowned in a small pool of water, 18 inches
in depth. This I learned from First Lieut. George E. Albee,

U.S. Army, retired in 1883. Albee knew him, and got the facts from Aspinwall's sister.

Capt. E. S. Godfrey wrote to me when I was at Fort McKinny, Wyoming, in 1886, about an article he was engaged at for a magazine concerning the 1876 campaign; my answer to him was to the effect, "That the greatest of these was charity," and asked him if he didn't think Reno had been sufficiently damned?

Pretty nearly ever since the stepping down and out of the more prominent actors in that fight of ours, June 25-26, 1876, Godfrey had been trying to make much capital for himself; and perhaps 'twas well that he didn't undertake to do it sooner, as 'twas common campaign rumor among the enlisted men that he was one of 3 officers that showed the white feather. You were in a better position to hear of this man than I was—but I heard it—and I made no mention of either of the three troop commanders in my battalion. Of course I knew a great many things about the fight that 'tisn't essential that the world should; now, "qui bono." but I shouldn't like to see Godfrey attempt to parade himself as an at all prominent actor in it; though I don't think that I am in a position to say anything about it; however, you could, and I'd give you the facts.

Of all the non-enities with which a troop of cavalry could be damned, as its head and front, Capt. E.C.M. fills the bill.

He was in charge of the "packs." (so he was at the battle of the Washita) (At that fight, having exchanged duties with Capt Louis McLane Hamilton of "A" Troop of 7th, who was the officer of the day, Hamilton was killed in the fight.) I don't suppose there was ever an officer of the army got such a "cussing out" as I have Mathey at the L. Big Horn on the eve of June 25th, and before crowds of enlisted men, officers and "packs." Personally, I brought three of the mules of the train back—the mules being loaded with ammunition, and had gotten quite a long way down toward the water, for which they were heading, before I could "round them up." I always knew he was one of the fellows that did Custer's dirty work, i/e., in part—and—though I thought of course Custer was alive at the time, still I metaphorically gave M. hell! And per consequence, made a life-long enemy; but of what use are such friends? I just cannot be friendly to such whelps! Everybody—I mean most of the captains and all of the subalterns in the 7th, seemed to be positively afraid of Custer. However, without parade, when he did anything that was irregular to me, or infringed on "regulations," where I was concerned, I always went to him in "propria persona" and had the matter adjusted at once. Custer liked me for it, and I always surmised what I afterwards learned, de facto, that he wanted me badly as a friend; but I could not be, tho' I never fought him covertly. With Godfrey, Mathey and such cattle, why, Custer did as he pleased with them; and that was more than he could do with John Aspinwall.

Reno and Weir were never friendly, but the cause of this I never inquired or knew.

What was the conversation between Reno and Weir on the little knoll on the bluffs? Weir belonged to my battalion, and, as I always thought, to "show his smartness" sallied out without orders on the march down the river; however, he was glad enough to have us pull his troop there and back, and he played a very humble part in the fight till 'twas well closed.

Should you see anything, or hear more of an article from Godfrey, be kind enough to let me know. Were I dead, I think he might "parade", but just now I think he is afraid to.

Very truly yours
F. W. BENTEEN

[199]

P.O. Box 118,
Hermitage Heights,
Nov. 17, 1891

Dear Goldin:—

Yrs. of 12th inst. came duly.

I can give you another chapter of the unwritten history of the 7th Cavalry.

I brought the Fort Rice battalion of 7th up river from that post, and while in camp below Lincoln, General and Mrs. Sturgis drove down to my tent—and "A" without cot or any useless paraphernalia—the tent being so small I could not ask Mrs. Sturgis and her daughter in; so they remained in the carriage, being entertained by the usual throng of attendant "youngsters". The general came in, and there he told me that, though he was begged by Mrs. Sturgis to give me the command of a battalion, that he did not see how he could do it. Lt. Col. Otis and Major Merrill going on campaign, Otis must have six troops, and it would not appear well to divide the remaining troops into two battalions; but that he wanted me to "command the reserve."

I said, "General, do not bother yourself about any command for me, as I know it will come when the opportunity for doing something presents itself, and I really am more interested in my own troop than in the whole balance of the regiment."

You know with what a fan-farenade of trumpets we went up the Missouri to the Yellowstone. Otis and Merrill's battalions seemed to strive as to which could make the most clamor.

In camp opposite Keogh we lost Otis, and I shall always

be of the opinion that General Sturgis persuaded the doctor to give him a certificate of disability.

Gen. Miles then took away the other troops, leaving six for Sturgis; well, soon thereafter we started for the Crow Agency region; and when there I did little else but fish.

At Clark's Fork Canyon, I was up the canyon so engaged, feeling the while that I had no business to be out of the camp, and with such feeling on we returned to camp just as "boots and saddles" were being sounded.

I soon learned of the reports that were brought in by the detachments that had gone out under Lieuts. Hare and Fuller, and from the direction (course) taken by the column, pretty soon arrived at the conclusion that if we kept it up, the Nez Perces would not be "in it."

I "pumped" Hare, Fuller and the guides [?] and was the more convinced; so I went to the General on the march (it then being nearly dark) and told him that he was deliberately going away from the Indians. He said, "No, there is only one pass through which they can get; we will go up the Stinking Water and cut them off." My remark was, "General, when you know where Indians are, that is the very best place to find them, otherwise you may not find them at all."

Now this was pretty "brash" talk for a captain to give a colonel, and I soon saw I could not impress my convictions on him, but I at least persuaded him that no fires should be lighted in our bivouac that night, which caused the Indians to "feel around" for us—which they did, running into pickets of "L" Troop.

We went up the Stinking Water and crossed the mountain next day, but found no pass; Sturgis and Major Merrill both telling me during the early forenoon that we were going to have a hell of a fight pretty soon. "No," said I, "you'll find

[201]

an abandoned camp, and the Indians gone through the gap left by us."

You know how, step by step, we followed their trail through that d—d gorge through which both the Indians and General Howard's command had gone, though we did not find the latter part out till just before we struck Howard's camp.

As soon as I had put my battalion in camp, and before any tents were put up, fishing I went, to get a mess for supper. I soon came back with a beautiful lot, and my Lieut. told me that Gen. Howard had been over, and that Gen. Sturgis had sent for me often, as they were having a council of war; mine was Cambronne's word repeated, though a Saxon phrase. However, as soon as I had gotten outside of as many fried trout as I could carry, over to see the general (Sturgis) I went. He told me thay had agreed to "reveille" at 3:30, "forward" 4:30. I said, "General, you will lose time by so doing; it is drizzling rain now; by morning the ropes of the packs will be stiff, and at 3:30 it will be so dark that it will be utterly impossible to pack the mules properly." So he sent around, changing "reveille" to 4:30, "forward" 5:30, and then we marched through Howard's camp before their reveille had been sounded.

After we had followed the trail of the Nez Perces through that gorge, and had gotten into the scantily pine-timbered hills, the officers got into a general group with their respective luncheons, and while eating them, I asked, "Why in the name of all that's good, when we knew where the Indians were, did we not go to them?" General Sturgis's face got as red as a turkey cock's wattle, and he replied, "Colonel Benteen, that is not a fit question for you to ask; there will be too many people asking that same." Merrill (or some one) said "Well, they are gone now, and we can't catch them." Said I, "O, yes we can." Sturgis then wanted to know how I would do it. My reply was, "40 miles today, 50 miles tomorrow if necessary." Soon after this talk, Major Merrill took me aside, saying, Sturgis wanted to send him with his battalion to check the Nez Perces, but that he did not believe in separating the battalions. I said, "Merrill, get Sturgis to send mine; I'll guarantee that it will check them, and hold them, too, and we will not suffer any unnecessary loss. I asked Hare and Garlington to try and persuade the General to let me go, but I heard no more from it.

You know on reaching the Yellowstone on 2d morning how much time we "monkeyed" away, and how we were actually going into camp, when Howard's scouts alarmed the G.O. by stating that the Nez Perces were coming to attack us; so, off toward Canyon Creek we went, Merrill's battalion in advance. I then learned what the General meant by his Lincoln conversation of wanting me to command the reserve, as order after order came for me to move slower. However, "Old Buckskin" had his war pace on, and I wasn't in a mood for letting Merrill's battalion get all of the glory; then, finding the pace wasn't lessened any, Sturgis came up to the head of my battalion—but I tell you "Old Buck" made his horse jog all the same.

Of course you know how we found Merrill's battalion, dismounted, fighting [?] on foot. The herd of the Nez Perces were on the other side of the canyon. "General, do you want those?" "Can you get them?" "Yes." "Well, do it." I had already sent Lieut. Graham over near the foothills with a platoon of "M" Troop. "B" Troop was guard for the packs; so we, "C" Troop, and one platoon of "M"—but we got the horses, didn't we?

In making the movement, one of Howard's scouts coming up from the canyon showed me where the lock of his Winchester had been struck with a bullet and rendered useless,

[203]

asking me to give him a carbine. Reply: "Can't take a gun from a soldier to give a scout." He told me the canyon was alive with Indians, and to go there we would all be slaughtered —but we were not, were we?

Well, Merrill's boys couldn't "foot it" fast enough to render us any service—other than through moral effect.

My feint through the gap threw the "reds" off, and consequently in the canyon I had time to strip my fine silk fishing line from the pole; yes, and I did not throw the gun leader away, either.

My fishing pole of birch was my spear on that ride.

From the fact of having struck the reds at Canyon Creek, what was left of Sturgis's reputation was saved; but he wanted me to make a hullabaloo of a report; but I couldn't. The whole facts of the case came, or should have come under his immediate observation; so, other than complimenting Wallace, Graham and Nicholson in battalion orders, I said naught.

Sturgis got Gen'l Howard to order him to Lincoln to prepare for coming in of the regiment, and he also wanted Howard to give Merrill a "grave" to keep him from nagging the regiment. This latter, however, Howard would not do, as he thought he had already exceeded his right—but Miles did for Merrill what Howard declined, viz: sending him in charge of wounded to Lincoln.

Sturgis was never very warm with me after the Canyon Creek affair. Why? Because he knew that I thought he was a coward.

So, after all the music, clamor of trumpets, made in coming up the Yellowstone, we went as quietly down as the conditions of our limping horses would permit; and froze and froze, awaiting the coming of the Cheyennes at Buford. I started out with one troop, but got the whole twelve troops back to Buford, and that must have been the "reserve."

[204]

Those were pretty rollicking gay days, old comrade; but I tell you in the matter of "dollars and cents" I suffered for my devotion to the clamor of the trumpet.

I lost all of $10,000 by neglect of my property interests here during those years; but I've enough, and I don't regret a day I spent in the saddle.

Mathey knew, and I knew that Custer did, that I never fought Custer in any but the most open-handed manner; always going face to face for it. However, Mathey was a man I never at any time noticed, and doubtless that fact might have riled him to the lying point.

I have been solicited time and again to write up reminiscences of the war, and of Indian campaigning; but I've written more to you tonight than I ever wrote before, and I think, too, more than I shall ever write again; for if there is anything I detest it is writing. I shall always be pleased to hear from you.

Do you know that your name "Theodore" attracts me, for I had a dearly-loved brother of that name, a bright, talented fellow, and it was also the name of my father.

You must excuse any writing on this kind of paper, as it is the only kind I have on the farm.

I have 170 acres of land close to the city limits, and I sometimes spend the night on it, though my home is in the city.

In connection with the '77 campaign, Wallace will never know now the premeditated meanness Sturgis intended him when he relieved him as Adjutant, and appointed Lieut. Garlington in his stead, intending to give my 1st Lieut. Gibson the command of "C" Troop, vice Garlington, however, I persuaded Gen. S. not to do it, telling him, too, that I should greatly prefer Wallace to Gibson as Lieut. in my troop. I never told Wallace about it, for I didn't want him to know how mean G was.

[205]

I've been a loser in a way, all my life by rubbing a bit against the angles—or hair—of folks, instead of going with their whims; but I couldn't go otherwise—'twould be against the grain of myself.

Yours very truly,
F. W. BENTEEN

P.O. Box 118,
Atlanta, Ga.
Jan. 6, 1892

Dear Colonel Goldin:—

Yours of the 31st ulto. just received. I am also indebted to you for a nice long resume of old times with the 7th Horse, which absence from home has prevented answering, and thus the seeming neglect.

Yours of the 31st informs me that Captain Godfrey has fired the train at last.

Now I haven't seen the article, but shall do so tonight, but I know the facts to a demonstration, and when I read the article I can comment on the same with a thorough knowledge of what is correct or incorrect in the same, and so can you.

Current camp rumor or talk at the time was that Moylan, Godfrey and Gibson did far from well. I know what Gibson did—which was all I told him to do, which wasn't much; but having nothing to do with Moylan or Godfrey, I gave them no orders. At the same time, however, I did not fail to notice that they were pretty well protected from grave danger.

How men of a command "tumble" to facts so speedily,

you have been in a position to know far more of, and better, than I; but they do get them.

Absence from home has multiplied work for me, so excuse this short answer to your last. When I have read Godfrey's narrative—which for 15 years he has been longing to "spring" on N. America—I can tell you—well, not much more than you know—but what I think about his "cheek", if any of the same exhibits itself.

Very truly yours,

F. W. BENTEEN

ADDENDUM TO LETTER OF JANUARY 6TH:

I expect Godfrey to say in his article that Reno recommended the abandonment of the wounded on the night of 25th, and of "skipping off" with those who could ride; well, so he did, to me, but I killed that proposition in the bud. The Court of Inquiry on Reno knew there was something kept back by me, but they didn't know how to dig it out by questioning, as I gave them no chance to do so; and Reno's attorney was "Posted" thereon.

P.O. Box 118,
Atlanta, Ga.
January 16, 1892

Dear Colonel Goldin:—

Your nice long screed of 9th inst., came along last night.

A conundrum suggests itself to me, viz: If Lieut. Godfrey or 7th Cavalry could—and did—so much by himself in 1876, why was it that when sent from Cedar Creek, M.T. in spring

of 1877, after hostile Indians that had robbed the U.S. mail—
taken it in too—that he did not pursue them at all, tho' they
were in sight, almost?

This occurred while we were lying in camp at the point
referred to, and I know when the detachment which Godfrey
commanded returned to camp, that the commander of it was
thought to be—well, not fitted to command cavalry after
Indians. Lieut. Eckerson was, I think, along with him, and
Eckerson's report of Godfrey was far from being in the vein
that Godfrey's report of his own conduct is in the January
number of CENTURY Magazine for 1892. In fact, Eckerson
said he was a coward.

Now as for facts as to the holding of the hill in 1876:
I had posted French's troop on the ridge at right angles from
the river, and told him to send his horses to the rear, but hold
the point at all hazards until I could find a place to check
the onset of the Indians. I designated the point also for
Godfrey to hold. Well, French's command, by some means or
other, "flunked" after my leaving there, seeing which I sent
word to Godfrey to hold his vantage point, and everything
would soon be "O.K." Godfrey can't remember the fact,
though, now!

The searching for a good, very good place, was vain, and
I had no such idea, but simply a place to form, where the
river would, in a measure afford some protection for that flank,
and to be as near it as possible for water, as I was impressed
from my sight of the village that we had at least bitten off as
much as we could readily chew, and that the chewing was
bound to consume some considerable time.

Godfrey was not far away, almost in hailing distance.

When I saw French "give way", and knowing that there
had been no occasion for his so doing, I grabbed Lieut. Wallace, the first officer I saw, and said, "Wallace, put your troop

here!" Wallace replied, "I have no troop—only two men." Well, then, put yourself and your two men here (I designating the spot) and don't let any of them get away. I will look out for you." And so I went, gathering them in as they came, and had formed the line to the river bluffs nearly where I met Reno. Godfrey, somehow or other, if my remembrance is good, got down to his part of the line about as soon as anybody else. Godfrey, Moylan, Mathey and Gibson all know (I am inclined to think) what was said of them then, and Godfrey, now that pretty nearly all of the old fellows have dropped out, intends to sound his horn a bit for the benefit of the bunch.

From the fact that Reno specified me so in his report of the battle, and leaving the balance with, "though they all did well," etc., it has stuck in the craw of everyone of them from that time till now.

Now, personally, Reno, I know, respected me, but I believe had no great regard for me, from the fact that I once slapped his face in the club room of a post trader's establishment before quite a crowd of officers, telling him he was a "S.O.B." and if I hadn't given him sufficient, that I would be pleased to do so; so therefore 'tisn't to be supposed he was at all dying with love for me that he made me a special mark in his report of the fight; and he certainly didn't consult me about the matter of report.

When midway of the line, or still close even to bluffs of river than the center of line, I came across Major Reno, who seemed to have been forming a line to meet the one I was forming, though there had been no understanding of the kind between us relative to the matter. And that is how the line was formed.

Answer to query 3d: Reno's line did change position somewhat during the night, Capt. Moylan's troop being changed to left and rear of pack-mules, and facing up the river,

[209]

and the other troops were "drawn in" somewhat to better positions; all of which I know nothing of, having had nothing to do with such changes, and having quite sufficient to absorb my undivided attention in the trying position in which I had placed my own troop, which, my dear boy, had by far too much of Montana Territory to look out for; and per consequence, I insisted on Lieut. Gibson keeping me company in assisting to keep the men who were on post from falling asleep, and all the night through (and though I hadn't slept a wink for two nights before) did I, with Gibson, do this act, having to fairly kick the worn-out sleeping sentinels to their feet.

Mathey paid no attention to his pack-train on the hill until I gave him a square heel-and-toe "cussing out" in broad Saxon, which was when I returned to him two mules, loaded with ammunition (4 boxes), which mules I had personally caught while they were hell-bent on getting to the blue water which was so plainly in sight.

Answer to 3d query is this.

To 4th query, my answer is, yes, I am quite sure that the theory of Godfrey is absolutely correct as to the route Custer pursued and to the very point where the Indians consummated their "surround."

My dear Goldin, I regret to have to say that my son has not as yet recovered, and though I am of the opinion that his mother is perhaps unduly excited as regards his condition, still, she may be correct. Women, as a rule, arriving at facts intuitively or instinctively that we men have to get at through slow logic; but nevertheless, notwithstanding his mother's doubts, I'm impressed with the belief that the boy will pull through O.K.

As the mother has lost four children in touring around the continent, following the music of the cavalry trumpet, she of course clings the more tenaciously to this lone chick of ours

—and he is a good son, and a good cavalry-man, too, having twice consecutively won the championship of the state of Georgia in tilting tournaments.

I trust that Captain K will be able to place your article with the CENTURY Magazine, and though it will not be God-fathered by so able a writer (and prolix, too) as General J. B. Fry, U.S.A., still, my boy, it will make a stir, and you can just bet your last peso on it. So round the edges to your level best, and have it as entertaining as you can make it.

I was talking with an officer of the army—two of them, yesterday, both quartermasters, but one of them, Col. Scully was Q.M. at Fort Rice in '76 at time of our defeat, and he knows that 'twas common rumor with everybody, as we know, of Godfrey, Mathey, Gibson and Moylan.

Scully had not seen nor heard of G's contribution to CENTURY for Jan. '92, but proceeded to purchase same at once. Scully knows Capt. Godfrey at his full value.

If you can decipher this scrawl, why, 'tis OK, but really I've been slashing her off in haste.

> Very truly your friend,
> F. W. BENTEEN.

> *P.O. Box 118,*
> *Atlanta, Ga.*
> *Feb. 22, '92*

Dear Col. Goldin:—

Yours acknowledging receipt of maps duly rec'd.

Sickness in the family and multitudinous rounds of duties combined, have thrown me out of all touch with my correspondents, but I trust that "Richard will soon be himself again," then I'll gladly make the comments on the screed sent to me by you. There are few if any changes however to be made in it, and as sent by you is near enough the whole true story.

I would prefer not being known in the matter at all, and this from the fact that the opportunity to make any speeches, were, first, when I made my official report of the part borne by my battalion up to time the battalion joined Reno's; and secondly, before the Court of Inquiry called for by Reno.

Had I not been quite ill when I made the first report alluded to above, I should have had more to say than I said in it; but as to queries before the Court of Inquiry, these I would answer now as I did then, and shield Reno quite as much as I then did; and this simply from the fact that there were a lot of harpies after him—Godfrey not the smallest of the lot.

I regret to hear of the accident to your hand, and trust that you will soon recover from it.

My son has not recovered from la grippe—or whatever 'tis; in fact, grows worse.

Very truly yr. friend,
F. W. BENTEEN

P.O. Box 118,
Atlanta, Ga.
Feb. 24, '92

Dear Colonel Goldin:—

I've been on a slight "jag", so am not in good trim for writing, but having a little leisure time now will give you a few comments on the "screed" sent by you to me some time ago.

From where the battalions were formed—the point from which I struck out at about a left oblique with my battalion of three troops, to the spot where Custer's body was found, is estimated by me to be fifteen (15) miles. Now if I had carried out to the letter the last order brought to me from General Custer by the Sergeant-Major of the regiment— which was, to the effect, that if from the furthest line of bluffs which we then saw, I could not see the valley—no particular valley specified—to keep on until I came to a valley (or per- haps *the* valley) to pitch into anything I might come across and notify them at once. Now I don't know how much farther I should have had to go in the direction I was headed to have found the valley of the Little Big Horn river, but think per- haps that six or seven miles more would have brought me to it. What I want you to deduce from this is: supposing I had found up that valley what Reno and Custer found lower down the river—how in the name of common sense was Gen'l Custer to get back to where I was in time to keep the troops from being chewed up as it were by the combined reds?

Now, isn't that the whole and sole reason that we were so badly beaten? i.e. the regiment being broken up into four columns, and none of the four within supporting distance of either of the others, (without any orders even to be such a support to any) true? In right obliquing back to the trail Custer and Reno had gone on, I overtook the pack train and Capt. McDougall's troop, but I didn't stop, and, as I am sure you will allow, got to Reno's assistance in the very nick of time. Tell me, please, was there any generalship displayed in so scattering the regiment that only the merest of chance, intervention of Providence—or what you will—saved the whole 12 troops from being "wiped out."

That is all that I blame Custer for—the scattering, as it were, (two portions of his command, anyway) to the—

[213]

well, four winds, before he knew anything about the exact or approximate position of the Indian village or the Indians. Now, don't forget the fact that when Custer descended from the mountain where Varnum and the scouts had passed the night of June 24th, he told the assembled officers that the scouts had told him that they could see the location of the village, ponies, some tepees etc., but that he didn't believe it, and that he looked through the field glass—a telescopic one I believe—belonging to the Indians (Custer had none), and he couldn't see anything, and didn't believe that the Indians could.

Well, right then and there, I, for one, did believe that the Indians had seen and could see all that they had told Custer of; however, I said nothing to anyone, but was convinced that we would see plenty of them before the night came, without the remotest idea though that there would be quite so many of them.

I see nothing in your screed to change, but if you want any special information, why, ask for it, and I'll give it, to the best of my knowledge and belief.

My time is up now. I close with best wishes &c.

Very truly yr. friend
BENTEEN

March 1st, 1892,
Atlanta, Ga.

Dear Colonel Goldin:—

Yours of the 26th ult. I'll proceed to answer as if under oath.

To 1st inquiry: Yes, Nick Boyer (Mitch Bouyer) the half-breed interpreter and guide, certainly informed Gen'l Custer that he would find more Indians at the point where they had located them, than he, Custer, would care to "handle" with the force he then had; and 'tis just as true that Custer said, "he didn't believe there were any Indians at the point our scouts indicated."

As to the number of able-bodied Indians at the Little Big Horn fight, my belief is that there were eight or nine thousand—8,000 or 9,000—of them.

2d query: Ans. to—viz: "as to what was done when we advanced to pull Weir out of his hole."

I followed, with the remaining two troops of my battalion, the trail that Weir had "sallied on", he having no orders to proceed—some ten minutes later perhaps; anyway, just as soon as I learned of his insubordinate and unauthorized movements. While enroute to the highest point on the river bluffs in that vicinity, Major Reno kept his trumpeter pretty busily engaged in sounding the "Halt" for the purpose of bringing my command to a stand. However, I paid no heed whatever to the signal, but went to the highest point of bluffs, the battalion being in columns of fours. On arriving at elevation I then had my first glimpse of the Indian village from the height. Still I saw enough to cause me to think that perhaps this time we had bitten off quite as much as we would be able to well chew. Then I got the guidon of my own troop and jammed it down in a pile of stones which were on the high point, thinking perhaps the fluttering of same might attract attention from Custer's commands if any were in close proximity. Reno had then gotten up to the point where I was. However, I ordered French to put his troop in line on a bluff near, which was at right angles with the course of the river, and then for the purpose of showing where our command was, if there were any other bodies of our troops in sight.

Weir's troop then "showed up" midway in canyon, coming in hot haste toward us, and, as it seemed, myriads of howling red devils behind him. Of course I knew that Reno's retreat from the bottom had been a rout—a panic—and I made up my mind then and there that there was no necessity of having a repetition of same. So I ordered French to dismount his troop, keep his dismounted men on the bluff, send his lead horses to rear, let Weir's troop through, then slowly fall back with his dismounted men, and I'd tell him more when I found it out myself. Well, French "weakened" (no doubt of it!) though he let Weir through; but ye gods! how he came, (no doubt of it!) though he let Weir through; but ye gods! how he came, too! 'Twas then I ordered Godfrey to take position on the point he writes of.

I was intent, of course, on getting the best position we could possibly attain, though I felt the urgent pushing, prodding necessity that was causing the hasty backward movement; but arriving at the conclusion that forming a line couldn't be longer postponed, I grabbed Wallace, then 2d Lieut., saying, "Wallace, put your troop—the right of it—here, facing there." Wallace said, "I have no troop, only two men." "Then," said I, "put yourself and your two there, and don't let any of them get away. I'll look out for you."

That was the nucleus of the line—Wallace on the right, with his brave set of two men (hurrah for G!) I then gathered the procession in as it came, stringing it around an arc of a circle, as it were. Had Reno consulted me about his report, I should have requested him as a favor to eliminate the special reference to me in it; and this from the fact that I had little regard for his opinion in any manner, shape or form, and I had a sufficiency of commendation, proof already established,

[216]

of what I had done with cavalry commanded by me on many fields during stirring war, to which the episode of 1876 was a mere incident. However, as I've said, he didn't consult me, and the appearance of his report brought out the remark from Capt. Weir: "But he didn't mention me!" Others were in same category. Now, really, when a man quietly and serenely composed and all that, thinks of it, what could Reno have said of Weir, confining himself strictly to the truth, that would have been at all complimentary to him? If I had been forced to mention him, there would have been nothing special, other than he exhibited a very insubordinate spirit, which came very nearly bringing disaster on himself and troop.

In your reference to what Godfrey says about the charge made by Reno's line on the 26th—I went over to the line and persuaded him to consent to it—the charge. This was after I had driven the Indians from the ravine in my front; but I don't remember the "get back" part of it.

I am writing this in great haste from the fact that I haven't time now to scarcely think of it, but I really should like to hear the story told again from the standpoint of an enlisted man of "Ours." And I know of no one so capable of doing it as yourself, so give it to us. Spare no one! Not even the dead, as they, through their living friends, have assailed everyone who could not think with them, from President U. S. Grant down.

I shall be pleased to see your friend the druggist, and if I do so, shall recommend him to go to Thomasville, Ga., near the Florida line.

Thanking you again for your good opinion, kind, I should say perhaps, and trusting to hear from you at your earliest leisure, am your friend &c.

BENTEEN

P.O. Box 118,
Atlanta, Ga.
Mch. 19, 1892

Dear Colonel Goldin:—

Am happy to state that my son Fred has gotten well enough, and on the recommend of his physician, has gone to Florida. Both of his parents' minds are much relieved at the change for the better in his case, and trust that time, the great physician, will complete the cure begun. Thanks for your sympathy. On the 27th of the month, he will be 25 yrs of age. He was born on the day we started with the 7th Cavalry, Major Gen. W. S. Hancock in command, from Fort Riley, Kans., on the expedition against the Cheyennes, viz: March 27, 1867. On that expedition we burnt Roman Nose's village on the Pawnee Fork of the Arkansas. Fred was born on my plantation near Atlanta, and was eleven months old before I saw him. Doubtless you have seen him many times at both Rice and Lincoln. He was even than a fearless rider, always well mounted, and the darling escort of the young girls of the two posts. I think I told you that he has for two consecutive years won the championship of the state of Georgia for cavalry tilting, which is very much practiced by the mounted militia of the state, and they have been having annual contests, with quite a handsome prize for the best team (5) and also another prize for the greatest score made by any tilter, viz: "champion."

Well, I am rejoiced to learn that an account of the battle of the Little Big Horn, from the standpoint of an enlisted man, who was in the field, has been injected into the varied accounts of the same to the great American people; but, my boy, I think "the packs" will be after you. However, then,

[218]

if you want my corroboration of your account, 'tis at your service. I am quite confident that your version of the affair will be the most correct that has ever yet been unfolded to the G.A.P. McDougall, (French, Weir dead) Mathey, Moylan, Godfrey, Gibson, Varmun, Edgerly, Hare—in fact, everyone, save Wallace, were—well rabidly incensed at Reno at not mentioning them by name in his official report of the battle, and they, in some measure, seemed to hold me responsible for such action on his part, when however, the fact is known that I was scarcely on good terms with Reno, and knew no more of what he intended reporting than you did, and cared as little, too! It can readily be seen that I was in complete ignorance of what he intended reporting to the Asst.Adj.Genl.Dept. Dakota; at any rate, too, I was really ill with a malarious dysentery. However, I was well enough, too, to tell Col. Weir before a dozen or so officers that he was a d——d liar, and this was occasioned by some remarks he made about Custer and Reno, and the fight at Little Big Horn, and occurred while we were in camp opposite mouth of the Big Horn river in August, '76, about the 4th or 6th. Col. Weir said that meant "blood." "Well," said I, "there are two pistols in my holsters on saddle (near him); take your choice of them; they are both loaded, and we will spill the blood right here!" The crowd went off, Weir with them, and the next time I met him he shoved out this hand to me to shake! Aha! I scarcely knew what to make of it, but at same time had his accurate measure. At the organization of 7th Cavalry, Weir had been my first lieutenant.

These old reminiscences are of no manner of interest to anyone, but I doubt if you ever heard of the one I have just given, ere this.

The syndicate you have consigned your account of the

battle to did, at Charlie King's request, invite me (some time ago) to furnish them an account of same. However, as I couldn't do it, I didn't even answer the communication from them.

In conclusion, I shall be pleased to see your account in print. However, it is the replies to same from which I expect the greatest source of amusement.

Very truly yr. friend
F. W. BENTEEN

P.S. You will know before the Ex. of Knights Templar comes off pretty well how the Riley garrison i.e. officers of same, will have taken your comment on the affair of '76; but I am of the opinion that you have pretty well diagnosed the treatment you may expect to receive. Well, what of it? They are but a fraction of this G.R.

P.O. Box 118,
Atlanta, Ga.
April 3, 1892

Dear Colonel Goldin:—

I cannot begin to understand the cause for bringing two troops of Indian cavalry to vicinity of Chicago, perhaps other than this: that it takes them from the "tee-pee" locality, shows them some little of the world and shows the Chicago denizens some of their wild friends.

I have known General Miles since he transferred from

the web-footed brunettes to the 5th Infantry, and to date; and I am of the opinion that you are not but a little way off in your diagnosis of the "build" of the man. Too much circus, too little brain! In the—or after the—Nez Perce campaign of 1877, Gen. O. O. Howard gave Col. S. D. Sturgis a leave of absence, and Colonel S. requested of Gen. Howard that he would send Major Merrill home that the command of the 7th might devolve upon me. The sending of Merrill home was too much of a pill for Howard, as he had already exceeded his prerogatives in giving Sturgis "a leave", and—so he told Sturgis. However, Col. Miles sent Merrill off, and through such an excuse as to exercise his soldierly abilities in supervising the care of sick and wounded on the boat.

Miles' idea was to make a winter campaign against the Sioux and settle a grudge he had against the Milk River halfbreeds, expecting me to cooperate therein with him in true cavalry spirit; but you see, I knew the man, and knew his antecedents, too (only too well!) and we couldn't pull together worth a nick. So, when Gen. Terry floated down the muddy Missouri in a mackinaw (finding us above the Musselshell) I deliberately knocked Miles' combination into pi, because I informed Gen. Terry of what machinations he was "up to", and so we went Bufordwards instead of camping on the north side of the Missouri, perhaps near Fort Peck, for that winter. I feel that Miles bears me the grudge for that as yet. However, I will compromise with him by not voting for him for President—no, not even for president of a football club!

My son is "home again", and has commenced buckling down to business. However, his natural bent is for the Army, but as the Probs. are that he will be very well off in this world's goods at no very remote date, why should his life be wasted in army cliques?

I am expecting him on the farm in a few minutes, where with his large kodak he intends taking some views. We have a beautiful place of 170 acres just out of city limits, and the kodak depicts views with greater facility than does a pencil or charcoal sketch, and the working of same perhaps keeps him from mischief which youngsters are prone to fall into.

I will be pleased to see your (our) side of the "Narrative of the Big Horn Battle", and as soon as you can get copies of same, please be kind enough to send me at least two of them. I do not think there will be a necessity for "doubling teams" to "stand off" anything the disgruntled folks of the 7th may have to say about your history, but should it come to that, then count me with you. As to taking any kind of notice of what bereaved widows have to say, then I'm "not in it." The game isn't worth the candle.

I think you are correct about the chances the Milwaukee Troop would have in a game of sabers with the Georgia cavalry, but don't forget the fact that we are getting up some points for cavalrymen besides the sabre and spur elementary principle.

Georgia's mill is fast grinding out patriots.

Very truly yr. friend,
BENTEEN.

I underscore to show you that after 19 years of waiting, the U.S. has showered upon me, drenched me with the Bvt. of Brig. Gen'l, for the Little Big Horn and Canyon Creek. *Same to Col. Merrill.*

Dear Colonel Goldin:—

I thank you very much for having sent me the "Army Magazine" containing first installment of your Big Horn narrative. It is to be regretted that you have had to put it through such a simmering process as it has evidently undergone, for justice cannot be done to the subject in a few columns.

Should not "Sunset Peak", as it appears in June number, be Sentinel Buttes? as *that* is where we were in the '76 June snowstorm. That, however, is a trifle.

A Mr. Squiers, formerly of 1st U.S. Inf. and who was transferred from that regiment to the 7th Cavalry with Barry of '77 I think, has agreed to put up the l'argent to pay for the getting up of a superfine, double gilt-edge history of the 7th U.S. Cavalry, and per consequence I have been solicited to send a photo for the projected volume and a reminiscense of some of my years of service in the regiment.

I gave Benn, of '78, adjutant of the regiment—sec'y of com., a chit of some 11 pages of "cap", and this bore solely on the "Affair at the Washita", Nov. '68. Ten thousand to one, they don't dare to publish it! Custer was to be the frontispiece. I vote for putting Forsythe "Tony" there.

Squiers married a Miss Fargo of Ex. Co. fame, and besides being a "C.P." he was a "B.F." of first water. I believe he is a stock broker now in N.Y. Evidently he wants it to appear on Change that he was once a warrior [?] God save the mark!

I would be obliged to you for the continuation of your narrative in July number, as I cannot purchase it here.

Very truly yr. friend,
BENTEEN, *Bvt. Brig. Gen. U.S. Army*

39 Pavilion St.,
Atlanta,
Aug. 23, 1894

Dear Colonel Goldin:—

What's the matter with the Army Magazine's 2d chapter of the Little Big Horn?

I send you the prospectus of the forthcoming history of the 7th Horse, in which you "rough it" for 6 years (see next page).

How should you like to write a "skit" of the fight at Canyon Creek, M.T. Sept. 13, 1877, and from our leaving Clark's Ford Canyon to the beginning and the end of the fight?

I will insure its finding a place in the book under your name, but should like to revise it, as I kept a diary from 1861 to 1888.

I don't think the story of that fight will be truly told by any officer who was in it, excepting one only. He is Capt. John C. Gresham, and 'twas his first fight, and he didn't know much then anyway. You will note on front that 7th heading is put in by me.

Very truly yours friend.
F. W. BENTEEN

Send your photo in Col's "togs" if you write it.

Fort Riley, Kansas

——————— *1894*

My dear Sir:—

Mr. Herbert G. Squiers of N.Y. City, formerly an officer in this regiment, has made a proposition to its officers to publish at his own expense a handsome history to contain:

1. A history of the regiment from its organization to present time.

2. A sketch of the battle of the Washita

3. Of the battle of the Little Big Horn

4. Battle of Bear Paw Mountain

5. Of Wounded Knee

6. Short sketches of every officer who has ever belonged to and served with the Regiment, setting forth service with it as shown by the records. Each sketch to be accompanied by a portrait of its subject.

7. What General Merrill saw at Canyon Creek. [No. 7 apparently inserted by Benteen.]

The history will not be a mere recital of the official facts connected with the Regiment's yearly existence, but will be gotten up in a descriptive narrative style, with a view to its being readable by the general public.

The frontispiece of the book will be a portrait of Gen. Custer. [Apparently Benteen inserted the following: "This is in doubt."] Remington will contribute a few sketches for the work, and Dr. Holmes will be requested to write the dedication.

Mr. Squiers purposes to present to each person whose sketch appears in the book with a copy. The remainder of the edition of about 250 copies to be presented to libraries or disposed of as he may see fit. At the request of Mr. Squiers a

[225]

committee has been organized which is authorized to add members to itself and to solicit aid from all interested.

It is assumed that every person who has ever been an officer of the Seventh Cavalry will be as much interested in this history as Mr. Squiers or the committee, and the cooperation of all is therefore earnestly solicited in forwarding it to a completion. Mr. Squiers is particularly desirous that everyone should feel as free to offer suggestions and contribute aid as if financially interested in the undertaking. He desires it to be a monument to the regiment and purposes, if duly assisted, to produce a work in every respect worthy of its subject.

No difficulty is anticipated in gathering the necessary material except possibly as to producing pictures and facts pertinent to the history and antecedents of some of the members of the regiment in its early days; cooperation is especially asked in this regard.

Will you kindly forward to the secretary of the committee a photograph of your self (preferably one taken in uniform while a member of the regiment), such a one as you would like used in the preparation of a portrait to accompany sketch of yourself. Should you already have sent a picture to the secretary of the Seventh Cavalry Mess. 4 for the regimental album, will you be kind enough to state whether you desire to have it used for the portrait?

The Committee earnestly urges the freest correspondence and cooperation, not only in order to forward the work to a completion, but in order to manifest due appreciation of this very munificent generosity of a former comrade.

Very respectfully, THE COMMITTEE
Per J. F. Bell,
1st Lieut. & Adjt. 7th Cavalry
Secretary

Dear Colonel Goldin:—

Yours of the 25th inst. rec'd, and I am somewhat inclined to think the committee in charge of preparation of
sketches for "Squiers" 7th Cav. book is somewhat on the close
corporation biz., but the hot-shot I threw in protesting against
Custer's ugly phiz being shown in front of book, is having its
effect, and I think the volume will come out without any
frontispiece in shape of a portrait.

Squiers is a "Canuk", and was appointed 2d Lieut. in 1st
Infantry, I think from Minnesota. He had sufficient influence
to get appointed or be sent to the Artillery School at Fortress
Monroe, and while there he eloped, or married secretly, a Miss
Fargo—of the Express Company of that name. She was not
pretty, but was a nice girl, and had a very plump, well-rounded
"dot", which of course was what Squiers was after! The mother
was a widow, and died not long after the marriage, being
followed not many years later by Mrs. Squiers—she leaving
two children I believe. I think S. is a broker in New York,
and wants to see himself in print as having belonged to the
7th Cavalry, and moreover, I think, sees a chance of getting
sales for more than 200 vols. of book, the work on which will
have to be done by other people. Good trick, isn't it? The
Canuks as a rule are not born blind. He has been dining and
wining the young cubs of the 7th when he picks them up in
N.Y., and per con. they think he is a H—— of a fellow, and
for perspicacity he is.

I can give you no idea as to the amount of space, nor do
I think I could get at what space would be given to the

Canyon Creek fiasco. Never mind, though. If you can spare the time, fire away at it, simmering as much as you can, and send same to me, and I'll revise and return to you. I'll get her in or know the reason why thru Tony Forsythe, but I want "Togs" complete, too, let up on modesty. I want to see the rank and file represented.

Very truly your friend
BENTEEN

39 Pavilion St.
Atlanta, Ga.
Oct. 11, '94

Dear Colonel Goldin:—

Yours of the 8th inst. in your perfectly legible address, sent to Macon, Ga. P.O. mistake.

Thanks for the address of poor Aspy's sister. They want it you know in that grand (?) history of "ours." I've sent it.

Rather wondered why you hadn't received copies of the Army Magazine. It is one of the magazines that cannot be purchased here, and the only way I know of seeing a copy would be by going to Fort McPherson, and then most likely only thru one of the army and navy unions, and I haven't had the time to prosecute that.

I haven't had the gall to send "ours" anything as yet on the Canyon Creek—what shall I call it—fiasco? Waiting, rather, the report of Supervising Board on my first "chick of the Washita", then, if they are seeking history sure enough why, 'tisn't a bit of trouble for me to sling it at them; but

I'm going to squeal if there's any garbling done. At the Washita we lost Major Elliott, Sergt. Maj. Kennedy—a fine
young soldier, and 16 enlisted men, and damned if any search
was made for them till a fortnight after. Now, as ever, I want
to get at who was to blame for not finding it out then? 'Tisn't
really worth while to know now, but I am not ready to sub-
scribe to any effort of the public's opinion to convince me that
Custer was a great man or great warrior; au contraire, he was
quite ordinary.

Very truly &c yours
BENTEEN

When I see your second article I will know exactly whether
you said too much or too little. Without having seen it, I will
wager 'twas too little. I trust that you may have an overwhelming majority in your political endeavor.

*39 Pavilion St.
Atlanta, Ga.
Oct. 19, '94*

Dear Colonel Goldin:—

I have just rec'd, and have twice gone over your continuation of Little Big Horn story in double number of Army
Magazine, and I cannot for the life of me, see how anyone can
take exception to your recollections of that affair.

I think Godfrey has endeavored to make more out of it
for himself than impartial history from onlookers could grant
him, though had I anything to say in the matter, I should

[229]

have recommended for brevets, first, Hare, then Varnum, and lastly, Godfrey, yes, Wallace, too, before Hare, then I think I should have stopped. Reno brought the wrath of the regiment on me—commissioned officer part, on account of special mention. Well, Lord knows I couldn't help that, and up to the time my battalion joined Reno of course nothing had been done for which to mention anybody. Thus I couldn't do it, and from fact of not being on best of terms with Reno, I rarely ever went near him unless sent for, and then at no time was my opinion called for on any subject. I do not see one thing to be altered in your statement, and I am of the opinion that perhaps that is the last that will be heard from the Little Big Horn.

Charles King may have talked with some of those would-be B.H. heroes, but by the gods of war, we were there, and know just what we say.

Had Godfrey wanted to show the mettle of which he was made, he had from Sunday on Cedar Creek in 1877 a fine opportunity so to do it; but he hadn't lost any Indians then, and didn't look for them when sent to do it! Later on, same year he got plugged by Nez Perces, but that was an illy-managed affair. I haven't heard a word from anyone concerning your article, although I correspond pretty regularly with Lieut. Bell, Adjt. 7th Cav., and it cannot be that at Riley your comments haven't figured among them. Other than to get notes into shape I have done nothing on the Canyon Creek affair, than which I can recall no more thoroughly disgusting campaign, though on few other trips have I ever had such a wonderful lot of amusement in fishing, hunting and the like. For instance, when we change camp at mouth of Musselshell River on the Missouri, who will ever see again the same number of antelope together at any one time again that we saw and killed during that change of camp?

You will remember that Gen. Sturgis besought Howard to give him orders to proceed to Lincoln in person, which he did, taking Garlington, Hare, the Sergt-Major of the regiment, and every scrap of paper, leaving nothing behind but the 12 troops of the regiment, with a captain in command. Sturgis besought Howard to order Merrill in, but H. didn't like to interfere so much in a department in which he had no control; so Sturgis got Miles to send Merrill to Lincoln in charge of sick and wounded.

A man with one eye—if he is at all a thoughtful fellow—can see a good many things in the army in even five years, can't he? It seems to me that all of them "soldier for revenue" simply now.

Thanking you for the magazine, and trusting you have won your political fight, I am, very truly yr, friend,   BEN-TEEN

*39 Pavilion St.
Atlanta,
Sept. 14, '95*

Dear Colonel Goldin:—

Glad to receive your letter of 9th inst., and pleased to know that you got the clerkship of Court.

Should Knights of Pythias movements—or any other scheme ever waft you southward, we shall be glad to entertain you.

Mrs. Benteen sends thanks for kindly remembrance of her entertained by the old warriors of the 7th.

By last A. & N. Register I see that the four troops of 7th Cav. in Texas go to Fort Logan, Colorado.

Well, DeRudio will not hail that for one with thanks, as Aug. 26, '96, he retires at 64, and any long move means a sacrifice of much to a man with as many "hangers on" as De R. has.

I don't think Hare would have had any ill feelings about anything you might have said about Godfrey, for Hare was essentially a cavalryman, and G.—well, he was anything but!

Hare should have been breveted for L.B. Horn, and would have been had I any say about it. Bell was breveted Lieut. Col. for Canyon Creek, Sam D. Sturgis should have been tried by G.C.M. for the Clark's Ford Canyon idiocy. I labored the best part of the night we moved from there to get him to go where we knew Fuller had seen the Indian Camp, but I couldn't phase him. Merrill was "working" him then, and from Aug. 10, '61, I knew neither of them would fight. They had never lost a Reb or an Indian!

I suppose you saw enough of Merrill at Shreveport to glean something of his disposition. Good luck to you. May the C. of C.C. live long and prosper. Kind remembrances to Mrs. Goldin from all.

Very truly yr. friend
BENTEEN, 7th.

39 Pavilion St.,
Atlanta,
Oct. 12, '95

Dear Colonel Goldin:—

I was not surprised at the information contained in your last letter that Hare acquired a fondness for bug-juice, but I am surprised that he should exhibit so little charity for his Lieut. who got a drop too much, for Hare was a level-headed fellow. Anyway, it's $ to doughnuts nothing comes of it.

One of the Tompkins married Col. Barr's daughter. Barr is a Judge Advocate—high up.

Now, if people think there is no chicanery—or whipping the devil around the stump, in military law, why, they are not in it, so to speak. I know it, for I've seen it.

You can write it on your tablet that Capt. Wallace would have done nothing of the kind!

Miles is at the head of the army. Well, 'tis to be hoped he has gained much wisdom by experience. He is a man I never had any use for. I've known him since he was transferred from the Mokes to the 5th Infantry.

The Cameron & Sherman influence isn't to be sneezed at, and he's got it. But he will never warm the presiding seat in the cabinet of these United States.

I haven't been to see our much-heralded Expo. as yet, tho' my better half tells me "'tis pretty good, but worlds behind the Chicago exhibit" which, of course, was to be expected.

[incomplete]

39 Pavilion St.
Atlanta,
Dec. 28, '95

Dear Colonel Goldin:—

I was very much gratified at receiving your photo on yesterday. I have often wondered if I knew your face; but I didn't know it, though doubtless we have been side by side many a time, and as you know, might be again for years without a chance of your features being photographed on my brain unless some special act brought it about.

The five years you "put in" following the 7th Cavalry guidon were surely years of experience, and I really do not believe you can think of them as wholly lost, tho' in a pecuniary sense they were all of that.

My, my! Did it ever occur to you what a crowd of chumps the 7th Cavalry had among its field officers in 1877? Sturgis, Otis, Tilford, Merrill and Reno. Could a finely-toothed comb, well dragged have pulled out of the whole army a sorrier set? All "M.A.'s" too! On leaving the mouth of the Musselshell at Missouri River, however, they had all "skipped", and the whole 12 troops there were saved "a heap of worries." Weren't we in horrid shape then, though?

I had endeavored to acquaint Gen. Terry several times of the exact condition of the regiment, but I haven't a doubt but Gen Miles "hived them" from the scouts by whom they were sent.

Well, 'twas a dandy campaign, anyhow—that of '77, and I only wish I had known you then, as I might have made the lines easier for you.

Again, thanking you for your photograph, I am,

Very truly yr. friend,
F. W. BENTEEN, 7th

If I mistake not, I've sent you a photo of myself.

Major Benteen,
Dear Sir:

Pardon liberty in writing you, but am very much interested in the particulars of the Custer fight of the Big Horn
river, June 25, 1876. Knowing you were the Captain in Custer's cavalry regiment, would you kindly inform me if it was
on Sunday, May 17th, 1876, you and the others left Fort
Lincoln on your march after the Indians? Also, if it was the
Springfield rifle that you used? Also, what was done after the
arrival of Terry and Gibbon? I saw in a Wisconsin paper of
last summer an account of the shooting of one Philip Spinner
who had joined the 7th Cavalry in Dakota in '75, and who
was in the fight on the bluffs with your and Reno's commands,
which will send you a copy if you wish. Hoping to hear from
you soon.

Very respectfully yours
J. P. Grimes
Cor. Cherrie & Calder Streets
Answered   Grand Rapids, Mich.
Jan. 13, '96

Jan. 15, '96

Dear Colonel Goldin:—

Wrote you on yesterday. Received this (the Grimes letter) today. Answered the fellow by this mail.

He evidently must be in his salad days to be asking such questions.

To me this seems much like a "decoy" real estate agent's "pull-out". How does it strike you? Is he on a cold trail?

I respectfully referred him to you for any other information he might want, telling him you had written an article fully covering the ground, and thinking perhaps you could tell him where he could purchase the Army Magazine containing your articles.

Fred Calhoun, 1st Lieut. retired, lives, I think, in Grand Rapids. His brother James married Custer's sister. Is there meat in the nut?

> Very truly your friend
> BENTEEN, 7th

39 Pavilion St.
Atlanta,
Jan. 11, '96

Dear Colonel Goldin:—

Your very complimentary letter of late date came duly.

Well, there's no denying that it warms the cockles of one's old heart to know and have told to him by one of the formulaters of history who was on the spot, that my actions were such as Uncle Sam expects from all of his employees.

As I didn't know you, of course I didn't know that you knew anything about my fishing rod, but she was a daisy, and I wanted to put it to use that night in the Yellowstone, but I didn't, as I need not remark.

Of course you didn't know how cussedly mad I was when I saluted those Nez Perces.

You see, we had quite a lot of daylight left, and had two of Howard's mountain howitzers with us that had gone thru the gap, and were not quite up. Well, I wanted to put 20 or 30 shells thru the woods where those N.P.'s shot at us, but the most peremptory orders came from Sturgis to hustle back to him with all the haste possible—which order was followed up with another to same effect. Therefore I had to leave our red friends with due form.

I wanted to get some more practice with those little bull pups, because in 1862 I was an expert with them, and at Pea Ridge, Ark., March 7th, when the Rebs had broken E.A. Carr's brigade, I withstood three separate charges of Mc-Intosh's Indian brigade on my four-gun battery of mountain howitzers, gave Carr time to form in rear; pulled my "little pups" out by hand, and saved the evening at "Elk Horn" and lost no gun. With double-shotted canister I staggered them.

Now, my dear Colonel G., if you think I'm giving you anything of the fairy-tale order, just look, when you get a chance, at the Vol. XII, Series 1, Part 1, Reports Price's Missouri Expedition etc. "Rebellion Records, July 1st to Dec. 31, 1864, Serial No. 83.

At the close of that expedition, Major Gen. Blunt was commanding the 1st Division of Cavalry, and Lieut. Col. F.W.B., the 2d Division of Cavalry which comprised all of Gen. Sam. B. Custis' Army, Army of the Frontier, which was cavalry wholly.

Doubtless you can find the same (Vol.) without much

trouble in your city. Any retired officer or active officer above grade of Captain will have it.

Those were the days, Colonel! You'll see that I didn't have to form the acquaintance of Custer to know something about fighting cavalry—and as to Indians—I fought against them in 1863 and 1864 long before he ever had a whack at them. I know that Custer had respect for me, for at the Washita in 1868, I taught him to have it.

I had received the Jan. copy of Military Service Inst. the day before I received your letter. Colonel Hughes evidently had more in reserve than he paraded at that review. "Tony" Forsythe was the officer on Sheridan's staff who met Custer at R.R. Station in Chicago, and Tony told me that "he put him in arrest" (a fact which Hughes knew but didn't tell.)

Gen. Fry and Godfrey have the mystic characters "M.A." after their names in the Army Register, and, think as you please about it, Colonel, those fellows think that no one had a right to know anything quite as well as they do. (Law as well as soldiering goes.)

In the 1864 Price raid in Mo. Col. Lewis Merrill might have been commanding the 2d Division of Custis's cavalry (not Custer's), but, Colonel Goldin, he preferred the flesh pots of St. Louis, and I don't know but in the long run, terrapin and Madeira is the first choice, and you can see from this that Sturgis and Merrill were old compadres of mine, and I knew their full value in 1861.

Sorry for troubling you to read so much chicken tracks. Mrs. B. will send you a photo as soon as she gets one.

Yr. friend,
BENTEEN

This letter doesn't come near paying you for yr. nice long one, but just now I'm quite a busy man in looking after my son's business, he being in Chicago.

That I'm obliged for your nice, kind, long letter goes without saying.

F. W. BENTEEN

39 Pavilion St.
Atlanta,
Jan. 19, '96

Dear Colonel Goldin:—

In answer to Mr. "Grimes" letter, I told him about what you said in yours to me, only I added Colt's revolvers as a portion of the arms carried by the 7th.

As to what was done after junction of Terry and Gibbon with our battered fragment, simply intimated that the querist must still be in his salad days to know so little of what occurred less than 20 years ago.

I expressed a desire to receive a copy of the article he spoke of being willing to send me, but as yet have not been so favored.

Doubtless I might have "played him" a bit, but I didn't think the fish large enough to toy with.

Varnum, of 7th, after poor Aspinwall's downfall, came to me one day when I was on a visit to Lincoln to have me sign an application to have Fred Calhoun appointed Lieut. in 7th in "Jack's" place. "No, no," I said to Varnum, "this is premature. Aspinwall, by the statutes is allowed 3 months to "show up", and in any event, Varnum, don't you think that we have quite a genteel sufficiency of that clique at present in the Regiment?"

Of course this decision of mine was soon known at Custer and Calhoun houses, and such decision kept others from signing. At all events, Calhoun didn't get appointed in 7th, but did in 14th Infty., where he got his first lieutenancy, and soon afterwards was retired (A something I look on as a kind of swindling of the Govnt). How does it strike you?

On our trip of '73, with Stanley, Custer got Rosser to give Fred Calhoun a job which necessitated Calhoun's being mounted. "H" Troop was short of horses. Custer had a clay-bank horse for which I was responsible and which I had assiduously endeavored to have returned to troop, but without avail.

Lieutenant Ray, commissary of expedition, from lack of horses, had to content himself with riding a poor mule from his train, so Ray said to me one day, "Benteen, can you not do better for me than this?" "Yes, I think I can," I said, "now I have fourteen dismounted men in troop, but you see that claybank? Well, I'm responsible to U.S. for him, and cannot get him. Custer gives him to that young man to ride, and now he is employed by Gen. Rosser for the N.P. Get the horse if you can."

The correspondence about that horse got Custer in arrest. Stanley got drunk, so the game was thrown into Custer's hand, and thus he "got away with Stanley." Of course the Calhouns never had any use for me; I was not pliable enough.

Moylan married Calhoun's sister; "Jim" C. married Custer's ½ sister; and they played things in general to suit themselves.

Lord, Colonel! We have known for lo, these many years that Custer disobeyed orders, and had not Col. Hughes been the bro.-in-law of Gen. Terry, it is one hundred to one odds that history would never have gotten at the bed-rock facts.

I have been taking so much quinine that I can scarcely write—breaking up a cold, you see; but I thought this quiet Sunday eve I would send you a few chicken tracks, because I owe you many thanks for your complimentary thoughts of me. See the Reb. records I referred you to, and I hope you'll find that my cavalry breast was exposed to the storm for 4 years, 4 mos. and 22 days to help bring my deluded Southern brothers back into the fold.

Always truly yr. friend,
F. W. BENTEEN

39 Pavilion St.
Atlanta,
Jan. 24, '96

Dear Colonel Goldin:—

I received another installment from Mr. Grimes, which I enclose for your amusement.

I told him about the number of "for duty" and "wounded" that Reno had, after Terry got to us, and that we moved the wounded on mule litters to the boat at mouth of river.

I am still of the opinion that there is some hocus-pocus in his modus operandi.

[241]

However, I plainly told him to divest himself of the idea that there was one or any concealed points concerning the Little Big Horn. If there was one, I didn't know it, and had there been one I should certainly have known it.

As to Custer having been a Michigander, why, that's pure rot. He went to West Point from Ohio, and from the M.A. to the war.

He commanded a Michigan brigade, and had it afterwards in his division, and his father had removed to Michigan. That's all; other than Gen. Custer married Miss Bacon of Monroe.

From his handwriting, the fellow evidently doesn't do anything in the line of manual labor to speak of.

Some time or other you may perhaps learn who Mr. J. P. Grimes of Grand Rapids, is.

Can it be that "Grimes" is a woman? I should judge the writing to be a man's.

> Very truly yr. friend
> BENTEEN

> *39 Pavilion St.*
> *Atlanta,*
> *Jan. 31, '96*

Dear Colonel Goldin:—

Your welcome screed came duly. From the tone of my last to "Grimes" I scarcely think he'll pursue his investigations to a greater extent, i.e., from me.

I don't know the men of the regiment had such an

aversion to Mylie Moylan, but my! how correct they were in so having!

On 25th June, 1876, when my battalion got to crest of hill where Reno took refuge from his "charge" from bottom, the first thing which attracted my attention was the gallantly-mustached captain of Troop "A" blubbering like a whipped urchin, tears coursing down his cheeks.

Now, I knew he hadn't much of what we call in the South "raising", but I had accredited him in my mind with having some nerve, though I had never seen him in a position before to display it; but as sure as you are born, the bottom tumbled out—and all the nerve with it, before he reached the crest of the hill.

Lieut. Jack Aspinwall and Moylan had a little conversation together on '74 trip, of which I'll tell you at some time, though to write about Moylan is a great waste of time.

I have just received your letter from Grimes. The varmint is proceeding to develop, isn't he? I'll keep the letter you sent of his for awhile. Something for a foundation for attack on Hughie [Hughes?] is in preparation, I'm beginning to think. They'd better not!

Another family line existed in the 7th of which you are perhaps unaware. Jackson, captain of "C" Troop, married Miss Calhoun, a cousin of Mrs. Moylan, Jim and Fred Calhoun.

Afraid of bothering you with my epistles, I'll quit this for the nonce.

Truly yr friend, Benteen

39 Pavilion St.
Atlanta,
Feby, 5th, '96

Dear Colonel Goldin:—

Yrs. of 3d inst. received. Without a doubt Grimes knows about the article written by Col. Hughes, and there can be no reply to the facts there set forth that will help the fame of Custer.

If the youth knew more of the world, this would be self-evident.

When I accepted a captaincy in the 7th Cavalry I had no idea whatever of remaining permanently, but was taken to it from the fact that the Indians seemed to have things pretty nearly their own way, and I knew that cavalry, well handled, should more then "stand them off", which wasn't then being done.

Well, I have never heard of anyone accounting for the fact how the profession of arms grows on one, but it certainly does, so I stuck; but it was a pecuniary loss to me all the time.

Moylan didn't get a captaincy till '73, but from thence till the time he was retired, he saved in round ducats, $30,000 —'67 till retirement.

I know how he did it. Aspinwall knew how he did it, and many others knew the same, but other than officially we never had anything to do with him.

Mrs. Moylan was, and is, a very nice woman, and she certainly helped him amass. I have often wondered how she could "stand" him, but she seemed to, and I believe did look on him as the apple of her eye, "De Gustibus" &c.

I had thought of acquainting Col. Hughes of the tenor of

[244]

Grimes' writing, but think I'll await further developments;
Hughes being rick-ribbed needing no help.

[not complete]

39 Pavilion St.
Atlanta,
Feb. 10, '96

Dear Colonel Goldin:—

Your announcement of the death of Gen. Gibbon came
at time of receipt of A. & N. Register, but I learned it first
from your letter.

I knew Gen. Gibbon well, and I suppose he was attached
to me somewhat from the fact that my cousin, Gen. E. S.
Bragg, succeeded to the command of the famed "Iron Brigade"
of Wisconsin.

Gen. Gibbon was not only a brave and faithful soldier,
but he was far, far better than that. He was an honest and
conscientious man, which often brought him in conflict with
the staff of the army who notoriously attempted when oppor-
tunities offered, the government of the whole; and this Gibbon
wouldn't stand in silence—a fact which affected his promotion
very seriously, all of which he knew.

Peace to his ashes! The U.S. has need for millions of
such men.

"Grimsey" is beginning to develop in "first class" shape!
The item of its all being "for his own personal information"
is getting somewhat threadbare from usage—is it not?

[245]

I had thought of sending the matter to Col. Hughes, but would not until I had gotten your consent.

If those defenders of Custer's fame only knew what I know of that man (and not only I know, but can prove), they would be willing to let him rest with the grand aura around him which the public now recognizes, and I know not of anyone who cares to attempt to dispel the ignis fatuus.

Col. Hughes let him down very easily. I would, I think have been scarcely so considerate.

Having been sent off from the command some 15 or more miles from Custer's field, and leaving the whole command dismounted, no other disposition of any part of it having been determined upon by Custer, how could McDougall's rear guard become part of my battalion? After getting with Reno, not that I didn't feel free to act in opposition to Reno's wishes, and did so act, but then, what more could be done than we did do?

Like ostriches, we might have stuck our necks in the sand, only that Custer had galloped away from his reinforcements, and so lost himself.

I am firmly of the opinion that Mr. Grimes will still continue to develop. Your handling has been masterly.

Can "Grimesey" be playing it that he didn't know of Hughes' article?

I am always pleased to hear from you, but I fear I tire you with my chicken tracks.

Very truly yr. friend
BENTEEN

Dear Colonel Goldin:—

At the risk of tiring, and perhaps disgusting you, I have come to the conclusion of giving you a dissertation on the Seventh Cavalry from the time I joined it in winter of '66 and '67, to death of Gen. Custer.

I think someone in the Great West should have a just opinion of that man, and therefore I give my unbiased view of his character, which you can take as if they were sworn to on a stack of Bibles.

I had never seen Custer before joining at Fort Riley in '66.

At my first formal call at his private quarters, he paraded his orders and books of the old Cav. Div. in the Cav. Corps, as if endeavoring to impress me with the magnitude and eminent success of his operations in it.

I remember his orders shown me said, "No gun has ever been pointed at that Division but what they captured it," etc., etc.

Well, the impression made on me at that interview was not a favorable one. I had been on intimate personal relations with many great generals, and had heard of no such bragging as was stuffed into me on that night.

Col. A. J. Smith, a general who had done far greater work than Custer ever thought of, was the Col. of Regt. and stationed at Riley at the time, commanding the 7th Cavalry and the District of the Upper Arkansas, including Ter. of New Mexico; Custer comdg. post of Fort Riley, Kas.

[247]

Gen. Smith, with whom I had served, knew a good deal of my record, and Capt. Noyes, now Lieut. Col. of Cav. was Smith's A.A.A.G., and having been an A.D.C. to Cavalry Wilson in our raid through Ala. and Ga. in '63, so I wasn't at the Post quite an orphan and unknown, but with people who knew what I had done with a cavalry regiment and a division of Cavalry regiments, when war was red hot.

My 2d appearance at Gen. Custer's house was by invitation, given after tattoo roll-call, "to come and play dime ante poker." The result of that "call" and game was that I won every cent of money at the board, and Weir, who was my first lieut. at the time, insisted on giving me his "I.O.U." for $150. Weir never got out of my debt.

From 10¢ ante the game was, at Custer's request, in which Weir acquiesced, swelled to $2.50 ante, which, with "no limits" is apt to make a pretty steep game, and it was, many having to go up, no "cuff" went.

The "swell" of ante sent two of the players out of the game, they not having any money.

At dime ante one can play the game and have some friendship for another player, but at $2.50 ante—well, all "friendship" has got to cease, or one is apt to find himself pretty well begrimed, and a long way from water quite early in the game; so I went for those Heathen Chinese!

Being officer of the day, I had to quit at Reveille, and that broke it up. Weir came to my qtrs. before Guard Mounting, tendering the I.O.U. for $150, which, as I've intimated, is yet unpaid.

I started in with my troop to make friends and soldiers of them. I would treat them like men, and everybody else had to; so they got to love me.

The four troops at Riley left that post under Custer on

the 27th March, 1867, the same day and year my son Fred was born on my farm in Georgia.

Gen. W. S. Hancock, Commdg. Dept. of Mo. went in command of the expedition in the field. From him, Custer performed his first "cutting loose" act.

Hancock didn't relish it, and "rounded him up" at old Fort Hayes, Ks. At this point, Custer began his first exploitation with trying to blackmail the post sutler.

We had captured the empty village of Roman Nose on the Pawnee Fork of the Arkansas, Hancock present, and in command some days before. Our pursuit of Indians took us via old Fort Hayes. The "hard-tack" left over from the war— and bacon too, perhaps—wasn't of the best, and men were tired and hungry. Gen. Custer camped within a base-ball throw of the flagstaff of the post.

What, if any, inducements were held out at this camp to the post sutler, I don't know. This, I know: A cordon of sentries were put around the camp of battln. of 7th Cav. and orders were issued "that no enlisted men would be allowed to visit the post without a written order", which appl. must be sent in with Morning Report Book, and was to be signed by the Adjt. of Battln.

Just at this time I was summoned to return to Fort Riley to take with me five enlisted men of my troop to report as witnessed in the case of a deserter from my troop to the Judge Advo. of the G.C.M.

On return to old Fort Hays with my party of five, Custer had gone toward the Union Pacific R.R., my troop going under command of First Lieut. "Tom" Custer. I was held back with party until news from Custer was gotten, then I was to take a four-gun battery of Gatling guns to the regiment, which I did, joining at Fort Wallace, Kans.

[249]

From this point, Custer having received an anonymous letter via the U.P.R.R. that he'd better hustle back and look out for family interest, did so, I meeting him one day's march before getting to Wallace.

Custer had 50 picked men (and picked horses also) as escort. Capt. Hamilton, 1st Lieut. Tom Custer and Lieut. Cooke being along.

On arrival at Fort Wallace next day I received a great awakening.

At old Fort Hayes, two of the men of my troop, one of them troop farrier, other just off guard, either or both of which could perhaps have obtained passes by asking, but who had "Frenched it" in preference, were, with many others, arrested at the post for being without passes.

The gang of prisoners were marched thro' company streets preceded by trumpets sounding the "Rogue's March"; their heads were then shaved, and the poor devils were "spread-eagled" on the plain until they cried "Peccavi."

Now my immediate interests were in only two of those men, so I took down their affidavits, the affidavits of responsible witnesses, on which I based my report to Dept. Hdqtrs.

I will say here that on leaving the post of old Fort Hayes, Major Wyckliffe Cooper being some days from post, and out of whiskey, shot himself—suicide—because the d——d fool Dr. (Lippincott) acting under orders from Custer, wouldn't give him even a drink of whiskey to "straighten out" on. Cooper was 2d Major of Regt. and a most gallant soldier during the war, Col. of a Ky. Cav. Regt. This occurred when I was on G.C.M. duty.

The other awakenings I got on arrival at Wallace were, that on arrival at Fort McPherson, the same orders issued at Hayes were carried out. Men of the command arrested were soused in the Platte River, a lariat having been tied to their legs, and this repeated till they were nearly drowned.

Next, and worst of all, the dismounted deserters that were soon on the march from McPherson, and who were shot down while begging for their lives, by Major Joel H. Elliott (2d Major of Regt. vice Cooper), Bvt. Lieut. Col. Tom Custer and Bvt. Lieut. Col. W. W. Cooke (executioner-in-chief).

One of the deserters was brought in badly wounded, and in extreme agony from riding in wagon (over the Plains without a road), screamed in his anguish. Gen. Custer in passing by, rode up to the wagon, and, pistol in hand, told the soldier "that if he didn't cease making so much fuss he would shoot him to death!" How's that for high? Now these things are gospel truth!

On the arrival of Custer and his 50 picked men and horses at Fort Harker, Kansas, Custer was, by order of Major-Gen. W.S. Hancock, placed in arrest, and the party were ordered back to regiment.

Custer, after leaving me one day's march from Wallace, kept on toward Hays, but at Ellis Springs, a stage station, it was reported to him that a man belonging to him had escaped, so a party of 10 men and non-com. were sent to catch him. They did so, but were jumped by Indians, some being killed, and one man of my troop badly wounded, but who saved his life by tumbling from his horse in a huge buffalo wallow. The Indians seeing the horse going off to command with others, didn't notice that it had no rider on it.

So, Capt. Carpenter of 17th Inf. Comdg. Co. at stage station, was requested by Gen. Custer to send out and scoop in his wounded debris, bury dead, etc., as he, Custer, hadn't the time to stop. Carpenter made a report to Dept. Hdqtrs. by telegraph, which report preceded mine by mail, and Custer was arrested, tried and dismissed, which sentence was commuted to suspension from rank and pay for 12 months by Gen. Grant, or Pres. Johnson I believe it then was.

At all events, we were free of Custer till autumn of 1868, then by verbal recommendation made by J. Schuyler Crosby, A.A.A.G. for Sheridan, who came to me from that General, offering me the command of the 7th Cavalry in the field. Major Elliott and Capt. Wm. Thompson, who were my seniors, were to be given leaves of absence.

I politely but firmly declined the compliment of being so selected, recommending to Col. Crosby that Sheridan secure the remission of unexpired portion of Custer's sentence, and let him join command, saying that perhaps he would have, and exhibit, more sense and judgment than he had during his former short tour in command. So Custer came!

At the battle of the Washita my Fort Harker squadron broke up the village before a trooper of any of the other companies of 7th got in, and we protected the fifty-five squaws and children we captured.

1st Sergt. Duane of M. Troop, 2 privates, "California Joe" and myself surrounded and drove in the ponies that were killed on that field by Custer—some 800. Custer, in his "Life on the Plains" gives Calif. Joe the credit; but as surely as there's a sun, I conceived, and we carried it out, and Custer knew it. I turned the herd over to Col. West, who had his squadron intact, and was enroute to find something. Godfrey was 2d Lieut. of K, West's troop, at that time.

Elliott, like myself, was "pirating" on his own hook; allowed himself to be surrounded and died like a man. Elliott was a captain in a brigade I commanded during the war.

Elliott and West, the latter being a Div. Comdr. under Butler and Kautz (pro tem) and was a distinguished man, but given at times to hellish periodical sprees. Those two had, in underhand ways been "peppering" Custer, thinking he was not aware of it, but he was. Elliott being out of the way, and upon arrival at the present site of Fort Sill, Okla., West, feeling that Custer would catch and salt him away surely, at same time succeeded in getting promise from Sheridan—who was with us—of the sutlership of the new post of Sill. He got it. Officers of Regt. Hall, whom it promoted Captain, and all the juniors, chipped in a "pot" for West and everybody signed an application that West be allowed to go around with regiment in the field as Trader. When such application was presented to Custer, he declined signing, saying, though, that he would do so soon.

However, West learned differently, but went on East to purchase goods, did so purchase and brought them to camp of 7th Cav. before his experience was available. The difference there was that he had written to old "Pop" Price sutler at Fort Leavenworth, who was at camp, and informed him that Custer had tendered the appointment to him, and that he was there to buy him out—which he did. On arrival at Camp Supply from site of Sill, via El Ilano Estacado, in spring of 1869, we (the regt.) met Major Smith, paymaster U.S.A. waiting for us at Supply, having been ordered to do so by Dept. Comdr. At Fort Meade, Dakota, in winter of '81 and '82, I met the bookkeeper of the firm who were sutlers at Supply in the spring of '69. He was then cashier of First Nat'l Bank of Deadwood, but suffering with sciatica; was the guest of Lieut. Garlington at Meade, and I frequently went to see him to cheer him up.

He said one time to me: "Benteen, do you remember when the regiment was at Camp Supply in spring of 1869 that Major Smith, P.M. had been sent there to pay off regi-

ment, and had been ordered to await the arrival of it there."
"Yes," said I "of course." "Well, then, you remember that
the regiment was not paid, and that it was taken off at daylight the day after arrival?" "Yes, of course." "Well, do you
have any idea of the cause of this?" "Not the slightest," said I.

"Then I'll tell you," said Thumb. "Custer issued his
regular pronunciamento on arrival of regt. at Supply, this time
the lines being more rigidly drawn, to the effect that neither
commissioned officers, non-coms, or privates could visit the
post without written orders from Custer. Why was this? A
stone's throw from the post?" "Give it up," said I.

Well, an officer of the 7th Cav. presented himself to
Tappan (the trader) saying he came from Gen. Custer, and
that if the firm would give Custer $3,500 for which Custer
would give them a bill of sale for an (U.S.) ambulance,
4 mules and horses, he would then keep the regiment there
for payment, otherwise he'd march the regiment off at daylight, take the paymaster with him and pay off at Fort Hayes."

"Tappan and Weichelbaum wouldn't agree to it, so the
7th marched.

"Now," said Thumb to me, "can you guess the name of
the officer bringing the proposal?" "Well, if it wasn't Tom
Custer, Cooke or "Fresh' Smith, I'll have to give it up." "No,
to save you trouble, 'twas First Lieut. Wallingford", (who,
by the by, had been dismissed from the regiment and had
died in the Kansas State Penitentiary, serving sentence for
horse-stealing.)

Now, Col. Goldin, this was the first inkling I had as to
the cause of the issuing of those orders on arrival at the
different posts. 'Tis quite apparent now that we know!

We will skip over now that we are skipping so much, to
the time when "Salt" Smith, his Regt. Qr. Mr. lost so many

U.S. Gov. Qr. Mr. checks to the "Custer gang" in playing draw poker, in which game Lieut. Aspinwall, just making his advent in the regiment, autumn of 1869, thought perhaps as it seemed so very easy, to see what he could do at pulling in $300 or $400 at a whack with a pair of deuces. "Salt" Smith deserted at once.

The end was, the "Custer Gang" skinned him, and I'm told Jack's poor old father squared up some $1600 in debts to those damned cormorants! Oh, if I only could have known of it and seen him before he did it—but I wasn't there, but was in Colorado.

From this time on, I had never seen Aspinwall play cards, and was the unwitting instrument of putting temptation in his way, and this from fact of being in command of post of Fort Rice, and having the highest opinion of his honor and integrity, made him by appointment Asst. Commy. of Subsistence of the post.

Being "snow'd up" a greater portion of the winter left large amounts of money in his safe. On all of the inspections this money was there, all correct. When Major Tilford relieved me of command I'm inclined to think he might have been neglectful of his duties in that respect, and so the sutler store employes got all the money wasted by poor Jack.

Now, whether Capt. Harmon got any of it I don't know, but I believe that he did. Aspinwall deserted some time after Tilford assumed command, and went on to Bismarck with Tilford, the latter going on leave. Jack followed without leave.

I'll skip now to 1873: At Memphis, Tenn., Baliran was the proprietor of a restaurant and gaming establishment, doing a good business, and a gambler by profession. Having some money, Custer induced him to come with 7th Cav. as Sutler telling him the officers of the regiment were high players, and he could make a big thing, "catch them going and coming." Baliran told all this to DeRudio on '73 trip, and DeRudio told me Custer had put in 0, but had drawn out to that time $1,100.

A few weeks thereafter Baliran and old Vet. Honsinger were killed. What became of the effects of the firm I never heard.

I know that third day out from Rice, that Col. Fred Grant informed Custer that on next day a search of the whole train was to be made; train halted enroute, for whiskey. Baliran's whiskies and wines were put in 7th Cav. troop wagons, and Baliran's wagons carried grain belonging to same troops. Ketchum & Ray, A.C. & C.S. for Stanley, evidently did not inform Fred Grant of the fact that they were going to swoop down on the store in camp of 7th, or they might have been again spirited away; but with the earliest dawn, the two members of Stanley's staff came, axes in hand, and spilt the good red liquor on the dry alkaline soil of Montana at the "Stockade" camp.

Grant, Gibson, Weston and myself had procured a quart about one-half hour before destruction. We were owling!

Now Stanley was stupidly drunk at the time, and that is how Custer got away with him.

In 1874 Custer was in partnership with John Smith through the Black Hills picnic. As I have this from the original J.S. he ought to know.

In 1873 Custer didn't leave Lincoln; in 1876 he did, but he didn't have any opportunity to speak of to organize the sutler dept. of his campaign. However John Smith was out, on the "Far West"; but I think in the interests of Joe Leighton & Co. of Buford.

Now, if such a man as Custer was, is deserving of the

good opinion of this great republic's people, then so does the worst criminal in any of its many penitentiaries.

I haven't given you any of his worst crimes, but if any inquiring "Grimes" wants them badly, why, I have them pretty well in mind, and certainly they can be proved—and they can have them.

If I have tired you as much as I have myself, then it's a stand-off.

Very truly yr, friend
F. W. BENTEEN.

39 Pavilion St.
Atlanta,
St. Valentine's Day, '96

Dear Colonel Goldin:—

I omitted saying, in the long scrawl sent you lately, that it was my purpose to exhibit to you what course led to the very, very frequent desertions from 7th Cav. from '67 to '69, at which time Col Sturgis relieved Custer from command of the regiment.

Those men of my troop who were punished for going to old Fort Hayes '67, (a baseball's throw from camp) were wholly sober, having purchased nothing but fresh bread from post bakery, and some canned fruits from sutler, having these in their hands at the time of arrest. This evidently was their offense, only ascertained too late, to make mention of at the proper time.

When Sturgis arrived at camp of 7th below New Fort Hayes, in summer of '69, Gen. Custer had a hole deeply dug in ground about 30x30 square feet, about 15 feet deep, entrance by ladder, hole boarded over. This was the guard-house, and a man even absent from a "call" was let down. I don't know how the prisoners laid down.

It had been discontinued before I joined at that camp by Gen. Sturgis.

At Camp Supply in spring of '69, Weir and Robbins (Capt.) owed the sutler $1500 each; even 2d Lieut. Gibson owed over $500; other officers proportionately, except myself (who never purchased from anyone in my life, save for cash.)

The men of Regt. had not been paid for about six months, and the sutler held checks for a great amount on the men of all the troops, 11 of them present, so Custer thought he had an easy $3500 cinch on Weichelbaum & Tappan, Sutlers.

Capts. Weir, Robbins, Lieut. Tom Custer, Dr. Renick, et al. went to Supply with passes from Custer.

Weir & Robbins played even on their $3,000 debt with the post sutlers at faro; the sutlers having a game in operation for the occasion, a 2d Lieut. of 3d U. S. Inf. being the dealer.

Custer started from (at daybreak) camp, leaving Capts. Weir, Robbins, Lieut. Custer and A.S. Surgeon Renick, drunk at Supply, they being sent to our next camp in a post ambulance the same afternoon. All of them, Dr. with them, were placed in arrest, but for some reason Tom Custer was released.

As they all messed together, the captains and Dr. said to Tom: "What does your brother mean by putting on all those frills? Doesn't he know that Dr. Renick has seen him "not only" sleeping with that Indian girl all winter long, but has seen him many times in the very act of copulating with her!"

"Now don't you think, Tom we can stand the general off?"

Tom, of course told his brother, and he thought a speedy release in order, which was done.

Weir & Robbins raised merry hell to their heart's content after that, and by Custer's advice, orders for one troop having been received, to be sent to Fort Scott, Capt. Robbins was sent by Sturgis.

When Custer's two years were passed, preventing bringing charges against him (per Art. War) he forced Capt. Robbins to resign, which fact gave Moylan his captaincy; Gibson, first lieut, to my troop, and I must say that I don't think there was a poorer lieutenant in the Army.

A fact which you may not be aware of is: there were many officers in the 7th who wouldn't have believed Gen. Custer on oath!

Of course, being in a regiment like that, I had far too much pride to permit Custer's outfit driving me from it, the more particularly as I had taken the initiative to have Gen. Custer disciplined accordingly with Army Regulations, which was done.

The suspension of arrest, however, and return to duty, was a mistake, as it made him worse instead of better.

Colonel Goldin, you never had the remotest idea what a villain that man was, and of course if you hadn't, under a five-year blanket, how in the name of common sense can the great majority of people know anything as to his character? That he was a murderer, the first campaign of Regt. proved; on same we found him a liar (from crown of head to sole of foot.)

Gen. Sturgis served in Texas as Lieut.-Col. 6th Cav. under Custer commdg. Cav. Division-after war. When Custer was mustered out of Vols. as Major General, Sturgis remained in Texas. He found the contracts let by Custer for grain, hay, &c., &c., stupendous frauds. Sturgis notified the authorities: the

contracts were annuled, and when Sturgis joined the 7th
Cavalry he brought all the papers connected with that affair
with him, and two weeks after I joined the Regt. under Sturgis
at Fort Hayes, Sturgis showed me all of the documents, as
Custer had commenced war on him through his minions (not
showing his own hand then, however). Sturgis knew all
about it.

It isn't worth while to tell you all of these things about
Custer, a dead man, but I think some other body than myself
ought to know something of his true character; therefore, I
trust I haven't disgusted you.

If you want more, I can give it to you "ad infinitum"

Yrs. very truly,   F. W. BENTEEN

Of course I cannot have any notion in rehearsing these
things to you, only to show Custer was a bad, bad, man! This
goes without saying.

I think I've given you enough to show that Custer was
a sure enough dandy! But I've gems yet untold!

No. 39 Pavilion St.
Atlanta,
Feb. 17, '96

Dear Colonel Goldin:

I am pleased to know that I haven't disgusted you in the
relation of what I know of Custer's character. Moylan is the
only living party that can know of what concerns Custer
that I've been giving you in details, and it is presumable that

he'd never tell. Neither Mrs. Custer or Mrs. Calhoun or Fred C. know anything about those things, and others who might have known are all dead.

I intend giving you a few more details concerning the S.O.B. and not in one word that I extenuate, nor ought set down in malice, because I had and have none, and showed him through all the history of the Seventh Cavalry that I was amply capable of taking care of myself, and never did I attack him in any but a soldierly manner and through military channels.

In 1869, five (5) graduates of the M.A. came to 7th Cavalry ranks, as in following order, viz: Ray, Porter, Craycroft, Braden and Lieut. Aspinwall.

Lieut. Ray was the brightest man, and in every way the best fitted for a cavalry soldier. He was stationed in late autumn and winter at Fort Leavenworth, which was regimental Hd. Qtrs. Gen. Sturgis comdg. 7th Cavalry and post of Leavenworth.

In city of Leavenworth, Ray became infatuated with a most charming member of the demimonde, and paid her assiduous court—on C.O.D. order. He became so "stuck" on her that he took her out horseback riding one afternoon, Ray having no sign of a uniform on but his chasseur cap.

On one of the main roads, outside of city limits, Ray saw behind him another party of cavaliers and ladies, mounted, from the post.

Not caring to be recognized by the party, which consisted of Gen. and Tom Custer, and among others of the ladies (?) composing it, was one, a guest of Custer's who afterwards, along with her mother, were arrested for shop-lifting in a western city, but by some turn of the law evaded the execution of justice by paying out—and the crime was yclept kleptomania. By ocular demonstration it was known that Lieut. Cooke was criminally connected with this girl, and the popular supposition was that Gen. Custer had long been having such connection with her. Lieut. Ray, however, knew nothing of all these facts, so put to his horses. The sudden jump threw his cap from his head, but not stopping for cap or girl, made way for the post, bareheaded.

Custer came along, picked up the cap and afterwards persisted in demanding the resignation of Lieut. Ray, and the fellow was so terrified that he submitted the same. He was afterwards a 1st Sergt. in the 7th U.S. Inf. in Montana.

Now at this time it was notorious that Custer was criminally intimate with a married woman, wife of an officer of the garrison; besides, he was an habitue of demimonde dives, and a persistent bucker of Jayhawker Jenison's faro game. These facts all being known to Mrs. Custer, rendered her—if she had any heart(?) a broken-hearted woman. From knowing her as well as I do, I only remark that she was about as cold-blooded a woman as I ever knew, in which respect the pair were admirably mated.

In October, 1868, immediately after his suspension was remitted, and he had joined the regiment, which was then in Bluff Creek, Ind. Ter., Custer cast around for some officer to send to Fort Harker, Kans. after 300 horses and 200 recruits there for the 7th Cav. I was selected, and with one orderly I was to go (overland, of course) 180 miles, through a country fairly alive with hostile Indians.

This didn't daunt me a particle, for I knew every mile of the district, and I knew my orderly, who, by the way, was a brother Virginian, had the fullest confidence in my plains skill. Funny, wasn't it?

This private of my troop was a major of artillery in the

Confederate Army, and born and raised a few miles from my native town, Petersburg, Va. Of course he was under an assumed name in the U.S. Army.

Before starting, which I did at night, Custer sent for me and solicited when I arrived at Harker, to be kind enough to send to his wife (Mrs. E.B. Custer) one hundred dollars (100) at Fort Leavenworth, Kans.

I then began to see why I had been selected! It was known that I always had plenty of money in the regiment.

I got to Harker O.K. First duty performed was to send to Mrs. Custer my check on First Nat'l Bank of Leavenworth for $100.

2d Lieut. Volkmar, 5th Cav., now Lieut-Col. and Deputy Adjt. Gen. U.S. Army, was the youth, (Kid) "Johnny" came later, who had the recruits in charge. I gathered them in, took Volkmar and one of his classmates along, his classmate's bride of few weeks, too, which portion of outfit went to 3d U.S. Inf. Fort Dodge.

We arrived at Ford Larned. A mexican train loaded with arms and ammunition was to be ordered to report to me, but by some means did not do so, and I knew nothing about it. The train pulled out some hour or so ahead of my outfit from Larned, and some mile or so from Big Coon Creek, I came in sight of the train watering the animals at pond of water (surface water) a short piece from roadside. I knew this was done on account of the terrible alkalinity of Coon Creek water; so on arrival of my detachment, I watered all stock at ponds.

Just as we had straightened out for the march I saw that the train ahead was attacked, surrounded by Indians, pouring the bullets into it, circling around the while. I took the leading platoon, telling Volkmar to bring up the 2d and 3d platoons which were on right and left flanks of my train, and off I pitched into the Indians with my one platoon, scattering them, and saving the life of the wagon-master who had gone out some little distance to procure a good camp ground for the night. When Volkmar got up, I had the red scamps run off. They broke for the Arkansas River, crossed, and 'twas worse than useless to pursue.

However, "the mills of the gods ground exceeding fine," for them, for 'twas this very party that by its trail through the snow, led us to the village of Black Kettle on the Washita.

I reached camp of the 7th, then Camp Sandy Forsythe, and on the Arkansas River, 10 miles below Fort Dodge, in fine fettle, my recruits having been in their first baptism of fire.

When I reached camp I learned that my fine mount of horses that Gen. Sheridan told me in August same year, "was the finest mount he ever saw a troop of cavalry have," had been distributed around promiscuously to other troops. In fact, the troops of the regiment had been "colored" in the field at the beginning of the severest campaign that ever cavalry underwent. Fine bays and brown horses taken—other bays given in place.

And all this going on with my first Lieut. W.W. Cooke, looking on, permitting—or at least acquiescing in it.

My $100 and horses went about the same time.

Well, this was in October, 1868. In November, 1869, Custer was to march the battalion that went to Fort Leavenworth to winter at that point. I drove my wife and son out to see the regiment start from camp, standing at the head of horses to keep them from scaring at the band in its passing. Custer rode up, shook hands with, and told Mrs. B. goodby, but to me said never a word about refunding (or even spoke of) the borrowed $100 I had sent to buy fuel and groceries for Mrs. Custer. This had been due something over one year, and Mrs. Custer was in want, dire straits, before receipt of it.

In the winter of '69 and '70, I learned from an army officer just up from Leavenworth, that Custer had made a haul at Jenison's faro bank. I wrote him that if he had the money convenient it was high time the debt was paid, telling him it was $91—nine dollars having been absorbed in "calling him" for small amts. when I knew he had the winning hand, and save putting up cash to his pile to ascertain fact. He replied immediately to my dun, sending his check for $92, which he said was his account of it.

Now, as one dollar would scarcely be living interest on a hundred doll. for fourteen months and over, and as I was not a Shylock, lending money at interest anyway, I coolly returned on same day a one dollar bill, thanking him for his promptitude in discharging the debt!

Reno, who was president of the G.C.M. at Hays, where I was then stationed, and at which Court of Justice doubtless at time some fellow, some 1st Sergt. was putting in big licks of testimony to convict some "Johnny come lately" or other for getting too full on "20-rod" 25 cts.a dram, sutler whisky, [He asked] was I doing this work and mailing the $1 in letter. Reno had the curiosity to ask me what I was doing. I related the circumstances in toto. He wanted to know if that was the way they did business in the 7th Cav? I told him I thought if he had any business to do with Custer he'd find it so.

After that you can imagine what dealings I had with the S.O.B. He had proved to my entire satisfaction that he was a cur of "1st water."

1871—at Louisville, he, Tom Custer and Cooke, Adjt. came to train to endeavor to persuade me to choose going to South Carolina instead of taking Nashville as a station, Custer saying, "J.B. Fry, then A.Genl. for Halleck comdg. Dept. had informed him that the troop going to Nashville would only be there a short time. I knew what a liar Gen. Custer was, so

[265]

I told him I'd go up and see Gen. Sturgis, Comdg. Regt. about
the matter. Custer remarked to Mrs. Benteen, "that anything
he recommended to me I was pretty sure to choose the exact
opposite." His "guff" imposed on Mrs. B. and she thought and
said I was dead wrong, but she wasn't the poker player I was,
and she didn't know the scoundrel as I did.

I saw Gen. Sturgis. His remark was: "The lying whelp!
There isn't a word of truth in it. Custer is trying to keep
French's troop, in which his brother Tom is 1st lieut., from
going to South Carolina." But Tom had to take S.C. in his!

On return of the regiment from Washita—El Llano
Estacado—campaign of 1868–69, and on arrival at our sub-
depot of supplies on the Washita River, Custer found in the
Missouri Democrat a letter criticising his management of the
battle of the Washita.

Custer had gone ahead with band—one troop of Regt.
taking the "Sharpshooters" under Lieut. Cooke, Moylan, Tom
Custer, &c. I was to bring in the remnant of the starved
command.

I was about frozen when I dismounted, so not caring
to hunt of Moylan, the adjutant, thinking it his business to
put the battln. in camp, I rushed into the first tent I came to
to warm myself. In a moment or so, Tom Custer and Lieut.
Cooke came in, Tom with a newspaper in his hand, showing
it to me, saying, "Isn't that awful!" I looked at it, reading
down a line or so, and said, "Why, Tom, I wrote that myself,"
and so I had. The Civil War turned out no three brighter
enthusiasts and able soldiers than the brothers Frank, Wm. J.
and Jacob De Gresse. Frank was captain of H. Battery Chicago
Artillery—20 lb. Parrots—and his battery threw the first shells
into Atlanta with Sherman in 1864. Wm. J. was a captain in
my regiment, the 10th Missouri Cavalry. Jacob was a captain
in the 6th Mo. Cav. and A.A. Gen. on same staff.

The letter in Mo. Democrat written by me to Wm. J. DeGresse from Fort Cobb, I.T., was about the first report received there after the Washita affair.

De Gresse was in the life and fire insurance business in St. Louis then, and of course an active man, knowing everybody, and besides, being greatly interested in me; was interested in the description of the country we had been going over for last year or so, as it was on the same line of march he, as an enlisted man of the Montana Rifles, had gone over in 1855 to New Mexico.

I suppose DeGresse came across a lively newspaper report and the letter then got to the public, i.e., only the portion affecting the Washita fight—I wasn't ashamed of it; didn't care a d——n for Custer, if he did owe me $100 debt of honor, and owned straight up that I was the miscreant who had given it to the world, though I hadn't the remotest idea it would be published—the glimmer of some truth about Indian fighting.

Well, Custer had given me a fair chance of getting scalped in sending me 180 miles alone, almost, for recruits and horses; had endeavored to the best of his ability to get Col. Myers and myself killed at the Washita, all of which close to death embraces I was thoroughly aware of, and I must say wholly careless of; but the intent was perceptibly plain "allee samee."

Custer paid me off for the letter in almost spot cash.

Col. Wm. Thompson's troop was and had been stationed at Dodge since the birth of regiment, and Thompson liked Dodge as a station, and he and his troop both desired to remain there. I did not want it; this, Custer knew. He also knew that I had had a child born and died at Harker since I left there, and that my wife was very ill, and came very close to death, and I'm inclined to think he hadn't forgotten that he

[267]

still owed me $100 I had sent Mrs. Custer, to purchase food, fuel and raiment with in 1868.

Nevertheless, when we arrived at Arkansas River crossing, opposite site of Dodge, I can still remember the fiendish gleam of delight that seemed to sparkle in the eyes of Adjt. Myles Moylan, as he appeared on south bank of the Arkansas River, and handed me the written order to await on that bank of river until all our train had crossed, though I wasn't in charge of the train, then to report to the C.O. of the post of Fort Dodge for duty at that post. Major Harry Douglas, 3d Ind. was C.O., but had been "put on" unassigned list. Philip Reade was 2d Lieut. and Post adjutant.

I reported to Douglas. His reply was, "Glad to see you, Benteen. I've been waiting arrival of somebody to receipt to me for the Ord. and Ord Stores. I'll turn over command of post and stores to you, and be off tomorrow." In those days Ord. and Ord. stores were all invoiced to the C.O. of posts, and he was the responsible officer.

I receipted to him for them, and Douglas skipped. Of course being then Comdg. Post, I took a seven days' leave and started for Harker, packed my "larea and penates" and sent my wife and boy to St. Louis.

In transporting my household and troop property from Harker to Dodge—155 miles overland—I had the pleasure of the company of Phil Reade back to Dodge.

I remember his exhibiting to me a gorgeous photograph of his intended bride—which he afterwards made her. I had known her long before, she belonging to an itinerant musical band that sang, played and gave concerts at mess-halls and chapels at posts which were unfortunate enough to have such an encumbrance.

"Phil" married her, and, Dame Rumor says, shipped her

to Italy for the training of her voice, spotless and untouched! However considerate in that regard Phil might have been, the same authority says some Dago over there got her with child, and she died in childbirth. Phil sought relief of the D.C.(?) Rumor says the woman didn't die also—but she died to Phil.

Guess this is all the newest of the new to you. Phil, at that, was just as full of crotchets as he is today.

A week or so after getting back to Dodge, Col. Mitchell, A.D.C. & Insp. Gen. for Gen. W.S. Hancock, Comdg. Dept. came to Dodge to inspect and report on some trouble Capt. Geo. Armes and Capts. Graham & Cox of 10th U.S.Cav. were having at camp of Battln. near Dodge. Col. Mitchell was surprised at finding me there in command, and asked me if I wanted the job. "Not by a d——d sight!" I remarked, but Custer banished me for punishment. I showed him the copy of letter in newspaper that caused it. "Well," he said, "I'll fix this up for you the first thing I do on my return to Fort Leavenworth. You can be making preparations to join regiment at Hays."

As soon as I got my orders I put out for Hays, meeting enroute Tom Custer and Lieut. Cooke, escorting the Inspector Gen. of the Army, with one troop of cavalry to Fort Supply. Custer, of course, didn't know business the Gen. was on, but he had fine spies as an escort to ascertain same.

I had just driven a fat buffalo cow up to the road; had killed her there, and was engaged in cutting her throat, when Cooke rode up with his advance guard, some distance ahead of Gen. Inspec's ambulance. Cooke said, "At your old business I see," "Yes," said I, "I can't keep out of blood."

Cooke was my first lieut. when I was left on S. side of Ark. at Fort Dodge. He was made aware of my troop's fate, but never intimated it to me, but his troops were put in another

[269]

wagon, and Cooke given seven days' leave, Custer taking off with him, and Cooke never said good-by even, nor did he ever ask the amt. of his mess bill!

He transferred with Brewster to Keogh's troop without any opinion from me; however, you can easily deduce what would have been.

Cooke informed me that Gen. Sturgis had arrived, and was in command of 7th at Hays. I gave 3 hearty cheers! and just then my troop wagons were up ready and men were putting aboard carcass of buffalo cow, while the Inspec. Gen's. ambulance and escort were passing. I didn't speak to him!

Had I then known what was told me by "Tom Thumb" at Fort Meade in 1882 about the $3,500 trade Custer offered sutler at Supply, in 1869, I might have prevented his being killed at the Little Big Horn. Tom Custer and Cooke were sent along to see that that proposal didn't crop out! (?)

You will remember that in 1873, Custer was placed in arrest by Stanley just on arrival at edge of Bad Lands, and I was ordered with G. H. and K Troops to escort R.R. engineers through the Bad Lands. I think 'twas G. and K. I had.

Anyway, we so thoroughly satisfied the chief, Rosser, that to please him and punish me for the grand time I had at Stockade in '73 while Custer was Mussell-Shelling, I was sent thru the Bad Lands again with them on return march to Lincoln.

He hadn't sense enough to know that nothing was too hard for me to do that took me away from his immediate proximity.

If you were along with Troop G, you will remember that we took five wagons through Lands, and broke only one tongue on way, and that just as we got in sight of camp on the Little Missouri river.

Of course you have heard of an informal invitation from Custer for officers desiring to avail themselves of the services of a captured squaw, to come to the squaw round-up corral and select one! (?) Custer took first choice, and lived with her during winter and spring of 1868 and '69.

To crown the marriage(?) the squaw "calved" at site of the present Fort Sill. The issue was, however, a simon-pure Cheyenne baby, the seed having been sown before we came down on their fold at Washita.

The husband presented himself at same camp, but "Custer's woman" gave him the marble heart in the finest of shapes.

She was senior wife (present) of the two-starred big chief, with lots of "chuck-away" in the lodge, and wagon upon wagon-full outside!

"Go away, you poor one-blanketed Indian man! You must swappy for some older squaw to keep your lodge-fire going and your back warm! Custer heap good!"

I cannot tell you any more than you know of affair at the Little Big Horn, as you know that we made the attempt to get through to where we thought Custer was, at the earliest possible moment, and you also know that the attempt was vain; in fact, impossible.

At my own request, Gen. Terry permitted me to mount what was left of my troop and go to Custer's field, soon after he joined us on the 27th. When I returned, I said to Lieut. Maguire of Engineers, "By the Lord Harry, old man, 'twas a ghastly sight; but what a big winner the U.S. Govt. would have been if only Custer and his gang could have been taken!"

The Lord, in His own good time had at last rounded the scoundrels up, taking, however, many good and innocent men with them!

You know enough of me to know I'd have gone through

[271]

to him had it been possible to do so. At same time, I'm only too proud to say that I despised him as a murderer, thief and a liar—all of which I can prove.

All this scribbling is only as a drop in the bucket to what I can tell you of my connection with Custer and 7th Cavalry, but, like Mercutio's wound, "'Tis enough," and what's more, all I've said is true as Holy Writ!

Yrs. Truly,
BENTEEN, 7th

39 Pavilion St.
Atlanta,
Feb. 19, '96

Dear Colonel Goldin:—

I gave you a long, rambling disquisition on yesterday which must have worried you, yet it did not exhaust the Custer subject by any manner of means. Enough was told you, however, to show that he was a bold, bad man.

I wrote it hastily, and was so much interrupted while jotting it down, that I paid little attention to arrangement, grammar or anything else.

I wanted you to know it, and through you, Capt. Charles King, when you see him that he will make no mistake as to the character of that man.

I have an idea that "Charlie" King was of the opinion that there was in the 7th Cav. a clique of insubordinates who were antagonists to Gen. Custer, because he was what is known as a "live man", and they were desirous of shirking their duties.

The anti-Custer faction—if there was such a faction—were the people in regiment which had all of the hard duty to perform, and who did it nobly, because they loved their country and the "Service."

No favors were ever asked for by them, and none would have been granted them by Custer had they been requested.

The fact of the matter is, the regiment was in terrible shape from the very beginning, and Custer was the grand marplot and cause of it all.

I'll not devote more time to him.

> Very truly your friend
> F. W. BENTEEN.

39 Pavilion St.
Atlanta,
Feb. 20, '96

Dear Colonel Goldin:—

Yrs. containing Grimes' latest effusion just received.

I don't think it wise to say anything to him just yet about "Calhoun." Give him a little more rope, and it will not be long before he begins to develop who are the investigators.

It is idle to think that a youth of less than 20 years is doing all this inquiring on his own hook.

Sergt. Brown of G. Troop was Sergt. Major of my battln. in '77.

He wasn't giving that hell-hole of a "guard-house"—at, or below Fort Hays, Kansas, in '69—any undue prominence in his relation of same to you.

I had known Brown for many years. He was a good clerk, and if we have the same man in contemplation, he was an excellent man but for the whisky habit.

In going from Mussellshell river to Yellowstone, in '77, on one of the marches, we passed through a swamp which was fairly alive with water fowl of all kinds. My battln. was in rear on that day, so I dropped out of column, Brown coming with me. He had only 11 cartridges for his carbine. I borrowed the carbine and 11 cartridges, and Brown held my horse. I got one Mallard duck for each one of the cartridges, having a fine string of 11 of them. I had, of course, shot them in the water.

Brown insisted on carrying the string of ducks.

I overtook and inspected the manner of march of the pack-train and joined at the head of my batt'ln.

We soon after camped, at which time Major Merrill saw the ducks, wanting to know how many cartridges they had cost the U.S. I told him I had only 11 cartridges, and I got one duck for each. Sergt. Brown's carbine was a strange one to me, but if he wanted any more knowledge of the shooting, he could apply to Brown who witnessed the whole of it, but that he could not have any of the ducks for the doubting propensities evinced—and he got none.

When we arrived at Mussellshell on our return march, on trail of the Nez Perces, as soon as I put my battl'n in camp, down I went with my fishing line. I had a scarlet fly, salmon fly: so I simply dropped the fly in a large hole or eddy, and in a surprisingly short time had caught about 15 or 20 "white fish" (a fish that in Va. we called mud-shad) of no great force as food fish, but as you know, just at that time, we were at our wit's end for "grub", so they went.

Met Major Merrill there, and he wanted to know where I caught them, and wanted me to give him some of them. "No, Merrill, you just take to hunting and fishing for yourself. I will not do it for you."

Now, if he had been a (good?) soldier, or a good "hail fellow well met," I'd have given him the whole string of fish, but the "sucker"—I'd known him since 1861—and he couldn't, just could not get anything from me.

Merrill and Reno should have been class-mates, 1855. R. was set back, '56 '57, but poor a soldier as Reno was, he was a long way ahead of Merrill.

You may perhaps think I have given you the worst phases of General Custer's (also Tom's) character that I know, but I haven't. I'm keeping them in reserve, as perhaps some blockhead in attempting post mortem history, will give me "slack" enough to make it worth my while to turn my budget of information loose on the world—and all supported with affidavits! And this would not be courageous. Sturgis treated Reno like a dog. Reno was a far better soldier than Sturgis, and that isn't much praise.

Give Grimes all the line he wants. Keep the top of pole well up, and reel him well up to the side of boat. We have sharp gaffs and nets that if Grimes once gets into, he'll wish he hadn't.

Very truly your friend,
F. W. BENTEEN.

39 Pavilion St.
Atlanta,
Feb. 22, '96

Dear Colonel Goldin:—

Yours of 20th just received.

As a matter of course, Mrs. Custer was aware of a great many of his peccadilloes, tho' of course not all of them.

But of the affair of the wife of the officer at Leavenworth, she must have known. The officer is dead, but the wife lives.

I know "Billy" Bartlett well. He was brevetted Brig.Gen. Vols.

At New Orleans in '74 and '75, Col. DeLancy Floyd-Jones was Colonel of the 3d Inf., and "Billy" kept on a perpetual "bat" while at Jackson Barracks.

In the city, before any and everyone, "Billy" was constantly inveigling against "Old Fluggins", as the 3d called Col. Floyd-Jones. I took occasion at many times to caution Bartlett, who was open to reasoning from those he liked. "Billy" Bartlett, you know, was a son of Prof. Bartlett (the father-in-law of Gen. Schofield) Ph.D. and teacher of Philosophy at West Point.

Well, Billy used to berate "Old Fluggins" scandalously, and Floyd-Jones I suppose shipped him up river to Col. Merill at the first opportunity that offered.

There he got after—among many others—said Dame R., Mrs. B. of 7th. McIntosh, Ben Hodgson and Wallace were there, and after Wallace was made Adjutant by Reno, he must have informed R. of what had been even proved by ocular demonstration concerning the woman in question.

This information R. attempted to put in practice, but

circumstances of which I am aware, led the woman to give the thing away, and pose as an innocent.

It cost Reno two years of suspension with loss of all pay, Hayes letting up on the dismissal, simply because the character of the woman was shown him unmistakably, but which could not be shown in evidence, as she wasn't being tried.

Sturgis caught Reno up soon after on the most frivolous of charges, and this time Mrs. Lucy Hayes had him sent to Coventry.

On the Maj.Gen. Hancock's expedition in '67, I became acquainted with 2d Lieut. Thompson, 3d Inf. and by the by, T. is still in my debt for "draw" played on that trip.

I was at Fort Larned, too, when the mad wolf ran amuck through the hospital in '68, and bit Thompson outside. His life was saved on account of wolf biting through pants, drawers and socks, thus getting rid of all the virus on clothes; but it scared Thompson "pissless", as we say in the cavalry, and well it might! All the others bitten by the wolf, died of hydrophobia.

I was stationed with 3d and 5th Inf. for many years, and knew them all, from "Shiny" William Hoffman down to the present Col. of 3d, then Bvt. Major Page.

Until latter part of August, '68 I was in command of the post at Fort Harker, and had H and M Troops, my squadron, out constantly, commanded by myself, scouting for Indians. After August, till about October, '68, I escorted with squadron Gen. Phil Sheridan from post to post, till Custer joined, as recommended by me, and then we made the Washita-El Llano Estacado campaign '68 '69.

Twenty men of my squadron and the 2d Lieut. of my troop, Eddy Emerson, was a guard for the same P.H. Sheridan, then a Capt. of 13th Inf. and who was the A.A.Qrmr and

A.C.S. of the army of the Southwest, in 1862, just before the battle of Pea Ridge, March 6,7,8th.

Sheridan declined to obey some of the orders of Gen.S.R. Custis, Comdg. Army of the S.W., so he was ordered to report to Gen.Halleck at St. Louis, in arrest, charges and spec's. as long as the moral law sent in against him, all of which Halleck paid no attention to, but put Sheridan to buying horses, taking him to Corinth, Miss. with him as Hdqtrs. Qtrmaster. There he got command of a Mich. or Wis.Cav. Regt. and went thereafter like a comet!

Sheridan always had an affection for me from the fact of giving him 20 such good men and such an efficient Lieut. to command his escort in '62.

They were employed in seizing mills, grinding corn, wheat &c by which means only was our army supplied, and as the mills and sources of supply were widely separated, Sheridan and escort were kept very busy. The Bushwhackers in Mo. and Ark. rendered it necessary to go with escort always.

There are many excellent ways of finding out the disposition and nature of a man. I know of no better way than having to live on shipboard with one for a series of years.

Next, in default of salt-water facilities in the great N.W., campaign with a man in the cavalry, for say 10 or 20 years, playing "draw" with him meanwhile, and if the investigator isn't a dolt straightout, he should garner some valuable statistics as to the matter in question.

Thus I became acquainted with Gen. Custer.

Ditto, in case of Gen. J.B. Fry, barring the campaigning; but in the game of "draw" Fry thought that no one from the Vols. had any right to down a Bvt. Maj. Gen. at the game: one who has studied philosophy and "math" at the great National School; but at the same time I used to down him regu-

larly, and he'd try to explain by philosophy why I should not
have "called him" on such-or-such a bet. "Oh, yes," said I,
"you play poker like the old fellow played the fiddle at the
cross-roads in Arkansas, and it wasn't until the Traveler came
along that he knew there was a change in the tune."

It is the change (turn) in the tune that I'm giving you
now. I hadn't a bit of respect for him if he was Adjt. Gen.
Dept. of the South, at last playing with him, A.G.Dept. of the
East.

He had been Provo Gen. U.S.Army, and by some hook
or crook had piled up a stack of coin of the realm. How?

Hon. Roscoe Conklin snubbed and in the U.S. Senate
denounced him, refusing always to speak to him, saying he
wasn't clean and honest. Fry was a finicky, cynical no end of
all'round d——n fool, with an unlimited amount of brass,
and little else, though he thought he was an author, genius
and all'round grand man. He and Rodenbough were active
in starting the Military Service Institution at Gov. Island, and
soliciting me to join. I said, I'd like to, but do not believe in
subscribing to lunches for you fellows in N.Y. while I'm
out in cactus and sagebrush.

I joined, however, though there were a lot of them there
I couldn't well tie to—a different gang from the present.
"Billy" Mitchell of Hancock's staff, however, induced me
to join.

Col. Mitchell was A.D.C. to Major Gen. Hancock, and
was the officer who rendered nugatory Custer's attempt to
banish me to Fort Dodge in Spring of '69.

From some cause or other, Gen. Hancock always seemed
fond of me, and was always kind, which was by no means the
rule to everybody, being at times quite over-bearing. I've been
told. I never had an axe to grind.

[279]

Mine was the only troop of cavalry left in New Orleans in '74 and '75, and when Sheridan came down to assume command, he rather surprised Gen. Emory, 5th Cav. (then in command Dept. of the South), and E's staff, by the way he threw his arms around and hugged me, telling me he was glad I was there, and I know he was, as I had made record in 1862, and he knew some of it.

I had a drag in N.O. at the time, and to pull it two grand Mambrino Chief mares, 16-2 high, as nimble as deer. I used frequently to take Sheridan and Tom Forsythe out to the race track in it. I had at the time two thoroughbreds at the track entered for spring races, neither of which I started from fact of not being sufficiently prepared, but the drive was a beautiful one, the springtime grand, and they used to enjoy themselves hugely; and so did I.

Custer, at the time was foaming at the mouth at Lincoln. He was shut out of showing himself up in the newspapers; however he had the relaxation of giving to the "Galaxy" his "Lie [Life?] on the Plains."

At Fort Cobb, Ind. Ter. in winter of '68-'69, officers call was sounded one night from Regt. Hdqtrs. I sauntered up, the other officers being mostly there when I arrived.

The officers were squatted around the inside of Custer's Sibley tent, (minus a wall), and Custer was walking around the center of tent with a rawhide riding whip in his hand. When all were assembled, he went on with a rambling story, stammering the while, that it had been reported to him that some one—or parties—had been belittling the fight at the Washita, &c., &c., and that if he heard any more of it, or it came to his ears who had done so, he would cowhide them, switching his rawhide the while.

Being right at the door of tent, I stepped out, drew my revolver, turned the cylinder to see that 'twas in good working

order, returned it lightly to holster, and went within. At a
pause in the talk I said, "Gen. Custer, while I cannot father
all of the blame you have asserted, still, I guess I am the man
you are after, and I am ready for the whipping promised." He
stammered and said, "Col. Benteen, I'll see you again., sir!"

Doubtless you can imagine what would have happened
had the rawhide whirred! The "call" broke up, sine die, in
silence, but no tears from whipping! I then went to Randolph
Keim, reporter from N.Y. Tribune (the only man I had
spoken to about the matter at all) and told him I wanted him
to go with me at once to Custer's tent, taking his notes with
him of all I had told him, as a whipping was due somebody,
and I didn't want a word I'd said omitted.

Keim went with me, and though I'd told him enough,
Custer wilted like a whipped cur.

He evidently knew whom to whip! Now all of this kind
of business was apt to result disastrously to me when Custer
could so work it, but I was determined to "stay right with"
him; then the other fellows got a little more of men than
formerly, and the Custer power can be said to have commenced to decline. Keim told Gen. Sheridan about the occurrence, and Sheridan gave Custer a piece of his mind about the
matter. (Sheridan knew that it was principally through me
that Custer was then along, and he was rapidly beginning to
learn to know more of the characteristics of the man, and I
really think he cared but little for him thereafter.)

In 1876, when Custer came to Fort Lincoln with Terry,
he found that Major Reno had divided the regiment into four
(4) battalions, captains commanding them.

Custer at once changed that order, dividing regiment into
two wings, Reno comdg. R.W. and I the left.

Custer sent for me one day after this division of regt.,
and when at his tent (Mr. Custer being there), he informed

[281]

me that my cousin, Lawrence Cobright, had called on him in Washington, in spring of 1876, and wanted to know how I was getting along, seeming, Custer said, to be wonderfully interested in me. "Yes," said I, "we've been very dear friends always."

Now Lawrence Cobright, during the whole war (and from the beginning of the Associated Press) had been at its head, its chief, and no dispatches were given to the public by him affecting the Union cause, until he had presented the same to President Lincoln and the Secretary of War, Stanton.

Cobright, though a Southerner, was a Union man to the core, a democrat, too, but as true as steel, and had the whole confidence of the President and Secretary through the whole of it.

I then began to scent out the cause of wing distribution by Custer. However, he had no idea of the pride of my race, for at no time did I seek any preferment through Cobright's influence, and no one knew better than he that I would apply for none.

However, he being the "head-monk" of such a power, Custer perhaps feared that I might possibly bring influence to bear at some time.

He was fully aware that I'd hold my own like a man and thought that perhaps he might need some such influence probably.

Well, after the disaster, when curs of every grade were hounding Grant, Reno and myself, never did I write one word to Cobright. Had I, the matter would have gone to the world straight.

You see, Colonel, there are wheels within wheels!

Very truly your friend,
F. W. BENTEEN.

Dear Colonel Goldin:—

Yr. leap-year letter came O.K.

The shadow behind "Grimes" may have thought it time to sound a halt, but I'm of the opinion that we shall hear more of that later on.

I have just come in from reviewing a battalion of the 5th Inf. out from McPherson for a practice march. The C.O. of battalion, knowing he would pass my house, sent me word by his Adjt. that he wanted the battalion to give me a marching salute, so down the terraces I bounded to get there in time.

It does rather brace one up to see again a lot of jaunty, well-set-up lot of soldiers, and I doffed my hat with pleasing alacrity to the young aspirants for fame at $13 per mo. They both looked and marched well, and the students of Hispania had better ponder deeply and well o'er it, before starting to ruffle the tail feathers of the eagle-bird; for in my opinion they are a bad lot of birds to monkey with.

Well, poor old Lewis Merrill has answered his last roll-call. If they have good inspectors in spirit world, heaven— and I believe they have, then L.M., in my opinion, will have to be re-"set up" before he joins the flying-squad.

I saw in the "World" that McBride, Miss Nina Sturgis— Madam Douseman, second husband (and Mc., by the by, was a bigamist), so that marriage with Mrs. D. was annulled, was ordered out of some little place in S.D., his press and materials having been purchased by some of the citizens previously for the purpose of getting rid of him; but as that didn't work, the gentleman-mob proceeded to destroy the stock, with the "pi" in flames, &c.

I have known all the Sturgis family since they were children, and I must say they all turned out better than one could expect, from the very worldly training they got as grown-up children.

Of course I could do nothing towards a "medal" for Gammon, J. E. Perhaps Nick Wallace forgot to put in the app. for medal for him. All of my app's for such were honored.

But in your case will state that Hon. Asst. Sec'y of War wrote me about the matter, and I thought that I had said sufficient to have insured the granting of it, not knowing till now that it had not been. I could not remember the names or faces even of those I saw spilling themselves over the brink for a camp-kettle of the liquid blue stuff—that was simply an impossibility; and then, my time was fully occupied in endeavoring to make it somewhat feasible to procure a drop of the dear stuff; and so I lamentingly told the Sec'y.

I trust a way may be found that I can render some assistance to you in the matter. You, I suppose, have a personal acquaintance with Gen. Doe, and I am only too willing to do all toward it that lies in my power.

As far as granting them to officers is concerned, and men also, I must say that in my opinion, in the cases of some officers and men to whom they have been given—and I knowing full particulars in such cases—that I'd scarcely give a tinker's dam for one to hand down to my son. That's where, perhaps, the "V.C." is better guarded.

Learn if I can do anything to help you in it (if you wish it) and only show me the way. I went through a lot of "cap" to demonstrate to Gen. Doe the general mixed state of affairs existing at the time in question, and I thought that though I didn't, and hadn't, known you personally, enough has been said to convince the Hon. Sec'y that I believed you were undoubtedly there, and recommended the "bauble" be granted, "or words to that effect." This, as you know, is all that I could say.

To jump to another strain; Is it within the bounds of possibilities that "Maj. B." could or did not scent out the musky mis-steps of Madam?

I, for one have my doubts on it! The affairs—from Dame Rumor's accts. have been too oft.

Little Benny H. told me on the shady side of a Montana bluff in '76, that when he got away from that La. town, he felt that the weight of a mountain had been removed from his shoulders, and though "Ben" and I were bosom cronies, I didn't ask him if he had hunted the musky fox (for I'd no right to, and he, as a gentleman, wouldn't have told me anyhow.)

My 5th Inf. friends having made their march to Mc-Pherson's monument, for practice, are now coming through the park, which my window overlooks, returning to Fort McPherson for supper.

I've been stationed at odd posts with that regiment since 1867, so, of course, know all of the old hands.

"The Johnny come Latelies" of these days I take little stock in, as they seem to think they know too much on graduation to be 2d Luffs.

A month or two of such work as hunting down Cuban insurgents would be of infinite benefit to them perhaps, as a stupid rancheria might at times give them points that Euclid did not embrace.

Grimes' long silence leads me to think that perhaps a

Council of War may be in session—and, notoriously, they never fight!

Thanking you for your nice long letter, & hoping I haven't bothered you with my reminiscences of old 7th, remain,

Truly yr. friend,
BENTEEN.

39 *Pavilion St.*
Atlanta,
March 14, '96

Dear Colonel Goldin:—

Yrs. of 12th inst. enclosing Grimes' queries &c. just recd.

For quite awhile I've had a "Pre"—a poker phrase, you know, and doubtless you know, too, that "Pres" do not always "pan out"; that perhaps 'twas Mr. Fredk. Whittaker of Mount Vernon, N.Y. the head and front of getting out W's life of Gen. Custer, mostly consisting of Custer's articles to the Galaxy Magazine, during a series of years, for the "padding" of the Vol., that was the puppet manager back of J.P.Grimes, Esq., and that Whittaker would get off some rapid-fire guns at Col. Hughes thereon, could he deduce argument sufficient from you or me. Whittaker is too wide awake to attempt to ask me for any information, as he knows I think him to be a pup.

Perhaps you may have read his book, "The Cadet Button." Well, if you haven't—don't! 'tis a waste of time!

I always thought of the distance lost by my battln. in left-obliquing from the trail, and getting back to same on the

morning of the 25th, as something between 10 and 12 miles—
perhaps more, as we went in hot haste both ways. From where
my battln. obliqued to left, to the spot where I found the body
of Custer, I put down as 15 miles. It is rather over than under
this estimate.

I think the "probs" very fair, that we shall hear from
both Godfrey and Whittaker on Hughes' dynamite bomb.
G. can have easy access to Mil. Service Inst. Journal. W.
would have to rely I think on some of the magazines; but as
he is a literary cuss, doubtless he'll find little trouble in getting
his work in one of the big ones, and perhaps in the "Century."

I think the information you gave Grimes in your last
as nearly correct as there was any necessity for, anyway, the
distance and time of day, and a great many minor details, have
to remain simply guess-work; which is just as well, as the
great fiasco was and is an accomplished fact; "done up" in
great shape by the noble aborigines to whom the disobedient
Custer had left all lanes open.

Of course Whittaker, an impecunious quill-driver, is after
"copy"—something that will sell. But he got "stuck" on "W's
Life of C," as the bookshelves of the publisher held them
nearly all for years, till recently they have been a bit revived,
re-edited and put on the market—a huge volume for 40¢, at
which price I got my first copy.

It is demnition strange that a lad of not 20 years complete
should be delving in this hurry-scurry age for what might be
termed almost antiquities—do you not so think? But I've quit
thinking 'twas "Fred Calhoun", as I'm of the opinion that,
firstly, he is too lazy; 2dly, he has sufficient "sabe" to know
there is nothing further to be gotten by following that trail.
But then, 'tisn't Grimes alone! That's pretty certain.

So, my advice would be to temporize with him a bit

[287]

longer, and he will let fall something soon that you'll get his exact bearings from. Whittaker would know that I am acquainted with his (W's) handwriting, and I shouldn't be surprised if Grimes copied W's queries.

You haven't done a bit of harm by the thrusts you have given him; in fact, believe those pokes will somewhat accelerate the development of the problem.

That the whole game is the worst of rot, goes without saying; but I'd like to know who the coon is that's drawing the woodpile around himself—wouldn't you?

The bulk of the work (all, in fact) is falling on you, but then, I could never "draw that coon", and now I'm bound to see Col. Hughes thru the balance of this game. Patience will trap them. Let's do it!

Very truly yr. friend
BENTEEN

That I'm obliged to you for your trouble in giving me the details of the game, you, of course, know.

39 Pavilion St.
Atlanta,
March 19, '96

Dear Colonel Goldin:—

Yrs. of 16th just recd., and as I have some spare moments, proceed to ans. I'll gladly give Gen. Doe an intimation to the matter in question.

Major Garlington was here on 16th inst. on a tour of inspecting accts. of disbursing officers, this station being in his bailiwick. I have seen him on his two different tours here, and he seems to stand prosperity very well.

I haven't written to Hughes on the Grimes inquiries, and this from fact of not having as yet gotten the true drift of the lad's inquiries, as he may be a harmless gossoon after all, acting under his own impulses, with some little desire to exhibit his delicate chirography. If there is anybody behind him, just rest; you'll develop it.

Godfrey, in my mind, is rather an obtuse fellow, and like the traditional Englishman, it takes him a good while to see the nub of a joke. That he'll rush up on that intrenched artillery you suggested, why, you can put it down as done. I have known him since he joined the 7th in '67, and am of the opinion that I've pretty well diagnosed his character and capacity.

I've known Major Bell, too, since '66. Bell was H.Q.M. at the Washita fight. 2d Lieut. Mathey took Capt. Hamilton's (Hamilton was killed) place as Officer of the Day, and Bell left him (Mathey) in charge of the train, and I heard Bell got up with some wagon or so of ammunition from train to scene of fight, but I didn't see him. The little racket at Canyon Creek in '77 was the only one fight I ever knew or heard of his being with the regiment. His time was put in in looking out for advancement to Qr. Mr.,Commy., Adjt.Gen. or any other berth that was in sound or sight, and his services were mostly on "leaves" of some kind of work in the 7th. He got none of the vacancies, and the disaster at L.B.Horn made him a Captain, and the War Dept. hustled Bell and Jackson to their newly-found troops; both of them (of same ilk, had to do some duty then.) [?]

Bell is a massive, fine-looking fellow, but I've no doubt the madam soon learned that her brain contained more gray

matter than did his, and as well took in all of his superficiali-
ties, and &c. She doubtless was a nymphomaniac.

Yes, McBride, a bigamist, "took in" Mrs. Douseman just
as easy! It must have been a terrible stroke to the family
pride, but it occurred, and with it a child by him—nameless
of course, i.e., in the eyes of the law.

Capt. Bowen, 5th Inf. who in '77 was 2d Lieut. on
Miles' staff, earnestly desired me to come to Fort McPherson
to hear his lecture, but having a move pleasing invitation
from Roland Reed to come to see Miss Rush and himself in
"The Woman Hater", I went to the latter and had some large
bottles with the girls and Reed in the latter's dressing room
between acts and after the play. That's what I deem putting
the time in to best advantage, don't you?

Thanking you for your nice long letter, and trusting to
hear from you every time you have the time to spare.

> Very truly your friend,
> BENTEEN, 7th

NOTE: I see by A. & N. Register that Col. Hughes has six—
6—months leave (Europe, I suppose).

> *39 Pavilion St.*
> *Atlanta,*
> *March 23, '96*

Dear Colonel Goldin:

Yrs. enclosing Grimes' latest just recd. I see nothing to
alter in your reply. "Grimesey" may be an inveterate yellow-

back story book reader, and thus have learned of "Reynolds." At all events, I am arriving at conclusion that he is getting somewhat puerile in his questions and remarks, and the gossoon may be acting in his individual capacity, as he has frequently remarked. If he is being "coached" we are just bound to find it out in time, and he may just as well get his chips ready for redemption.

Gen. Miles, through G.A.R. M.O.C.C. U.S. Public Press, A.&N. Register, etc. is moving things toward those (three stars), and I am greatly pleased at the stand of the Pres. & Secy. of War. I am of the opinion, too, that the present Adjt. Gen. doesn't view the promotion favorable. However, watch. If he, M. doesn't get it during this Ad. why, he will from next one. Everything, according to my lights tending toward a Republican Ad. for next term.

But I want to state right here, as a Democrat, that I infinitely prefer Thos. B. Reed to the "Young Napoleon" of Tariff fame(?).

I must say that I admired the man Reed czar's methods when in his first Speakership, as I don't believe in delaying legislation by minority tactics, as it gives cause for belief to the uninitiated world that we are not true patriots, and all as devotedly attached to our grand republic as we should be.

As an example of how Miles "did things" when he was in command of Dist. of the Yellowstone, in 1877, I give you this: I endeavored to get at least 3 communications through to Gen. Terry while he was on the Sitting Bull commission in '77, as when Gen. Miles left us on the Mo. river, at the junction of Squaw Creek (from which place I changed the camp to above the mouth of Mussellshell river.)

Believing it was the intention of Gen. Miles to use all of his best endeavors to retain the 7th Cavalry at that point, or some other, "peak" for instance on the Mo. River all winter, I stated the surmise to Gen. Terry, giving him the thorough condition of the men and animals of the 7th. Not one of the 3 communications got through. Miles' scouts took them to Miles. However, the accident of Terry's coming down the Mo. on a Macinac boat instead of via Buford, gave me the greater advantage of talking to him. Then I learned that he had gotten none of my missives. Gen. Terry asked me if I wanted to stay there at Musselshell and Mo. river. No, of course we didn't! He then asked me if I had any paper; I said Garlington with the non-com.staff of Regt. had taken off every scrap of paper, pen and ink connected with Regt. Hdqtrs, but I had a memorandum book that we could tear leaves from. "Well," said the Gen., "that's good enough isn't it to write an order to go home on?" "Yes, General," said I, "bum-wad is good enough for that purpose." Gen. Terry drafted the order in pencil, and his Aide made a fair copy in ink, which some zealous subaltern upturned for the purpose—Mathey, I think.

So we were free of Miles! With Miles still to wander ere getting to clean clothes; but it was something to outflank him, as he always had a grudge against the 7th Cavalry.

On nearing Buford, I sent Lieut. Brewer, Act.Adjt. ahead to learn where Col.Huston, comdg. post, would be pleased to have us camp, as I had to refit somewhat there, repairing wagons, get what clothing, buffalo shoes, coats &c that we could.

Col. Huston sent out his post Adjt. in hot haste with Brewer to the column, with a subsequent order to the one given me by Gen. Terry, viz: that I was to report to Col. Huston for orders, Jacobs the Adjt. telling me that Miles was then present at Buford, and Col. Huston feared I would report to him (Buford, you know, was an independent post, not in Miles' district.)

Well, there was no fear of my volunteering to go under Miles' banner!

However, I'm damned if Miles didn't induce Col. Huston to let him have 5 troops of the 7th Cavalry to help the troop of 2d Cavalry—Poole's—escort a portion of the Southern Cheyennes to Bismarck. I sent off all of the married officers of the regiment with that battalion, remaining at Buford to stand off Qr. Mr. E. B. Kirk, who was virtually "running" the post.

Well, you know how he played off the old rotten hay on us, rotten clothes ditto, and how we skirmished with our own teams through the snow, with the therm. 50 deg. to get fuel that would burn, and how, if we put in for 2 cans of condensed milk, tomatoes, or anything to purchase for cash, from A.E.S., why, perhaps we might get one can—if we were in luck!

Well, a blind man would see through the scheme. It was simply to force us to purchase from the sutler, and by the Lord Harry, I told them so, but I only made enemies of them, and we got no more of the milk or tomatoes by so doing!

Well, never mind. I've always known that I had the happy facility of making enemies of any one I ever knew, but what then? I wasn't found to be ground down by a besotted post C.G. or by a Capt. & A.D.C., and I, through the post comdr. proceeded to acquaint Gen. Terry of the whole lay of the land.

Taking my premises from the expected coming of the Cheyennes from Keogh to Buford (for the purpose of escorting same to Lincoln was the sole purpose for which we were ordered to report to Col. Huston).

Well, Major "Jim" Baker got down at last from Keogh with a battln. 2d Cav. having in tow the long looked for Cheyennes, and the same morning we were ready to pull out from Buford, back came the communication I had sent in to Terry's Adjt. Gen., the post comdr. at Buford being directed to have the same read to me before forwarding to Keogh.

Gen. Terry commenced by saying "That he was pained to see how constantly his orders were disobeyed", meaning by Miles' retaining Cheyennes even in disobedience of orders from the War Dept. from whence they originated. At that I thought "Well, General, were it my Dept. I'm inclined to the belief that would be 'tother fellow that would be pained. But at that juncture you see we really had the Cheyennes, and the snow was too deep for further comment.

At Knife River, Gen. Miles came into our camp by the huge haystack, alongside of which we remained during a snow flurry.

He came through in an ambulance, behind which was a fine cutter dragging. Well, when they went out of the camp, the cutter was being dragged by two of the finest black U.S. horses in "D" Troop, which had been presented by Lieut. Eckerson, Comdg. Troop! Months elapsed before I became acquainted with these facts.

I made it so decidedly warm for Miles while he was in that camp that he left us during the storm. Then it was that I drew on him his official report of the Bear's Paw fight, and convicted him by it of having dealt unjustly to the 7th Cavalry.

Now I have always known that such doings have invariably recoiled on me, but I cannot let them pass unchallenged. In Russia I'd be a Nihilist sure!

But none of that in America.

Gen. Terry, in his goodness of heart, perhaps, didn't want

[294]

to go roughshod over Miles; but maybe, too, he looked at the expense of a G.C.M., and it may be likewise at the strong backing Miles would have, and then, you know, Terry hadn't his twin stars yet. Further comment is unnecessary!

Take it all in all, though, the wintry blasts were keen and the snowdrifts deep, and the Missouri River plated with a full six feet of ice, I look back on that march down the Mo. in '77-'78 as a kind of test march of what animals, men and Indians can do when they've got to do it, and must say that I rather enjoyed the bonne homme that existed au haute, each and every one knowing we weren't there because we wanted to be, but each one doing his whole duty. Doesn't this strike you as being the facts of the occasion?

Were I a Czar—to which elevation truth compels me to say I haven't the slightest aspiration—I would have no regimental officer in the cavalry beyond the age of 45 years.

I tell you what, Colonel, they are "stale", too stale perhaps ere reaching it, for the real work the cavalry can do. I saw enough of that during the war to rivet it solidly in my mind. But then it worked to the advantage of giving me opportunity that otherwise would not have fallen to me; and so, for the good of our great republic, thank the good Lord!

I have gone on here in a rambling, harum-scarum screed, like unto as a backwoods Missourian would say, "A goose doing his mess by moonlight," but then, perhaps doubtless you have a waste-basket convenient, and if you don't like it, consign it to that receptacle.

Your letters always interest me, and as before, when you have the leisure and nothing better to do, shoot at me in volleys.

Very truly yr. friend,
BENTEEN.

[295]

39 Pavilion St.
Atlanta,
April 3, '96

Dear Colonel Goldin:—

Yours of 31st ult., enclosing excerpts from press concerning Miles' chances for stars, (3) just received. Ditto, presentation speech of Gen. Doe in turning over to you medal for
most distinguished conduct at the Little Big Horn, June 25,
'76. The presentation was well conceived, and I rejoice in it
that you rejoice in it, and I congratulate you most heartily
thereon.

Now as Capt. L.R. Hare has assisted you in that matter,
I shall take immediate occasion to interest myself in endeavoring to secure one for Hare, and I take this occasion to remark
that had I then been in command, Hare would have been in
possession of one long ago, if my recommendations could have
furthered such. The Army & Navy forever! Hurrah for the
Red, White and Blue!

Mind, now, should McKinley become president, then
Miles will secure the 3 stars triumphantly. But then, you see,
McKinley isn't going to wield the baton of Grand Marshal
over this grand Republic just yet, my boy; i.e., in my opinion.
Let us—as we'll have to—wait and see.

Gen. Miles would have been a grand, strong friend of
mine if I'd have let him be; this I know absolutely from
intimates of the Gen. But you see this d——d old stubborn
Democratic head of mine wasn't built to accept peace offer-
ings from newspaper people, and I never even met him a small
part of the way. It is easily to be gleaned from this that I've
never been at all politic, and would have made the poorest of
poor politicians. "Every one to his liking," or, to way he's built.

Poor Eckerson! The greatest fault of that kid was an over-weening vanity, and furthermore, he was not an honest man. He is now going over his accounts with his Maker, having died at Fort Hayes where he was forage-master over 16 years ago. If it will benefit any in t'other sphere, my testimony for him will go to the effect that he'd more grit than his captain. I believe, too, that in that other life, that "sand" when shown in defense of the Right, will have as great appreciation extended as it does here on our little handball of a globe.

What you say as to any reciprocation toward myself, my dear Colonel, I thank you for, but let me assure you that if my scrawl to Gen. Doe had any good effect in your case, then I am fully repaid, the debt canceled—and here's your receipt.

Ah, poor Grimesey! Perhaps the water was too deep for him, and where he hoped for pearls, got husks. Perhaps 'tis often so in everyone's life.

You are correct, Goldin, about poor "Nick"—Capt. George D. Wallace, and I must say that it gave me the serenest pleasure to "head off" my first lieut. when he was aspiring and conspiring to obtain the command of Troop G, 7th, at Cedar Creek in '77 when Garlington relieved Wallace as adjutant, and it was not that I value his services, for I really thought there was little of the true man about him; but I liked "Nick" better. But for me, you'd have had Gibson for Troop commander, and for that, I think you should burn an exra roman candle to my memory on the 4th of July next. Look to it that 'tis done! "Gib" has an extra good job now in Sanitary Street Cleaning Dept. under Waring, in N. Y. City, being "stable boss" I think.

Though I got out of going to hear Capt. Bowen's philan-derings on the L.B. Horn affair, given at barracks, I'm in for it anyhow, as he repeats his lecture for benefit of a church at theater in city, and my folks are tendered a box. Well, I'll anchor three beauties in it, perhaps, and then wander down toward the canopy, or rather, the under part of dress circle, among the pillars.

Always glad to hear from you.

Truly yr. friend, Benteen, 7th

39 Pavilion St.
Atlanta,
April 14, '96

Dear Colonel Goldin:—

It is really to be deplored if "Grimesey" has shed the lariat you have about encompassed him with, but then, I'm of the opinion that the first notes of "stable-call", or some such alluring strain, will find him ambling toward feed-trough.

Should "Grimes" fail to come up at grooming-time, I haven't the slightest doubt that Major Godfrey will parade in the next issue—April—of Mil. Service Instit. Let's wait and see!

I'm awfully off in my opinion of the latter if Col. Hughes' salt hasn't "struck in" on his tail feathers. As sure as you are born, "he's a man there's little to," but I think Hughes' next salvo; I believe H. has heavy metal behind, yet untouched. Then down will go "God's" craft out of sight! Am really of the opinion that Hughes didn't care to measure pens with such a lightweight. However, he can't get any heavy-

weights to war with on that threadbare subject. Hughes,
however, accomplished all he set to do.

Yes, I took in the lecture, placing my rosebuds three, with Mrs. B. for chaperone, in the place of honor, while I, as before indicated, sought deeper shade. My comments thereon were made to 3 of Capt. Bowen's friends, viz: to "call him off that trail," as really there was nothing in it. A parenthesis will state Bowen is a cruiser only—not a battleship.

I enjoyed you "inflection" immensely. It is not to be deplored that business in the clerk's office is booming, for that brings Louis d'ors, and those bring comforts if not always happiness galore. I am always delighted to hear from you, so, when business allows, go on with fusillade. Mrs. Benteen and my kid join me in kind remembrances to yourself and Mrs. Goldin.

Very truly yr. friend, BENTEEN.

39 Pavilion St.
Atlanta,
April 25th, '96

Dear Colonel Goldin:—

Your welcome letter just rec'd. Perhaps 'twas a little rough on the Madam to leave her with the rosebuds, but then, you see there were two sunflowers to keep them company, and my absence from box gave them all more room; moreover, none of them knew I intended *to vamoose.*

Only think I gave that Capt. of 5th Inf. yr. articles to Army Mag., he saying the show to be given at Fort McPherson was for an object lesson for his company. Well, I had better business on hand that night (Roland Reed), so the Capt. next gave his stereopticon exhibit for the benefit of a chapel being erected near post, putting in a proviso, I learned, that $100 was to go to the exchequer of the Capt. $34 went to the chapel.

And just to think the Asinus tonight gives another show at Grand Theater in city, "at the urgent request of numerous friends, the captain leaving for the north immediately; this is the last chance to hear the lecture and see the views."

Well, by gum, the idea of a Capt. of the U.S. Army becoming a showman! It is my opinion that Bowen is going north on leave to give this show and lecture. Now he cannot command good English; I don't believe he knows it when he hears it, therefore, the lecture part, though wholly compilation, is pretty twaddy and uninteresting from the manner of its delivery. Should you hear of his doing anything in the north of the kind, please write to the Hon. Asst. Sec'y and have the fellow saved from making a further d——d fool of himself. You know he can do it by revoking leave, if an intimation to leave off goes unheeded.

I have intimated to three of the captain's fellow officers that he ought to be choked off that lay, but whether they cared to inform him, I am at a loss to know. I think the dummy is really spieling for a position on the staff of Gen. Miles, having been one of the many 2d luffs Miles had savaging around him in '76-'77, and perhaps later.

Now I really am only guessing at his intentions when he gets north, but a dime to a peanut goes that I'm O.K. on it. I know one thing—that he wouldn't have gotten a word of information on the subject from me had I thought it was wanted for any other purpose than an object lesson in war for the benefit of officers and men of Fort McPherson, Ga.

If I should hear—see by newspapers is the only chance I'll have—that he is delivering the lecture north, I shall at once request Gen. Doe to have the business stopped as "conduct prejudicial" or on some other score—any other.

This 5th Inf. Capt. has no other object in berating Custer & Reno in public lectures than either for money-making or looking forward to duty on staff, as I've indicated. He cannot have, as personally he never saw Custer or Reno, and in a measure of brain is incompetent to judge of the worth of either of them. Both his stereopticon picture and talk are pretty near the ludicrous.

Kind remem. from all, to yr, family circle.

> Very truly yr. friend,
> F. W. BENTEEN

My son won two first prizes in tilting tour lately.

> *39 Pavilion St.*
> *Atlanta,*
> *May 26-*

Dear Colonel Goldin:—

Yr, last very interesting letter at hand. Always pleased when you can find time to drop me a few lines.

Poor Grimesey! I'd give a fip to know what the cuss was monkeying at. Preparing for a lecture doubtless. (Capt. Bowen of 5th Inf. may point a moral for him. Bowen—who cannot speak the best of English—hired the Grand Theater here for his 3d lecture on Reno, Custer & the Little B. Horn, the reduced hall rent being $100. Well, he had about twenty dead-heads as audience! Thus, R. and C. were avenged somewhat, and Bowen—'tis to be hoped, converted into a somewhat wiser man.)

The lecture abounded in compliments to me, but really, Colonel, I'm out of that whirlpool now; 'tis a dead, dead issue—stale, flat, &c., and I do not want a doughboy to speak in any but respectful manner of a dead cavalryman.

Had a letter from Major Godfrey a few days ago. He hadn't shown up in the Mil. Service Journal yet—but wait! G. said nothing about any such intention, either—but I know him.

As I hear the postman in the park, I'll let this go for the nonce and write you again.

Very truly yr. friend,
Benteen, 7th

St. Paul, Minn. Aug. 8, 1896

Mr. Theodore W. Goldin,
Attorney-at-law
Janesville, Wis.

Sir:

I have just heard that Reno's men while in the bottom, saw Custer's fighting on the bluff, or perhaps it was while his line was extended across the plain before he took to the timber, at any rate, the point is that sometime during Reno's stay in the valley, and before he made the wretched scramble for the bluffs, some of his men are said to have seen Custer fighting across the river, perhaps two miles or so away. I am told you were with Reno, if so, you may perhaps recall me, but in any event I should like to hear whether this story is true or not, so far as your observations went, and would you have been likely to have seen any action going on so far off while yourself engaged? I hear you have written something in a Chicago magazine about the fight. I should like a copy of the paper, or a reference that will enable me to get it. It seems hardly possible that such a material fact as Reno's knowledge that Custer was himself fighting but a short distance away, and his charging (which was of course expected, as it had been ordered) would have relieved him, should have gone all these years unmentioned, yet that is just what the Indians say took place—that Custer's first fighting was done in full presence of Reno's command, and notwithstanding not only was no charge made, but Reno did not try to hold his own in the timber—that is, the bottom—after you came in off the plain. Any light you may be able to throw on any of these matters will be very acceptably received.

Yours very truly,
R. E. THOMPSON
Capt. Signal Corps.

39 *Pavilion St.*
Atlanta.
Aug. 12, '96

Dear Colonel Goldin:—

Glad to hear from you again.

Your last inquiry on Custer Big Horn fiasco is from "Dick" Thompson, who was commissary on Terry's staff in the field in '76, Hdqtrs. on "Far West." Thompson was at that time a 2d Lieut. of 5th Inf. Grad. from M.A. of '68. I suppose Dick means at some time to give us a few lines concerning the whys and wherefores of the disaster.

Now 'twasn't physically possible for any of Reno's men to see Custer's men fighting on the bluffs, for no fighting was done by them till they were gotten into the corral into which they wandered in such hot haste, and "Gall" says 30 minutes settled the whole biz for them there.

True, Reno "didn't try to hold him on in the timber", but Custer deceived Reno in assuring him that he would support him "with the whole outfit". R. necessarily supposing that the support would come from the direction from which he

[304]

had come; in short, his rear, which was natural enough with no other explanation.

I am reckless as to whose feelings I hurt, but it is my firm belief, and always has been, that Custer's command didn't do any "1st-class" fighting there, and if possible were worse handled even than Reno's batt'n. 300 men well fought should have made a better showing.

"Dick" Thompson married a Miss Rice of St. Paul, when 2d Lieut. 6th Inf., and was stationed at several of the Upper Mo. river posts.

From the fact of Thompson having been in the '76 campaign in capacity of A.C.S. on Terry's staff, he may have some information about same, but 'tis by no means possible that he can have as great an amt. of same as had Hughes, who was General Terry's right hand confidential man. Hughes refers to "Dick" in his last article in M.S.I.

Let's hear from you when you can find time.

With kind regards to Mrs. Goldin and family,

Truly yr, friend, Benteen, 7th

This is the last letter in this collection, or at least the last letter to have come to light. Benteen died on June 22, 1898, thus ending any possibility of other exchanges.

INDEX